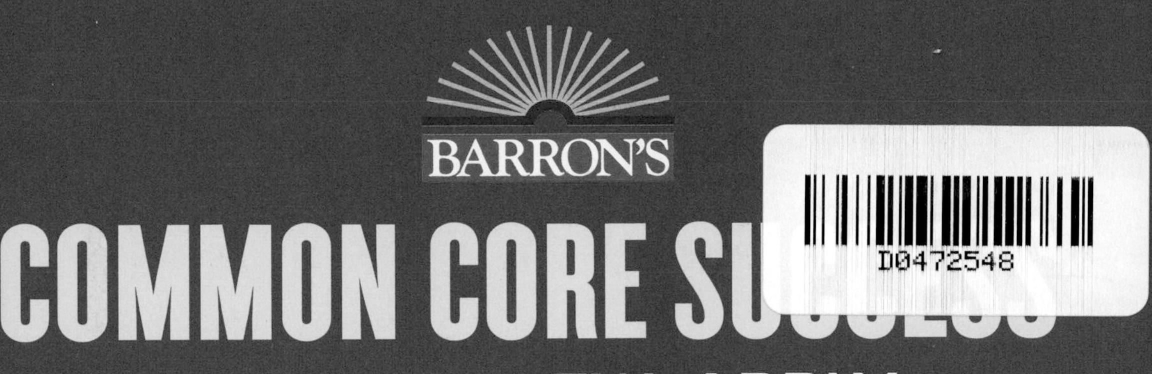

COMMON CORE SUCCESS

LEARN, REVIEW, APPLY

GRADE 4 MATH

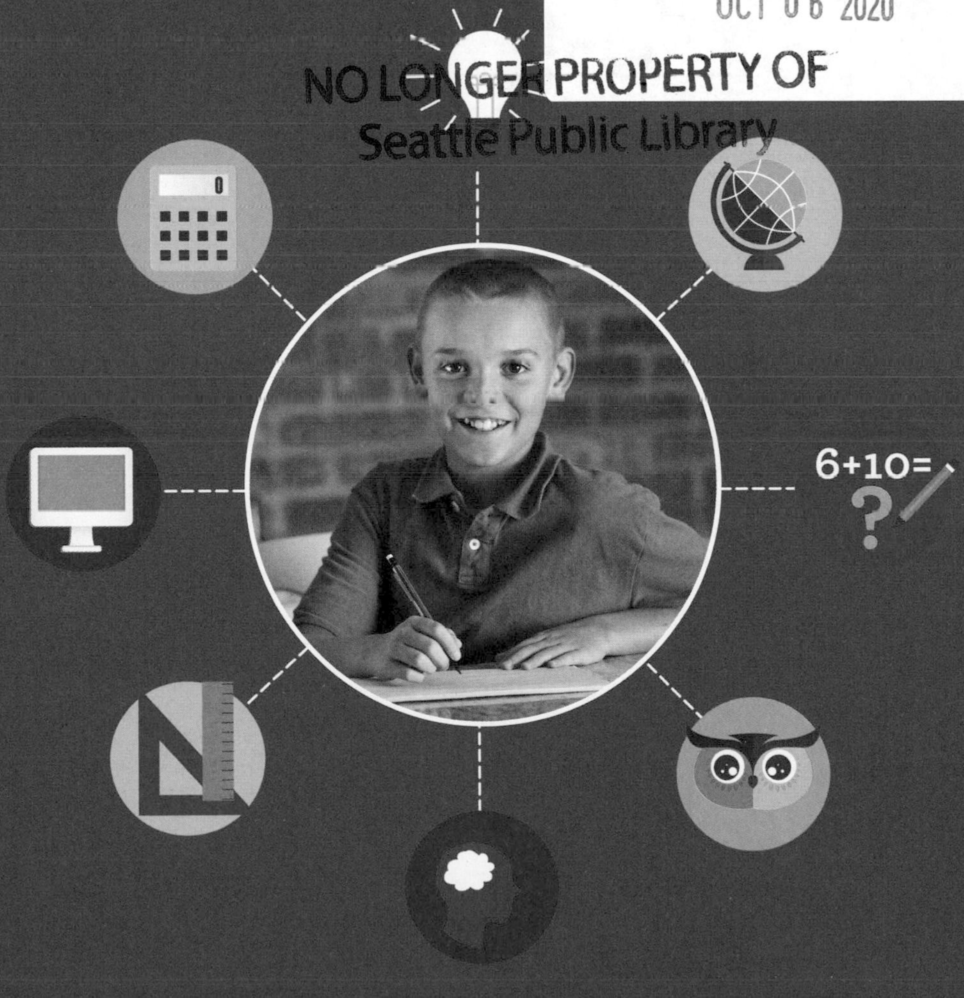

Elizabeth W. Moorhouse Abruzzo
Consulting Editor

All inquiries should be addressed to:
Barron's Educational Series, Inc.
250 Wireless Boulevard
Hauppauge, NY 11788
www.barronseduc.com

ISBN: 978-1-4380-0676-5

Library of Congress Control Number: 2015932211

Date of Manufacture: May 2015
Manufactured by: C&C Offset Printing Co., Ltd, Shenzhen, China

Printed in China

9 8 7 6 5 4 3 2 1

Title page ©Bocreative/Shutterstock, Page 5 ©AVAVA/Shutterstock Page 7 ©michaeljung/Shutterstock, Page 11 ©Monkey Business Images/Shutterstock, Page 14 ©lena Serdiukova/Shutterstock, Page 16 ©lena Serdiukova/Shutterstock,(fish) ©Nelson Marques/Shutterstock (tickets) Page 17 ©wavebreakermedia/Shutterstock, Page 19 ©Kalmatsuy /Shutterstock, Page 21 ©artiis/Shutterstock, Page 22 ©Nata-Lia /Shutterstock, Page 26 ©michelaubryphoto /Shutterstock, Page 27 ©Matthew Cole/Shutterstock (lighthouse), Page 29 ©Camek/Shutterstock, Page 30 ©graphic-line /Shutterstock, Page 31 © Markus Mainka/Shutterstock, Page 32 (girl) ©Victoria Kisel /Shutterstock, (money) ©Tiger Images/Shutterstock, Page 33 ©SLP London/Shutterstock, Page 34 ©abramsdesign /Shutterstock, Page 35 (colored pencils) ©Vorobyeva/ Shutterstock, (girl) ©Inara Prusakova/Shutterstock, Page 36©Mushakesa/Shutterstock, Page 37 ©margouillat photo /Shutterstock, Page 38 ©Naddya / Shutterstock, Page 39 ©KreativKolors /Shutterstock, Page 40 ©Lyudmyla Kharlamova /Shutterstock, Page 44 ©alkkdsg /Shutterstock, Page 45 ©Rawpixel / Shutterstock, Page 46 ©Grandview Graphics/Shutterstock, Page 47 ©wizdata1 /Shutterstock, Page 48 ©Passiflora/Shutterstock, Page 49 (girl with cards) © J2R/Shutterstock, (card suits) ©Torderiul/Shutterstock Page 50 ©Bragin Alexey /Shutterstock, Page 51 ©Macrovector /Shutterstock, Page 52 ©Seamartini Graphics/Shutterstock, Page 53 ©VL1/Shutterstock, Page 55 ©Macrovector /Shutterstock, Page 56 ©Macrovector/Shutterstock, Page 57 ©Luis Louro /Shutterstock, Page 58 ©Luis Louro/Shutterstock, Page 59 ©Julia Pivovarova /Shutterstock, Page 60 ©amirage /Shutterstock, Page 61 ©Elena Yakusheva /Shutterstock (painting), ©nexus7/Shutterstock (window), ©archideaphoto / Shutterstock (door), Page 62 ©goir/Shutterstock Page 63 ©Fat708/Shutterstock, Page 64 ©Viktor Kunz /Shutterstock, Page 65 ©inkwelldodo /Shutterstock (top guinea pig), ©Ase/Shutterstock (bottom guinea pig), Page 66 © PHOTO FUN/Shutterstock, Page 68 ©archideaphoto / Shutterstock, Page 71 ©Maks Narodenko /Shutterstock, Page 72 ©De Visu/Shutterstock (lunchtime), ©Tim UR/Shutterstock (grapes), Page 73 ©Oksana Shufrych /Shutterstock (bead pile), ©paulaphoto/Shutterstock (bead bracelet), Page 74 ©Oksana Shufrych /Shutterstock, Page 75 ©Nanette Grebe/ Shutterstock (girls), ©Nattika/Shutterstock (cookies), Page 77 ©iofoto /Shutterstock (girl on phone), ©Harper 3D/Shutterstock (green blocks), Page 78 ©TackTack/Shutterstock, Page 79 ©Panachai Cherdchucheep / Shutterstock (boy on books), ©Kiselev Andrey Valerevich/Shutterstock(girl on books), Page 80 ©iunewind/Shutterstock, Page 81 ©Xenium /Shutterstock, Page 82 ©Ian 2010/Shutterstock, Page 83 © Elena Schweitzer/Shutterstock (shell bucket), ©Ian 2010/Shutterstock (leaves), Page 84 ©Krailurk Warasup/Shutterstock, Page 85 ©Cherry-Merry/Shutterstock, Page 86 ©Maks Narodenko/Shutterstock, Page 88 ©Denis Cristo/Shutterstock, Page 89 ©Matthew Cole/Shutterstock, Page 90 ©Studiotouch/Shutterstock, Page 91 ©Studiotouch/Shutterstock (sandwich), ©Ruslan Guzov/Shutterstock (kids jumping), Page 92 ©Chuanchom Nuntamongkol/Shutterstock, Page 93 © verandah/Shutterstock, Page 94 ©Matthew Cole/Shutterstock, Page 95 ©Suzanne Tucker/Shutterstock, Page 97 ©Macrovector/Shutterstock, Page 99 ©John T Takai/Shutterstock (vacuum cleaner), Page 101 ©holbox/Shutterstock, Page 102 ©Carlos Amarillo/Shutterstock, Page 103 ©beta757/Shutterstock (flowers), ©Karen Roach/Shutterstock (button), Page 108 ©Iconic Bestiary/Shutterstock, Page 109 ©Stefan Holm/Shutterstock, Page 111 ©Goritza/Shutterstock, Page 112 ©Kim Nguyen/Shutterstock, Page 113 © Kalmatsuy/Shutterstock, Page 115 © Matthew Cole/Shutterstock, Page 119 © Catalin Petolea/Shutterstock, Page 122 © Mike Flippo/Shutterstock, Page 124 © Lorelyn Medina/Shutterstock, Page 125 ©Wong Sze Yuen/Shutterstock (boy), ©Cappi Thompson/Shutterstock (crumpled one dollar bill), Page 126 ©Cappi Thompson/Shutterstock, Page 127 ©GrigoryL/Shutterstock, Page 129 ©titosart/Shutterstock, Page 134 ©Rob Wilson/Shutterstock, Page 135 ©Hurst Photo/Shutterstock (salsa), ©Jaimie Duplass/Shutterstock (bowl of diced tomatoes), Page 138 ©BassKwong/Shutterstock, Page 140 ©Pete Pahham/Shutterstock, Page 141 © Masyanya/Shutterstock (watermelon), © naken2012/Shutterstock (shapes), Page 144 ©Anest/Shutterstock, Page 146 ©Brian Maudsley/Shutterstock, Page 149 ©michaeljung/Shutterstock (boy), ©Goldenarts/Shutterstock (letters), Page 150 ©Natsmith1/Shutterstock, Page 151 ©Natsmith1/Shutterstock, Page 152 ©Asier Romero/Shutterstock (girl), ©pringletta/Shutterstock (protractor, and triangle), Page 153 ©Chuhail/Shutterstock, Page 155 ©Jacek Chabraszewski/Shutterstock (girl) ©Piotr Rzeszutek/Shutterstock (middle boy), ©ER_09/Shutterstock (right side boy), ©Rafa Irusta/Shutterstock (pizza and wheel), Page 158 ©cristovao/Shutterstock, Page 159 ©Natsmith1/Shutterstock, Page 160 ©Picsfive/Shutterstock (water bottle), ©Preto Perola/Shutterstock (bread), ©Tatiana Shepeleva/Shutterstock (car), ©Africa Studio/Shutterstock (cup), ©Vlue/Shutterstock (gallon milk), ©Steve Cukrov/Shutterstock (orange juice), ©GooDween123/Shutterstock (thumb), ©Igor Lateci/Shutterstock (laptop), ©bestv/Shutterstock (oreo), ©tacar/Shutterstock (chocolate milk), Page 162 ©Olga Makhanova/Shutterstock, Page 163 ©Valentina Razumova/Shutterstock (apple), ©Hong Vo/Shutterstock (book), ©Picsfive/Shutterstock (bottle, paperclip), ©Tatiana Popova/Shutterstock (finger), ©AlexMaster/Shutterstock (guitar), ©Sergey Skleznev/Shutterstock (pencils), Page 164 ©donatas1205/Shutterstock (suitcases), © i9370/Shutterstock (tape measure), Page 168 ©Mostovyi Sergii Igorevich/Shutterstock, Page 170 ©Nicholas Gower/Shutterstock, Page 171 ©PHILIPIMAGE/Shutterstock

The recent adoption of the Common Core Standards now provides a distinct path to mathematic success. The standards are clear, the performance expectations are high, and the need for problem-solving is rigorous. The transition to this new method has been demanding for teachers, students, and parents alike. As a matter of fact, many parents, tutors, and even older siblings often think, "We never did it this way!"

Charged with the task of creating a parent-friendly mathematics handbook, we realized this was our opportunity to become the support that is critically needed. As classroom teachers for over forty-six years collectively, we have worked collaboratively for a number of years to improve our math instructional practices. Our math instruction evolved as a result of many research projects conducted within our classrooms. Using this research, we developed innovative ways to teach concepts otherwise viewed as extremely difficult by our students. We know what has to be taught, and we understand the struggles that students experience as they strive to achieve mastery.

The new Common Core Standards call for higher-level thinking and in-depth application of math content in multi-step word problems. Along with Common Core content standards, there are eight practice standards that dictate the behaviors required of our students as they engage in mathematics. As a result, we have implemented our **Ace It Time!** activity, or what Van de Walle refers to as a "math-rich" problem for each lesson. This is a rubric or checklist that will guide each student in the problem-solving process. It will also challenge him or her to explain his or her own thinking. This is often an element missing within most home resources. Parents will be able to turn to our product for support, insight, and assistance. They will have an invaluable resource that explains the standards in parent-friendly language, outlines the task required for that standard, teaches it in an easy-to-understand way, and provides adequate opportunities for practice. You will find that resource in our Barron's Common Core Success Math Series.

Parents, teachers, tutors, and other homework helpers—we wish you much success in your journey to help your student master the Common Core!

Lori K. Gaudreau, M.Ed.
Carroll Hutton, Ed.D.

Introduction to Problem-Solving and Mathematical Practices

This book will help to equip both students and parents with strategies to solve math problems successfully. Problem solving in the mathematics classroom involves more than calculations alone. It involves a student's ability to consistently show his or her reasoning and comprehension skills to model and explain what he or she has been taught. These skills will form the basis for future success in meeting life's goals. Working through the Common Core State Standards each year through the twelfth grade sets the necessary foundation for collegiate and career success. Your student will be better prepared to handle the challenges that await him or her as he or she gradually enters into the global marketplace.

The next few pages contain a listing of the fourth grade Common Core State Standards your student will need to master.

Number and Base Ten Concepts

CCSS.MATH.CONTENT.4.NBT.A.1 – Recognize that in a multi-digit whole number, a digit in one place represents ten times what it represents in the place to its right. For example, recognize that 700 ÷ 70 = 10 by applying concepts of place value and division.

CCSS.MATH.CONTENT.4.NBT.A.2 – Read and write multi-digit whole numbers using base-ten numerals, number names, and expanded form. Compare two multi-digit numbers based on meanings of the digits in each place, using >, =, and < symbols to record the results of comparisons.

CCSS.MATH.CONTENT.4.NBT.A.3 – Use place value understanding to round multi-digit whole numbers to any place.

CCSS.MATH.CONTENT.4.NBT.B.4 – Fluently add and subtract multi-digit whole numbers using the standard algorithm.

CCSS.MATH.CONTENT.4.OA.1.A – Determine whether an equation is true or false by using comparative relational thinking.

CCSS.MATH.CONTENT.4.OA.1.B – Determine the unknown whole number in an equation relating four whole numbers using comparative relational thinking

Factors and Divisibility

CCSS.MATH.CONTENT.4.OA.2.4 – Investigate factors and multiples.

a. Find all factor pairs for a whole number in the range 1–100.

b. Recognize that a whole number is a multiple of each of its factors. Determine whether a given whole number in the range 1–100 is a multiple of a given one-digit number.

c. Determine whether a given whole number in the range 1–100 is prime or composite.

CCSS.MATH.CONTENT.4.OA.3.5 – Generate a number or shape pattern that follows a given rule. Identify apparent features of the pattern that were not explicit in the rule itself. For example, given the rule "Add 3" and the starting number 1, generate terms in the resulting sequence and observe that the terms appear to alternate between odd and even numbers. Explain informally why the numbers will continue to alternate in this way.

Multiplication Concepts

CCSS.MATH.CONTENT.4.OA.A.1 – Interpret a multiplication equation as a comparison, e.g., interpret 35 = 5 × 7 as a statement that 35 is 5 times as many as 7 and 7 times as many as 5. Represent verbal statements of multiplicative comparisons as multiplication equations.

CCSS.MATH.CONTENT.4.OA.A.2 – Multiply or divide to solve word problems involving multiplicative comparison, e.g., by using drawings and equations with a symbol for the unknown number to represent the problem, distinguishing multiplicative comparison from additive comparison.

CCSS.MATH.CONTENT.4.OA.A.3 – Solve multi-step word problems posed with whole numbers and having whole-number answers using the four operations, including problems in which remainders must be interpreted. Represent these problems using equations with a letter standing for the unknown quantity. Assess the reasonableness of answers using mental computation and estimation strategies, including rounding.

CCSS.MATH.CONTENT.4.NBT.B.5 – Multiply a whole number of up to four digits by a one-digit whole number, and multiply two two-digit numbers, using strategies based on place value.

Concepts of Area and Perimeter

CCSS.MATH.CONTENT.4.MD.A.3 – Apply the area and perimeter formulas for rectangles in real-world and mathematical problems.

CCSS.MATH.CONTENT.4.NBT.B.5 – Multiply a whole number of up to four digits by a one-digit whole number, and multiply two two-digit numbers, using strategies based on place value.

Division Concepts

CCSS.MATH.CONTENT.4.OA.1.3 – Solve multi-step word problems posed with whole numbers and having whole-number answers using the four operations, including problems in which remainders must be interpreted. Represent these problems using equations with a letter standing for the unknown quantity. Assess the reasonableness of answers using mental computation and estimation strategies including rounding.

CCSS.MATH.CONTENT.4.NBT.2.6 – Find whole-number quotients and remainders with up to four-digit dividends and one-digit divisors, using strategies based on place value, the properties of operations, and/or the relationship between multiplication and division. Illustrate and explain the calculation by using equations, rectangular arrays, and/or area models.

Fraction Concepts

CCSS.MATH.CONTENT.4.NF.A.1 – Explain why a fraction $\frac{a}{b}$, is equivalent to a fraction $(n \times a)/(n \times b)$ by using visual fraction models, with attention to how the number and size of the parts differ even though the two fractions themselves are the same size. Use this principle to recognize and generate equivalent fractions.

CCSS.MATH.CONTENT.4.NF.A.2 – Compare two fractions with different numerators and different denominators, e.g., by creating common denominators or numerators, or by comparing to a benchmark fraction such as $\frac{1}{2}$. Recognize that comparisons are valid only when the two fractions refer to the same whole. Record the results of comparisons with symbols $>$, $=$, or $<$, and justify the conclusions, e.g., by using a visual fraction model.

Operations with Fractions Concepts

CCSS.MATH.CONTENT.4.NF.B.3 – Understand a fraction $\frac{1}{b}$, with $a > 1$ as a sum of fractions $\frac{1}{b}$.

a. Understand addition and subtraction of fractions as joining and separating parts referring to the same whole.

b. Decompose a fraction into a sum of fractions with the same denominator in more than one way,

recording each decomposition by an equation. Justify decompositions, e.g., by using a visual fraction model. Examples: $\frac{3}{8} = \frac{1}{8} + \frac{1}{8} + \frac{1}{8}$; $\frac{3}{8} = \frac{1}{8} + \frac{2}{8}$; $2\frac{1}{8} = 1 + 1 + \frac{1}{8} = \frac{8}{8} + \frac{8}{8} + \frac{1}{8}$.

c. Add and subtract mixed numbers with like denominators, e.g., by replacing each mixed number with an equivalent fraction, and/or by using properties of operations and the relationship between addition and subtraction.

d. Solve word problems involving addition and subtraction of fractions referring to the same whole and having like denominators, e.g., by using visual fraction models and equations to represent the problem.

CCSS.MATH.CONTENT.4.NF.B.4 – Apply and extend previous understandings of multiplication to multiply a fraction by a whole number.

a. Understand a fraction $\frac{a}{b}$ as a multiple of $\frac{1}{b}$. For example, use a visual fraction model to represent $\frac{5}{4}$ as the product $5 \times (\frac{5}{4})$, recording the conclusion by the equation $\frac{5}{4} = 5 \times (\frac{1}{4})$.

b. Understand a multiple of $\frac{a}{b}$ as a multiple of $\frac{1}{b}$, and use this understanding to multiply a fraction by a whole number. For example, use a visual fraction model to express $3 \times (\frac{2}{5})$ as $6 \times (\frac{1}{5})$, recognizing this product as $\frac{6}{5}$. (In general, $n \times (\frac{a}{b}) = \frac{(n \times a)}{b}$.)

c. Solve word problems involving multiplication of a fraction by a whole number, e.g., by using visual fraction models and equations to represent the problem. For example, if each person at a party will eat $\frac{3}{8}$ of a pound of roast beef, and there will be 5 people at the party, how many pounds of roast beef will be needed? Between what two whole numbers does your answer lie?

Decimal Concepts

CCSS.MATH.CONTENT.4.NF.C.5 – Express a fraction with denominator 10 as an equivalent fraction with denominator 100, and use this technique to add two fractions with respective denominators 10 and 100. For example, express $\frac{3}{10}$, as $\frac{30}{100}$, and add $\frac{3}{10} + \frac{4}{100} = \frac{34}{100}$.

CCSS.MATH.CONTENT.4.NF.C.6 – Use decimal notation for fractions with denominators 10 or 100. For example, rewrite 0.62 as $\frac{62}{100}$; describe a length as 0.62 meters; locate 0.62 on a number line diagram.

CCSS.MATH.CONTENT.4.NF.C.7 – Compare two decimals to hundredths by reasoning about their size. Recognize that comparisons are valid only when the two decimals refer to the same whole. Record the results of comparisons with the symbols >, =, or <, and justify the conclusions, e.g., by using a visual model.

Geometry Concepts

CCSS.MATH.CONTENT.4.G.A.1 – Draw points, lines, line segments, rays, angles (right, acute, obtuse), and perpendicular and parallel lines. Identify these in two-dimensional figures.

CCSS.MATH.CONTENT.4.G.A.2 – Classify two-dimensional figures based on the presence or absence of parallel or perpendicular lines, or the presence or absence of angles of a specified size. Recognize right triangles as a category, and identify right triangles.

CCSS.MATH.CONTENT.4.G.A.3 – Recognize a line of symmetry for a two-dimensional figure as a line across the figure such that the figure can be folded along the line into matching parts. Identify line-symmetric figures and draw lines of symmetry.

CCSS.MATH.CONTENT.4.MD.C.5 – Recognize angles as geometric shapes that are formed wherever two rays share a common endpoint, and understand concepts of angle measurement:

a. An angle is measured with reference to a circle with its center at the common endpoint of the rays, by considering the fraction of the circular arc between the points where the two rays intersect the circle. An angle that turns through $\frac{1}{360}$ of a circle is called a "one-degree angle," and can be used to measure angles.

b. An angle that turns through *n* one-degree angles is said to have an angle measure of *n* degrees.

CCSS.MATH.CONTENT.4.MD.C.6 – Measure angles in whole-number degrees using a protractor. Sketch angles of specified measure.

CCSS.MATH.CONTENT.4.MD.C.7 – Recognize angle measure as additive. When an angle is decomposed into non-overlapping parts, the angle measure of the whole is the sum of the angle measures of the parts. Solve addition and subtraction problems to find unknown angles on a diagram in real-world and mathematical problems, e.g., by using an equation with a symbol for the unknown angle measure.

Measurement Concepts

CCSS.MATH.CONTENT.4.MD.A.1 – Know relative sizes of measurement units within one system of units, including km, m, cm; kg, g; lb, oz.; l, ml; hr, min, sec. Within a single system of measurement, express measurements in a larger unit in terms of a smaller unit. Record measurement equivalents in a two-column table.

CCSS.MATH.CONTENT.4.MD.A.2 – Use the four operations to solve word problems involving distances, intervals of time, and money, including problems involving simple fractions or decimals. Represent fractional quantities of distance and intervals of time using linear models.

CCSS.MATH.CONTENT.4.MD.B.4 – Make a line plot to display a data set of measurements in fractions of a unit ($\frac{1}{2}$, $\frac{1}{4}$, $\frac{1}{8}$). Solve problems involving addition and subtraction of fractions by using information presented in line plots.

Making Sense of the Problem-Solving Process

For students: The eight mathematical practices outlined in the Common Core State Standards ask you to make sense of word problems, write word problems with numbers and symbols, and be able to prove when you are right as well as to know when a mistake happened. These eight practices also state that you may solve a problem by drawing a model, using a chart, list, or other tool. When you get your correct answer, you must be able to explain how and why you chose to solve it that way. Every word problem in this workbook addresses at least three of these practices, helping to prepare you for the demands of problem solving in your fourth grade classroom. The first unit of this book discusses the **Ace It Time!** section of each lesson. **Ace It Time!** will help you master these practices.

While Doing Mathematics You Will...

1. Make sense of problems and become a champion in solving them

- Solve problems and discuss how you solved them
- Look for a starting point and plan to solve the problem
- Make sense (meaning) of a problem and search for solutions
- Use concrete objects or pictures to solve problems
- Check over work by asking, "Does this make sense?"
- Plan out a problem-solving approach

2. Reason on concepts and understand that they are measurable

- Understand numbers represent specific quantities
- Connect quantities to written symbols
- Can take a word problem and represent it with numbers and symbols
- Know and use different properties of operations
- Connect addition and subtraction to length

3. Construct productive arguments and compare the reasoning of others

- Construct arguments using concrete objects, pictures, drawings, and actions
- Practice having conversations/discussions about math
- Explain your own thinking to others and respond to the thinking of others
- Ask questions to clarify the thinking of others (How did you get that answer? Why is that true?)
- Justify your answer and determine if the thinking of others is correct

4. Model with mathematics

- Determine ways to represent the problem mathematically
- Represent story problems in different ways; examples may include numbers, words, drawing pictures, using objects, acting out, making a chart or list, writing equations
- Make connections between the different representations and explain
- Evaluate your answers and think about whether or not they make sense

5. Use appropriate tools strategically

- Consider available tools when solving math problems
- Choose tools appropriately
- Determine when certain tools might be helpful
- Use technology to help with understanding

6. Attend to detail

- Develop math communication skills by using clear and exact language in your math conversations
- Understand meanings of symbols and label appropriately
- Calculate accurately

7. Look for and make use of structure

- Apply general math rules to specific situations
- Look for patterns or structure to help solve problems
- Adopt mental math strategies based on patterns such as making ten, fact families, and doubles

8. Look for and express regularity in repeated reasoning

- Notice repeated calculations and look for shortcut methods to solve problems (for example, rounding up and adjusting the answer to compensate for the rounding)
- Evaluate your own work by asking, "Does this make sense?"

Contents

CORE Problem-Solving Concepts

UNPACK THE STANDARD
You will make sense of word problems and use strategies to solve them.

LEARN IT: You are about to learn many different math strategies. This book will help you master multiplication, division, and fractions. Before starting, let's review some math tricks that work for all types of problems. You will use these tricks in the *Ace It Time!* section in each lesson.

STEP 1: UNDERSTAND

What's the Question?

Math problems can have many steps. Each of the steps is shown on the checklist.

The first step is to read the problem and ask yourself, "What question do I have to answer?" and "Will it take more than one step to solve the problem?"

When you find the question, underline it. Then check "Yes" on the checklist.

ACE IT TIME!

	yes	no
Did you underline the question in the word problem?		
Did you circle the numbers or number words?		
Did you box the supporting details or information needed to solve the problem?		
Did you draw a picture or a graphic organizer and write a math sentence to show your thinking?		
Did you label your numbers and your picture?		
Did you explain your thinking and use math vocabulary words in your explanation?		

PRACTICE: Underline the question.

Example: Mrs. Johnson is taking her fourth-grade class of 20 students and 3 adult chaperones to the aquarium. Admission for each student is $5. Admission for each adult is $7. What is the total cost for this field trip?

Will it take more than one step to solve the problem? **Yes**

STEP 2: IDENTIFY

What Numbers or Words Are Needed?

It is very important to locate the numbers you will use to solve the problem. When you find the numbers, circle them. Then check "Yes" on the checklist. *Hint:* Some problems might say "4" while others say "four."

PRACTICE: Circle the numbers you need to solve the problem.

Example: Mrs. Johnson is taking her fourth-grade class of 20 students and 3 adult chaperones to the aquarium. Admission for each student is $5. Admission for each adult is $7. What is the total cost for this field trip?

ACE IT TIME!

	yes	no
Did you underline the question in the word problem?		
Did you circle the numbers or number words?		
Did you box the supporting details or information needed to solve the problem?		
Did you draw a picture or a graphic organizer and write a math sentence to show your thinking?		
Did you label your numbers and your picture?		
Did you explain your thinking and use math vocabulary words in your explanation?		

STEP 3: RECOGNIZE THE SUPPORTING DETAILS

Name the Operation.

In every problem, there will be clues that help you figure out if you are adding, subtracting, multiplying, or dividing. Put a box around the clues. Then check "Yes" on the checklist.

Example: Mrs. Johnson is taking her fourth-grade class of 20 students and 3 adult chaperones to the aquarium. Admission for each student is $5. Admission for each adult is $7. What is the total cost for this field trip?

ACE IT TIME!

	yes	no
Did you underline the question in the word problem?		
Did you circle the numbers or number words?		
Did you box the supporting details or information needed to solve the problem?		
Did you draw a picture or a graphic organizer and write a math sentence to show your thinking?		
Did you label your numbers and your picture?		
Did you explain your thinking and use math vocabulary words in your explanation?		

When you have many groups of equal size, you use multiplication. The words "each student" and "each adult" are clues. When you need to combine amounts to find the total, you use addition. The words "total cost" are a clue.

STEPS 4–5: SOLVE AND LABEL

It is important to connect words in your problem to pictures and numbers. Before solving, you should draw a picture or write a math equation to solve the problem. Make sure to label your pictures and equations. Then check "Yes" on the checklist.

ACE IT TIME!

	yes	no
Did you underline the question in the word problem?	○	○
Did you circle the numbers or number words?	○	○
Did you box the supporting details or information needed to solve the problem?	○	○
Did you draw a picture or a graphic organizer and write a math sentence to show your thinking?	○	○
Did you label your numbers and your picture?	○	○
Did you explain your thinking and use math vocabulary words in your explanation?	○	○

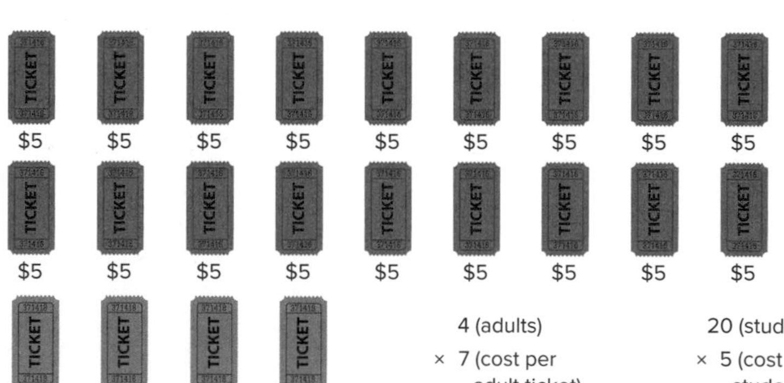

4 (adults)
× 7 (cost per adult ticket)
$28 (total cost of adult tickets)

\+

20 (students)
× 5 (cost per student ticket)
$100 (total cost of student tickets)

$28 + $100 = $128 total cost for the field trip

STEP 6: EXPLAIN

Write a Response. Use Math Vocabulary.

You are almost done! Explain your answer and show your thinking. Write in complete sentences to explain the steps you used to solve the problem. Use the vocabulary words in the Math Vocabulary box to help you!

Example: Mrs. Johnson is taking her fourth-grade class of 20 students and 3 adult chaperones to the aquarium. Admission for each student is $5. Admission for each adult is $7. What is the total cost for this field trip?

Explanation: First I drew tickets for 20 students, Mrs. Johnson, and the 3 chaperones. I knew each student cost $5 and each adult cost $7. I found the cost of the 20 students by multiplying 20 x 5 dollars, which equaled $100. Next, I had to find the cost of the 4 adults by multiplying 4 x 7 dollars, which equaled $28. To find the total cost of the field trip, I used addition. I added the $100 for the student tickets plus the $28 for the adult tickets, which equaled the total price of the field trip—$128.

ACE IT TIME!

	yes	no
Did you underline the question in the word problem?	◯	◯
Did you circle the numbers or number words?	◯	◯
Did you box the supporting details or information needed to solve the problem?	◯	◯
Did you draw a picture or a graphic organizer and write a math sentence to show your thinking?	◯	◯
Did you label your numbers and your picture?	◯	◯
Did you explain your thinking and use math vocabulary words in your explanation?	◯	◯

Math Vocabulary

- multiplying
- equaled
- sum
- addition
- total

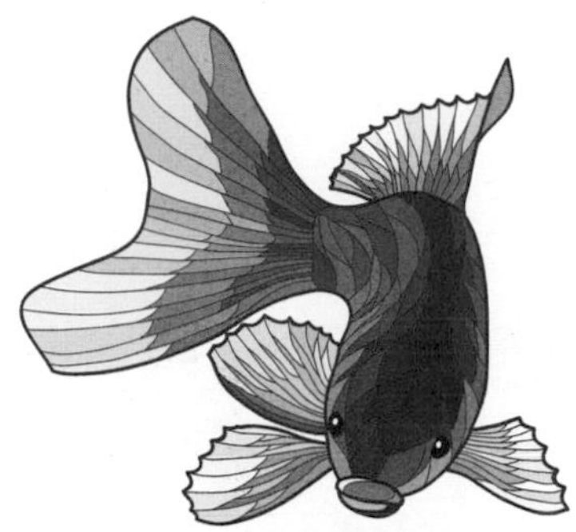

UNIT 2

CORE Number Concepts

Place Value Relationships

UNPACK THE STANDARD
You will understand that in multi-digit numbers, moving a digit one place to the left multiplies its value by 10.

LEARN IT: You count using the base-ten number system. ***Base-ten*** means that digits increase or decrease ten times in value when you move one place to the left or right. Digits to the left are higher in value. Digits to the right are lower in value.

Example: The value of 1,000 is _____ times as much as the value of 100.

Use blocks to follow the relationship between place and value.

Number	1,000	100	10	1
Model				
Name	cube	flat	long	block

One long has 10 blocks. A long is 10 times as much as a block.

One flat has 10 longs. A flat is 10 times as much as a long.

think!
What other patterns do you see in the blocks? How does the place of the 1 digit change from 10 to 1,000?

Use a place value chart.

Notice that as the positions move to the left, you are multiplying by 10.

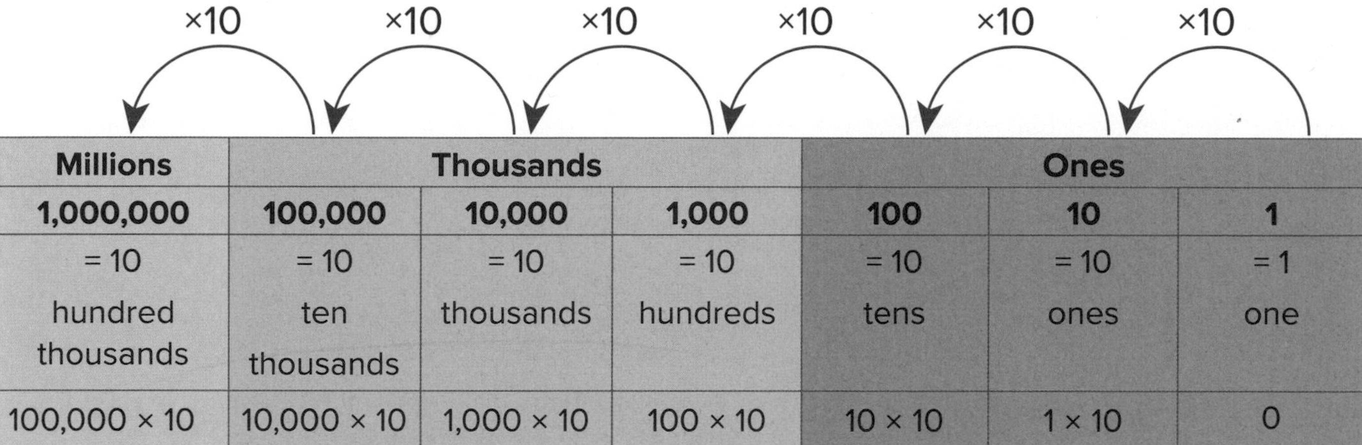

Millions	Thousands			Ones		
1,000,000	**100,000**	**10,000**	**1,000**	**100**	**10**	**1**
= 10 hundred thousands	= 10 ten thousands	= 10 thousands	= 10 hundreds	= 10 tens	= 10 ones	= 1 one
100,000 × 10	10,000 × 10	1,000 × 10	100 × 10	10 × 10	1 × 10	0

Let's compare the value of the 7 in 7,000 to the value of the 7 in **7**00 by writing the numbers in the place value chart.

Millions	Thousands			Ones		
1,000,000	**100,000**	**10,000**	**1,000**	**100**	**10**	**1**
			7	0	0	0
				7	0	0

Notice how the thousands place is one spot to the left of the hundreds place. This is the same as multiplying by 10 once (10 × 1 = 10). The value of the 7 in 7,000 is 10 times the value of the 7 in 700, because a thousand is 10 times the value of a hundred.

PRACTICE: Now you try

Write the value for the underlined digit in word and standard form.

Sample: 6,924 = 6,000 6 thousands	**1.** 3**2**8,591 = ______ ______	**2.** **7**46 = ______ ______	**3.** 9**8**7,522 = ______ ______
4. **3**56,276 = ______ ______	**5.** 2**9**7 = ______ ______	**6.** 59,34**1** = ______ ______	**7.** 22**5**,692 = ______ ______

PRACTICE: Now you try

Use the place value chart to help you solve.

1. Compare: **6**00 and **6**0 The value of 6 in 600 is ______ times the value of 6 in 60.	**2.** Compare: **3**,000 and **3**00 The value of 3 in 3,000 is ______ times the value of 3 in 300.	**3.** Compare: **5**00,000 and **5**0,000 The value of 5 in 500,000 is ______ times the value of 5 in 50,000.
4. Compare: **1**,000,000 and **1**00,000 The value of 1 in 1,000,000 is ______ times the value of 1 in 100,000.	**5.** Compare: **4**0 and **4** The value of 4 in 40 is ______ times the value of 4 in 4.	**6.** Compare: **2**0,000 and **2**,000 The value of 2 in 20,000 is ______ times the value of 2 in 2,000.

What if the digits are not right next to each other? Consider this problem.

Compare: **8**0,000 and **8**00 in the place value chart.

Millions	Thousands			Ones		
1,000,000	**100,000**	**10,000**	**1,000**	**100**	**10**	**1**
		8		0	0	0
				8	0	0

80,000 is 2 places to the left of 800, or 100 times the value. The value of the 8 in 80,000 is 100 times the value of the 8 in 800 because 10 times (thousands place) × 10 times (ten thousands place) = 100 times the value. The values continue to increase by multiples of 10.

Use the place value chart to compare **8**00,000 to **8**00. The value of the 8 in 800,000 is 1,000 times the value of the 8 in 800 because 10 times (ten thousands place) × 10 times (thousands place) × 10 times (hundreds place) = 1,000 times the value.

think!

800,000 is 3 places larger than 800, so we multiply by 10 three times!

PRACTICE: Now you try

Compare the value of the underlined digits:

1. 3,458 and 1,319	**2.** 86,792 and 4,561	**3.** 345,192 and 173,806
The value of 3 in **3**,458 is ______ times the value of 3 in 1,**3**19.	The value of 6 in 8**6**,792 is ______ times the value of 6 in 4,5**6**1.	The value of 3 in **3**45,192 is ______ times the value of 3 in 17**3**,806.

Sarah and Michelle want to know if the 5 in 3**5**6,798 is 10 times, 100 times, or 1,000 times larger than the 5 in 367,2**5**8. Sarah says it is 100 times larger. Michelle says it is 1,000 times larger. Who is correct—Sarah or Michelle? Show your work and explain your thinking on a piece of paper.

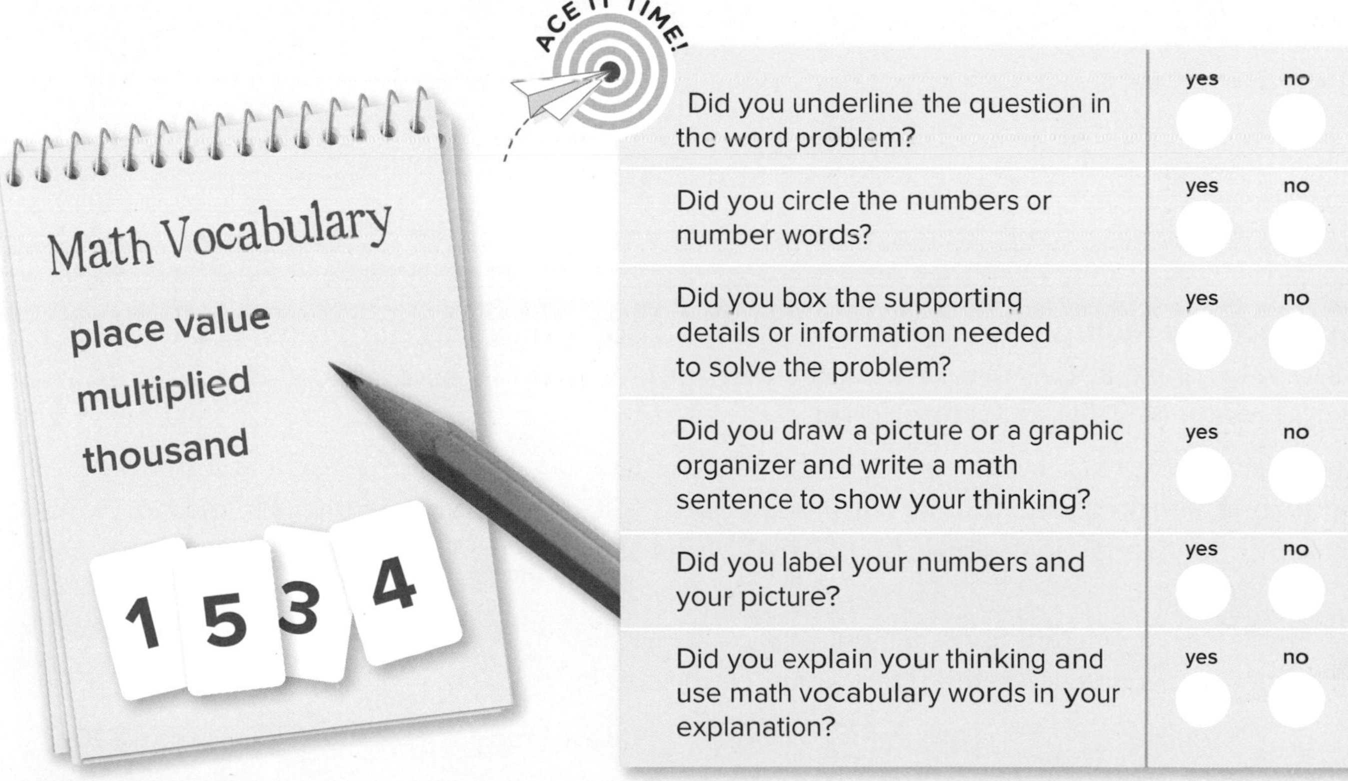

	yes	no
Did you underline the question in the word problem?		
Did you circle the numbers or number words?		
Did you box the supporting details or information needed to solve the problem?		
Did you draw a picture or a graphic organizer and write a math sentence to show your thinking?		
Did you label your numbers and your picture?		
Did you explain your thinking and use math vocabulary words in your explanation?		

MATH ON THE MOVE

How about a game of "Place Value War"? Using a deck of playing cards with the face cards and the tens removed, deal anywhere from four to seven cards to each player. Each player should then make the greatest number possible with the cards dealt. The player with the largest value wins the hand and receives 10 points. First player to reach 100 points wins!

Rename the Number

UNPACK THE STANDARD
You will rename numbers by creating equivalent values based on a number's place value.

LEARN IT: How would you rename the number 1,000 into only hundreds? Or only tens? You can use place value to rename numbers.

First way Use a place value chart: If you look at the digits in the thousands place (1) and the hundreds place (0), they make the number 10, or 10 hundreds = 1,000. If you look at the digits in the thousands place (1), the hundreds place (0), and the tens place (0), they make the number 100, or 100 tens = 1,000.

THOUSANDS			ONES		
Hundreds	Tens	Ones	Hundreds	Tens	Ones
1	0	0	0	0	0

one hundred thousands
10 ten thousands
100 thousands
1,000 hundreds
10,000 tens
100,000 ones

Second way Multiply: If you want to rename 1,000 using only hundreds, you could ask, "100 × _____ = 1,000?" You would count by one hundred 10 times to get to 1,000. So you could rename 1,000 as 10 hundreds.

To rename 1,000 using only tens, you could ask, "10 × _____ = 1,000?" You know that 10 tens equal one hundred, and that 10 hundreds equal 1,000. You would need to use enough tens to make 10 hundreds. So multiply 10 × 10 = 100 tens and rename 1,000 as 100 tens.

PRACTICE: Now you try

Rename the number. Use the place value chart to help.

Number	How many 1,000s?	How many 100s?	How many 10s?
Sample: 26,000	26	260	2,600
1. 74,000			
2. 890,000			
3. 93,000			
4. 307,000			
5. 650,000			

PRACTICE: Now you try

Rename the number.

Sample: 430,000 = 43 ten thousands	**1.** 82 hundreds = ___________
2. 129,000 = ___________ hundreds	**3.** 64 ten thousands = ___________
4. 780,000 = ___________ ten thousands	**5.** 1,578 tens = ___________
6. 120,000 = ___________ ones	**7.** 765 thousands = ___________

A video game store wants to order 2,000 copies of the latest video game. The store can order the game in sets of 10. How many sets of 10 does the video game store need to order? Show your work and explain your thinking on a piece of paper.

ACE IT TIME!

	yes	no
Did you underline the question in the word problem?	yes	no
Did you circle the numbers or number words?	yes	no
Did you box the supporting details or information needed to solve the problem?	yes	no
Did you draw a picture or a graphic organizer and write a math sentence to show your thinking?	yes	no
Did you label your numbers and your picture?	yes	no
Did you explain your thinking and use math vocabulary words in your explanation?	yes	no

Multiply the date of the month by 10, 100, or 1,000. Now make the product different ways. For example, on the 23rd day of the month, multiply 23 x 10 = 230. What are some different ways you could make 230? Try using 230 ones, 23 tens, or 2 hundreds and 3 tens. You could even extend the concept by making it with 23,000 pennies or 2,300 dimes.

Expanded and Word Form

UNPACK THE STANDARD
You will read and write numbers up to 1,000,000.

LEARN IT: You can use what you know about place value and expanded form to read and write numbers up to 1,000,000. Using a place value chart helps you to recognize the value of each digit in a number.

THOUSANDS				ONES		
Hundreds	Tens	Ones		Hundreds	Tens	Ones
5	2	4	,	6	1	4

There are three ways to represent a number: standard form, expanded form, and word form.

Standard form is a way to write numbers using digits 0–9. For example: **524,614**

Expanded form is a way to write numbers as the sum of each digit's value. For example:

The value of the 5 is 5 × 100,000 = **500,000**
The value of the 2 is 2 × 10,000 = **20,000**
The value of the 4 is 4 × 1,000 = **4,000**
The value of the 6 is 6 × 100 = **600**
The value of the 1 is 1 × 10 = **10**
The value of the 4 is 4 × 1 = **4**

So the expanded form of this number is: **500,000** + **20,000** + **4,000** + **600** + **10** + **4**

Word form is a way to write numbers using words. For example, five hundred twenty-four thousand, six hundred fourteen is the word form of 524,614. Note the hyphen that appears in "twenty-four." Remember to hyphenate two-digit numerals like this to avoid confusion.

PRACTICE: Now you try

Write the standard form for each number.

Sample: one thousand, six hundred forty-one Standard form 1,641	**1.** 200,000 + 30,000 + 7,000 + 10 Standard form ________	**2.** five hundred nineteen thousand, one hundred sixteen Standard form ________

Write the word form and expanded form for each number.

3. 3,807	**4.** 40,616	**5.** 924	**6.** 123,456

PRACTICE: Now you try

Match each number form in column A to its matching form in column B.

Column A	Column B
_______ **1.** 367,218	**A.** 400,965
_______ **2.** Two thousand, sixteen	**B.** 20,000 + 4,000 + 100 + 70 + 3
_______ **3.** 116,789	**C.** 14,473
_______ **4.** Six hundred thousand, two	**D.** Three hundred sixty-seven thousand, two hundred eighteen
_______ **5.** 10,000 + 4,000 + 400 + 70 + 3	**E.** 2,016
_______ **6.** 24,173	**F.** 600,002
_______ **7.** Four hundred thousand, nine hundred sixty-five	**G.** One hundred sixteen thousand, seven hundred eighty-nine

Students in Mr. Owen's classroom are working on writing numbers in expanded form. Kathryn says the expanded form of 507,840 is 500,000 + 70,000 + 8,000 + 4. What has Kathryn done wrong? Correct her answer. Show your work and explain your thinking on a piece of paper.

ACE IT TIME!

	yes	no
Did you underline the question in the word problem?		
Did you circle the numbers or number words?		
Did you box the supporting details or information needed to solve the problem?		
Did you draw a picture or a graphic organizer and write a math sentence to show your thinking?		
Did you label your numbers and your picture?		
Did you explain your thinking and use math vocabulary words in your explanation?		

Math Vocabulary

expanded form

standard form

word form

Creating place value charts can be time consuming. To save time, draw lines to separate the digits and use initials like "HT" for hundred thousand, "TT" for ten thousand, "TH" for thousand, "H" for hundreds, "T" for tens, and "O" for ones. The initials are meant to remind you which numbers are in which place, helping you to understand both expanded and word forms of numbers.

Compare and Order Numbers to 1,000,000

UNPACK THE STANDARD
You will compare and order numbers up to 1,000,000.

LEARN IT: ***Comparing and ordering numbers*** **involves comparing the value of each digit in order to see which is greater than (>), less than (<), and/or equal to (=) another digit. Place value charts can help you line up the digits by place value—ones, tens, hundreds, etc.**

Example: Compare the numbers 734,286 and 724,351.

Place the numbers into a place value chart. Make sure each digit is lined up in the correct place value: ones with ones, tens with tens, etc.

THOUSANDS		
Hundreds	Tens	Ones
7	3	4
7	2	4

ONES		
Hundreds	Tens	Ones
2	8	6
3	5	1

Beginning with the column furthest to the left, compare digits in each column until the digits are different.

734,286
724,351

700,000 = 700,000

7**3**4,286
7**2**4,351

30,000 > 20,000

So 734,286 > 724,351

Do you sometimes confuse the symbols for greater than and less than? Here's a little trick to keep them straight:

7**3**4,286 ⋮> 7**2**4,351

Think, "3 is bigger than 2," so put 2 dots next to 734,286 (because 2 is bigger than 1) and 1 dot next to 724,351. Then draw lines to connect like the picture shown above. Notice that the symbol is "open" to the greater number.

But what if the numbers were reversed? Follow the same rules, and now you've drawn a "less than" symbol! Notice that the symbol is still "open" to the greater number.

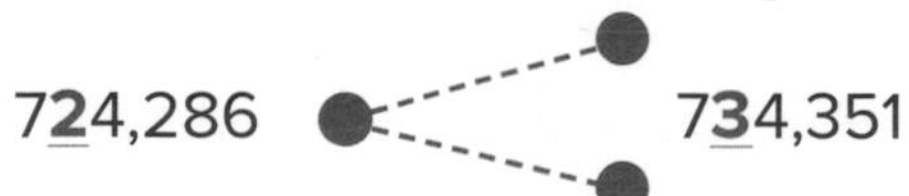

PRACTICE: Now you try Compare. Write >, <, or =.

1. 524,134  524,296	**2.** 78,437  79,645	**3.** 398,132  398,131

Order the numbers from greatest to least.

4. 45,761; 44,766; 43,765	**5.** 135,976; 142,894; 139,654	**6.** 796,538; 796,531; 796,539
_____, _____, _____	_____, _____, _____	_____, _____, _____

Order the numbers from least to greatest.

7. 26,750; 21,736; 23,798	**8.** 253,901; 253,904; 253,900	**9.** 521,755; 529,745; 524,763
_____, _____, _____	_____, _____, _____	_____, _____, _____

Micah is researching the number of seats in professional football stadiums. He wants to list the four NFL stadiums in order from smallest to largest. Micah lists the stadiums in this order: Sun Life Stadium, Arrowhead Stadium, Mile High Stadium, Superdome. Is Micah correct? Show your work and explain your thinking on a piece of paper.

Football Stadiums	Number of Seats
Mile High Stadium	76,125
Arrowhead Stadium	76,416
Sun Life Stadium	75,192
Superdome	76,468

ACE IT TIME!

	yes	no
Did you underline the question in the word problem?		
Did you circle the numbers or number words?		
Did you box the supporting details or information needed to solve the problem?		
Did you draw a picture or a graphic organizer and write a math sentence to show your thinking?		
Did you label your numbers and your picture?		
Did you explain your thinking and use math vocabulary words in your explanation?		

Use a deck of playing cards, but first remove the face cards and the tens cards. Play a game of "Greater Than" by dealing each player a certain number of cards: 4, 5, or 6 cards. Each player arranges his or her cards to make the greatest number possible and then lays the cards down. The player with the number "greater than" the other players' numbers wins the hand and all the cards. The game continues until one person has won all the cards—that player is the winner!

Rounding Multi-Digit Numbers

UNPACK THE STANDARD
You will round multi-digit whole numbers to any place through 1,000,000.

LEARN IT: You know how to read, write, and compare numbers up to 1,000,000. But how can you round a whole number up to 1,000,000? You can use what you know about rounding! The same rules apply for these larger numbers.

Example: Round 423,659 to the nearest ten thousand.

think!
When counting, first you pass 20,000. Then you count to 30,000. These are the closest ten thousands.

Rounding with Number Lines

Identify the digit in the ten thousands place. Circle it. 423,659

Which two ten thousands are closest to 423,659? Draw them on a number line. You can see that this number is between 420,000 and 430,000

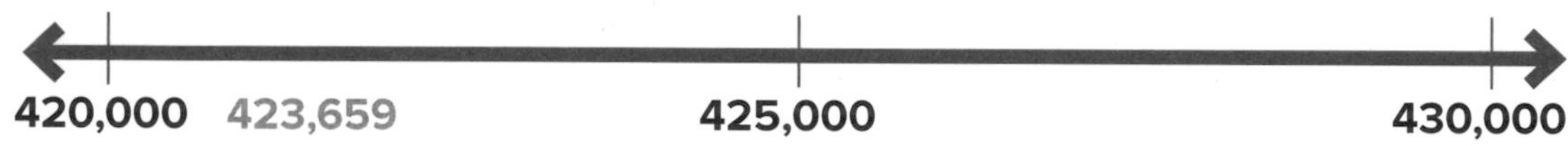

Look at 423,659. Is it closer to 420,000 or 430,000? Is 423,659 before 425,000 or after? It is before 425,000 and will round to 420,000.

Wait! What if you are rounding 425,000? You add 5,000 to get from 420,000 to 425,000. You add the same amount to get from 425,000 to 430,000. When you are rounding and the number is the midpoint, you round up to the *next* place value. So you round up to 430,000.

Rounding with a Shortcut

think!
5 and above—give it a shove! 4 and below—let it go!

You don't have to draw a number line to round. Look at the number 423,659:

4 2 3, 6 5 9

Find the digit in the ten thousands place and underline it. Now look at the digit to its right and circle it. If the digit is less than 5, round down. If it is 5 or more, round up.

Caution: You must include all of the digits to the left of the rounded place. After rounding a number, look at the original number and ask yourself if your rounded answer makes sense. For example, does 423,659 round to only 20,000? No, it rounds to 420,000.

PRACTICE: Now you try Round to the place value of the underlined digit.

1. Round 2<u>2</u>,145 = ________	**2.** Round <u>6</u>48,159 = ________	**3.** Round <u>3</u>8,614 = ________

Underline the place value in the number you want to round. Round each number to the place indicated.

4. 562,408 to the nearest thousand ____________	**5.** 12,890 to the nearest ten thousand ____________	**6.** 414,792 to the nearest hundred thousand ____________

Mrs. Peterson challenges her students to discover a range of numbers that, when rounded to the nearest hundred thousand, round to 600,000. Which student suggests the correct range of numbers? Show your work and explain your thinking on a piece of paper.

Joshua: 549,000 to 649,000
Jillian: 551,000 to 651,000
Marcus: 540,000 to 640,000
Mariah: 550,000 to 649,000

ACE IT TIME!

	yes	no
Did you underline the question in the word problem?	◯	◯
Did you circle the numbers or number words?	◯	◯
Did you box the supporting details or information needed to solve the problem?	◯	◯
Did you draw a picture or a graphic organizer and write a math sentence to show your thinking?	◯	◯
Did you label your numbers and your picture?	◯	◯
Did you explain your thinking and use math vocabulary words in your explanation?	◯	◯

Math Vocabulary

greater than
less than
number line

Ask an adult or friend to play a game. You will need a single die, 5 index cards, and a deck of playing cards with all face cards removed. On the 5 index cards, write the following rounding rules:

- Round to nearest 10
- Round to nearest 100
- Round to nearest 1,000
- Round to nearest 10,000
- Round to nearest 100,000

Shuffle and place the index cards face down. Draw a rounding rule card. Roll the die; the number rolled is the number of cards the player should draw from the deck. The player should rearrange his or her cards to round to the highest number possible. The player who makes the highest rounded number wins. Repeat until one player has won all cards possible.

Addition and Subtraction of Multi-Digit Numbers

UNPACK THE STANDARD
You will add and subtract numbers up to 1,000,000 using the standard method.

LEARN IT: When you add and subtract numbers write the numbers vertically. Line up each number by place value. Solve from right to left.

Place Value Strategy			Place Value Strategy		
Add the ones, then the tens, then the hundreds, thousands, etc.			Subtract the ones, then the tens, then the hundreds, thousands, etc.		
think! Since 6 + 5 = 11, that means there is 1 ten and 1 one. Why do we carry the ten to the next column?			**think!** When you borrow from the hundreds place, you are borrowing a whole hundred (100).		
1 623,466 + 82,615 81	1 1 623,466 + 82,615 6,081	1 1 1 623,466 + 82,615 706,081	4 16 47,567 – 34,285 82	4 16 47,567 – 34,285 3,282	4 16 47,567 – 34,285 13,282
Add the ones. Regroup. Add the tens.	Add the hundreds. Regroup. Add the thousands.	Add the ten-thousands. Regroup. Add the hundred-thousands.	Subtract the ones. Regroup to subtract the tens.	Subtract the hundreds. Subtract the thousands.	Subtract the ten-thousands.

PRACTICE: Now you try

Solve.

1. 583,201 + 327,218	**2.** 190,264 + 135,706	**3.** 71,920 + 6,773	**4.** 19,046 + 71,277
5. 416,317 + 152,748	**6.** 231,409 + 619,852	**7.** 54,255 + 3,280	**8.** 64,251 + 93,538
9. 456,912 – 37,500	**10.** 404,004 – 154,652	**11.** 11,659 – 10,583	**12.** 23,000 – 10,310

13. 798,980 − 248,659	**14.** 144,416 − 113,244	**15.** 23,148 − 9,164	**16.** 53,000 − 20,202

Find the missing digit:

17. 6,532 − 4,1□5 = 2,407	**18.** 247,219 + 364,□87 = 612,206	**19.** □08,665 − 659,420 = 149,245	**20.** 23,□67 + 46,859 = 70,426

Sharon wants to ride her bike to the library, which is 26,987 feet from her home. She rides 9,328 feet to meet her friend Maria. The girls then ride 8,629 more feet and stop at a park. How many more feet does Sharon have left to travel to get to the library? Show your work and explain your thinking on a piece of paper.

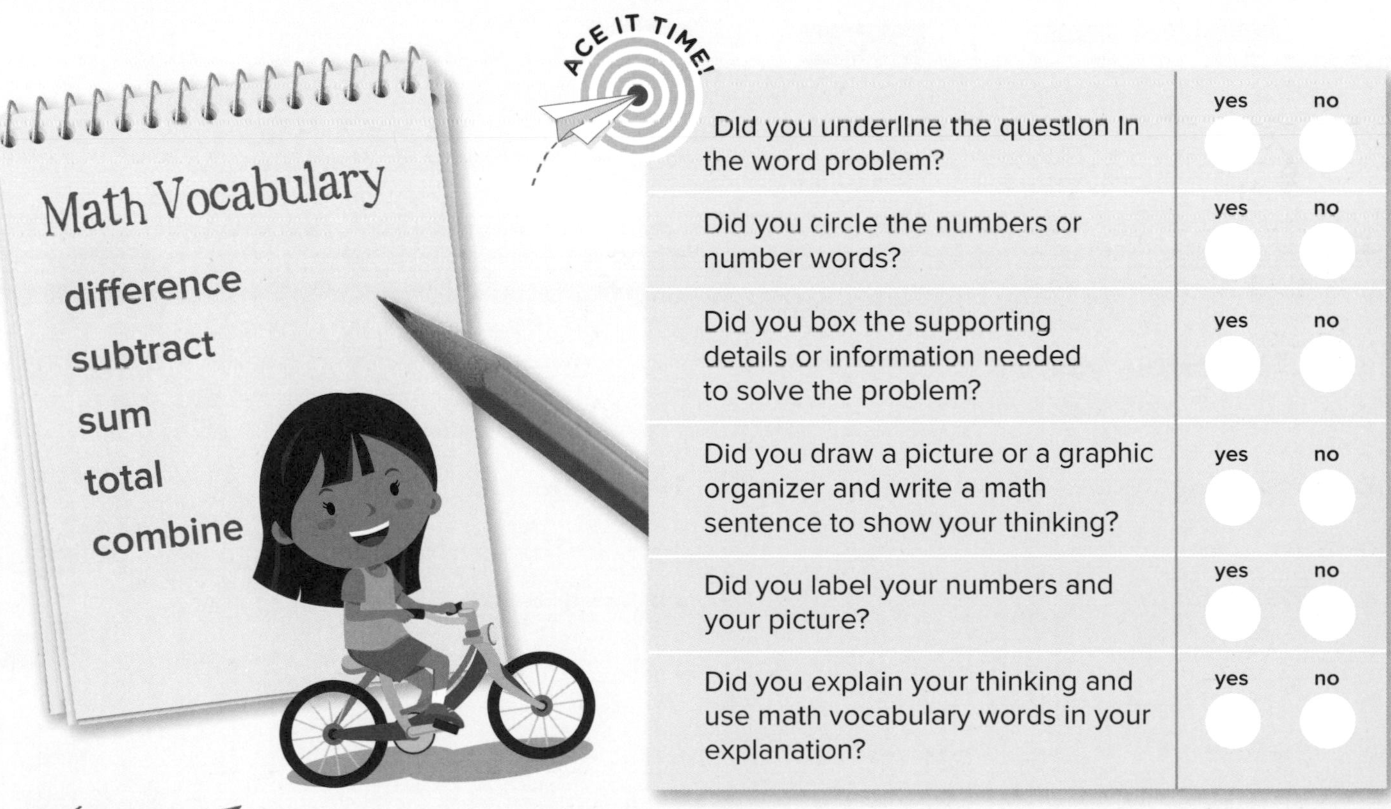

	yes	no
Did you underline the question in the word problem?	◯	◯
Did you circle the numbers or number words?	◯	◯
Did you box the supporting details or information needed to solve the problem?	◯	◯
Did you draw a picture or a graphic organizer and write a math sentence to show your thinking?	◯	◯
Did you label your numbers and your picture?	◯	◯
Did you explain your thinking and use math vocabulary words in your explanation?	◯	◯

MATH ON THE MOVE

Find advertisements in a newspaper or in the mail and calculate the total if you bought several of the items. Think of a dollar amount you would use to pay the bill and calculate how much change you would receive.

UNIT 3

CORE Factor and Divisibility Concepts

Factors

UNPACK THE STANDARD
You will find factor pairs for a whole number in the range 1–100.

LEARN IT: A ***factor*** is a number multiplied by another number to find a product. Numbers can be broken into factors in different ways. Every whole number greater than 1 has at least two factors: that number and 1.

Example: Model and record the factors of 12. Arrays are helpful:

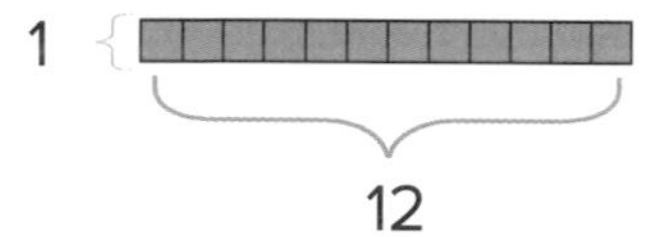

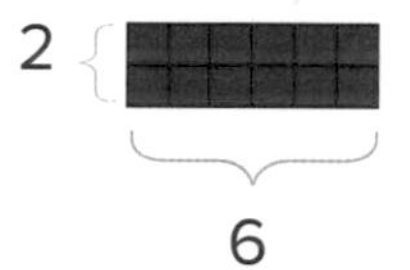

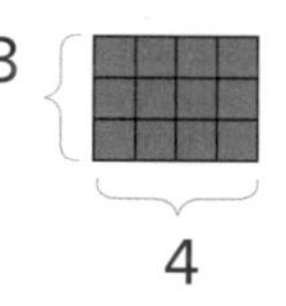

$1 \times 12 = 12$ $2 \times 6 = 12$ $3 \times 4 = 12$

think!
What numbers can I multiply together to equal each number in this section? Remember that 1 and the number always work.

The factor pairs of 12 are: 1 and 12; 2 and 6; and 3 and 4.

List the factors in order from least to greatest: 1, 2, 3, 4, 6, 12

PRACTICE: Now you try

Find all the factor pairs.

1. **10** has 4 factors. ____, ____, ____, ____	**2.** **14** has 4 factors. ____, ____, ____, ____
3. **9** has 3 factors. ____, ____, ____	**4.** **25** has 3 factors. ____, ____, ____
5. **16** has 5 factors. ____, ____, ____, ____, ____	**6.** **21** has 4 factors. ____, ____, ____, ____
7. **6** has 4 factors. ____, ____, ____, ____	**8.** **49** has 3 factors. ____, ____, ____
9. **24** has 8 factors. ____, ____, ____, ____, ____, ____, ____, ____	**10.** **18** has 6 factors. ____, ____, ____, ____, ____, ____

Allison believes that a larger number will always have more factors than a smaller number. She decides to test her idea by making a list of all factors for the numbers 30, 33, 36, and 39. Is Allison correct? Does the largest number have the most factors? Show your work and explain your thinking on a piece of paper.

ACE IT TIME!

Did you underline the question in the word problem?	yes	no
Did you circle the numbers or number words?	yes	no
Did you box the supporting details or information needed to solve the problem?	yes	no
Did you draw a picture or a graphic organizer and write a math sentence to show your thinking?	yes	no
Did you label your numbers and your picture?	yes	no
Did you explain your thinking and use math vocabulary words in your explanation?	yes	no

MATH ON THE MOVE

Counting money is a common way we use factors without realizing it. For example, four quarters make a dollar. Two factors of 100 are 4 and 25. A twenty-dollar bill can be exchanged for twenty one-dollar bills (factors 1 and 20), two ten-dollar bills (factors 2 and 10) or four five-dollar bills (factors 4 and 5).

Multiples

UNPACK THE STANDARD
You will determine multiples of a given number.

LEARN IT: The product of a number and a counting number (like 1, 2, 3, 4, etc.) is called a ***multiple*** of the number.

Example:

$$\begin{array}{r}5\\ \times 1\\ \hline 5\end{array}\quad \begin{array}{r}5\\ \times 2\\ \hline 10\end{array}\quad \begin{array}{r}5\\ \times 3\\ \hline 15\end{array}\quad \begin{array}{r}5\\ \times 4\\ \hline 20\end{array}$$

← counting number
← multiples of 5

A multiple of two or more numbers is a **common multiple**.

PRACTICE: Now you try

List the next 5 multiples of each number. Find the common multiples.

Multiples of 2: 2, (4), 6, (8), 10, (12)

Multiples of 4: (4), (8), (12), 16, 20

Common multiples: 4, 8, 12

1. Multiples of 5: 5, ____, ____, ____, ____, ____

Multiples of 10: 10, ____, ____, ____, ____, ____

Common multiples: ____, ____, ____

2. Multiples of 3: 3, ____, ____, ____, ____, ____

Multiples of 9: 9, ____, ____, ____, ____, ____

Common multiples: ____, ____

3. Multiples of 4: 4, ____, ____, ____, ____, ____

Multiples of 6: 6, ____, ____, ____, ____, ____

Common multiples: ____, ____

PRACTICE: Now you try

Is the given number a multiple? Write *yes* or *no*.

Number	Is this a multiple of the number?	Is this a multiple of the number?	Is this a multiple of the number?
Sample: 9	3 – no	18 – yes	45 – yes
1. 5	16 – _____	20 – _____	23 – _____
2. 6	18 – _____	36 – _____	52 – _____
3. 3	15 – _____	23 – _____	30 – _____
4. 12	22 – _____	48 – _____	60 – _____

Hot dogs come in packages of 6. Hot dog buns come in packages of 8. Randi wants to buy the same number of hot dogs and hot dog buns. How many packages of hot dogs should he buy if he has three packages of hot dog buns? Show your work and explain your thinking on a piece of paper.

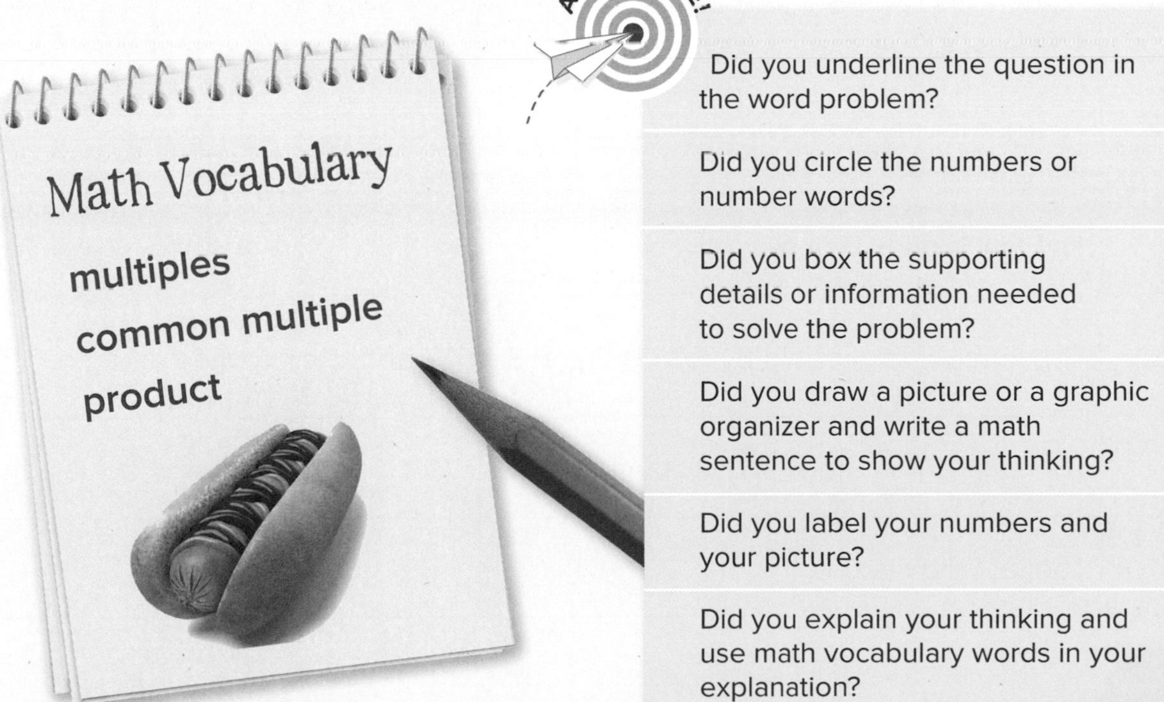

	yes	no
Did you underline the question in the word problem?	◯	◯
Did you circle the numbers or number words?	◯	◯
Did you box the supporting details or information needed to solve the problem?	◯	◯
Did you draw a picture or a graphic organizer and write a math sentence to show your thinking?	◯	◯
Did you label your numbers and your picture?	◯	◯
Did you explain your thinking and use math vocabulary words in your explanation?	◯	◯

MATH ON THE MOVE

Find a place in your neighborhood, home, or school where you can find multiples to count by. For example, to count the number of eyes you see on people passing by, count the multiples of 2. To count the number of wheels you see on cars, count the multiples of 4. What other things can you count by multiples?

Divisibility Rules

UNPACK THE STANDARD
You will use divisibility rules to help determine factors for larger numbers.

LEARN IT: A number is ***divisible*** by another number if the quotient is a counting number and the remainder is 0. In other words, it can be divided evenly by that number. Some numbers have a divisibility rule you can use to tell whether one number is a factor of another. These rules can help you more easily determine factors for larger numbers.

Divisibility Rules		
Divisible by	**If**	**Examples**
2	The last digit is even (0, 2, 4, 6, 8).	120, 122, 124, 126, 128
3	The sum of the digits is divisible by 3.	72: (7 + 2 = 9 and 9 ÷ 3 = 3)
4	The number is even and the last two digits are divisible by 4.	312 (12 ÷ 4 = 3)
5	The last digit is 0 or 5.	170 and 175
6	The number is divisible by **BOTH** 2 and 3.	48 (it is an even number, and the sum of the digits is divisible by 3)
9	The sum of the digits is divisible by 9.	108 (1 + 0 + 8 = 9 and 9 ÷ 9 = 1)
10	The last digit is 0.	150

PRACTICE: Now you try

Is the given number divisible by each factor? Write *yes* or *no* and show your work.

Number	Is this divisible by?	Is this divisible by?	Is this divisible by?
Sample: 27	3: yes 2 + 7 = 9 and 9 ÷ 3 = 3	5: no 27 does not end in 0 or 5	9: yes 2 + 7 = 9 and 9 ÷ 9 = 1
1. 30	10: ______	2: ______	6: ______

Cody has 20 pencils, 25 erasers, and 40 sheets of paper. He organizes them into groups with the same number of items in each group. How many items does Cody have in each group—4, 5, 8, or 10? Show your work and explain your thinking on a piece of paper.

ACE IT TIME!

	yes	no
Did you underline the question in the word problem?		
Did you circle the numbers or number words?		
Did you box the supporting details or information needed to solve the problem?		
Did you draw a picture or a graphic organizer and write a math sentence to show your thinking?		
Did you label your numbers and your picture?		
Did you explain your thinking and use math vocabulary words in your explanation?		

MATH ON THE MOVE

Design your own divisibility chart to help master these rules. Practice using the chart so you are able to quickly identify all factors a number may be divisible by.

Prime and Composite Numbers

UNPACK THE STANDARD
You will tell whether a number is prime or composite.

LEARN IT: You can use the divisibility rules from the previous lesson to help tell if a number is prime or composite. If the number has only two factors, 1 and itself, the number is ***prime***. If a number has more than two factors, the number is ***composite***.

Example: Is 27 prime or composite?

Is 27 divisible by 2? **No**

Is 27 divisible by 3? **Yes**

think!
So is 27 divisible by a number other than 1 and 27? Yes, it is divisible by 3 and 9. It has more than two factors, which makes 27 a composite number.

PRACTICE: Now you try

Tell whether the number is prime or composite.

Sample: 12 — 1 × 12, 2 × 6, 3 × 4 — composite	**Sample:** 7 — 1 × 7 — prime	**1.** 9 ______	**2.** 20 ______
3. 51 ______	**4.** 25 ______	**5.** 10 ______	**6.** 76 ______
7. 89 ______	**8.** 33 ______	**9.** 42 ______	**10.** 29 ______
11. 73 ______	**12.** 24 ______	**13.** 17 ______	**14.** 36 ______

PRACTICE: Now you try

Read each statement and think about what it means. Write *true* or *false* and give an example to support your answer.

1. All odd numbers are prime numbers.	**2.** Every composite number is an even number.
3. The number 1 is neither prime nor composite.	**4.** The number 2 is the only even number that is prime.

I am a number between 10 and 50. My ones digit is 3 more than my tens digit. I am a prime number. What number am I? Show your work and explain your thinking on a piece of paper.

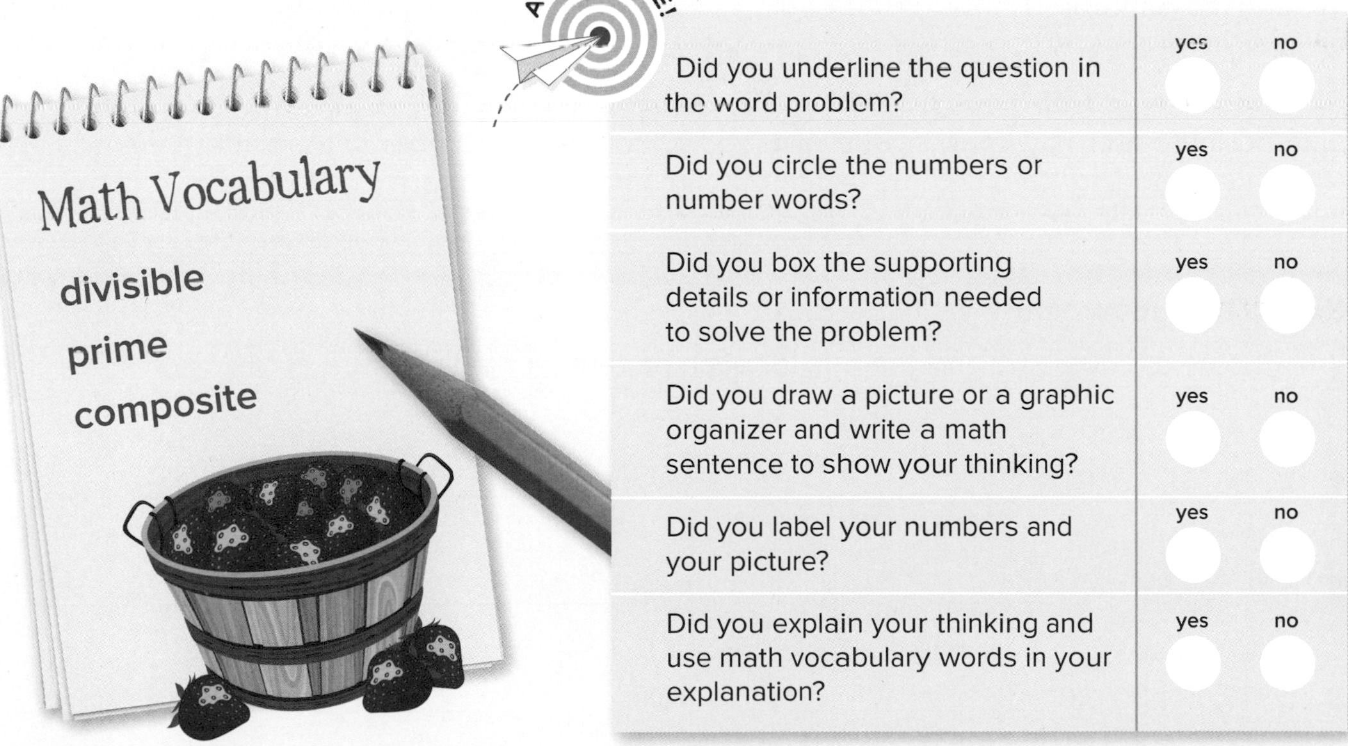

	yes	no
Did you underline the question in the word problem?		
Did you circle the numbers or number words?		
Did you box the supporting details or information needed to solve the problem?		
Did you draw a picture or a graphic organizer and write a math sentence to show your thinking?		
Did you label your numbers and your picture?		
Did you explain your thinking and use math vocabulary words in your explanation?		

MATH ON THE MOVE

Practice counting by prime numbers. See if you can count the first ten prime numbers. Can you count higher than that? Knowing these prime numbers will help you when it's time to reduce fractions to lowest terms.

Number Patterns

UNPACK THE STANDARD
You will make and describe number patterns.

LEARN IT: Let's look at number patterns. Every number pattern has a rule. A rule tells us what to do to each number to get the next number in the pattern. It includes both an operation and a number.

+ 10 + 10 + 10 + 10

Example: 13, 23, 33, 43, 53, _____, _____, _____

think!
How did 13 increase to 23 and 23 increase to 33, to 43, to 53? It increased by the same interval each time.

Every number pattern has a rule. The rule tells you how to solve the problem. Can you find the rule for this pattern?

The **rule** includes both the operation and a number interval that makes the pattern.

Rule: 13 + 10 = **23**; 23 + 10 = **33**; 33 + 10 = **43**; 43 + 10 = **53**

The rule is to add 10! If you add 10 to one number in the pattern, you get the next number. Extend the pattern by applying the rule (add 10) to the last number in the pattern. Then keep adding 10 to find the last three numbers of the pattern.

53 + 10 = 63; 63 + 10 = 73; 73 + 10 = 83

PRACTICE: Now you try

Write the next 3 numbers and the rule for each pattern.

1. 71, 66, 61, 56, 51, _____, _____, _____ Rule: ____________________

2. 4, 8, 16, 32, 64, _____, _____, _____ Rule: ____________________

3. 12, 18, 24, 30, 36, _____, _____, _____ Rule: ____________________

4. 100, 90, 80, 70, 60, _____, _____, _____ Rule: ____________________

Wait! What if there are two operations in a rule? Just follow the rule beginning at the first number. For example, Rule: Add 4, subtract 1: First number: 5.

5 (+ 4 = 9 – 1) **8** (+ 4 = 12 – 1) **11** (+ 4 = 15 – 1) **14** (+ 4 = 18 – 1) **17: 5, 8, 11, 14**

PRACTICE: Now you try

Use the rule to write the first 8 numbers in the pattern.

1. Rule: Subtract 2, add 3	First number: 4
2. Rule: Add 5, subtract 1	First number: 15
3. Rule: Multiply by 2, subtract 1	First number: 2

On average, a local art studio adds 4 new sculptures a day and sells 2 sculptures a day. The art studio currently has 50 sculptures in stock. If the pattern continues for the next 7 days, how many sculptures will be in stock on day 7? Show your work and explain your thinking on a piece of paper.

ACE IT TIME!

	yes	no
Did you underline the question in the word problem?		
Did you circle the numbers or number words?		
Did you box the supporting details or information needed to solve the problem?		
Did you draw a picture or a graphic organizer and write a math sentence to show your thinking?		
Did you label your numbers and your picture?		
Did you explain your thinking and use math vocabulary words in your explanation?		

MATH ON THE MOVE

Make a pattern of numbers and show it to an adult helper. Can this person determine the rule you used to make the pattern? Can he or she add the next number to the pattern? Switch roles. Let your adult helper create a pattern of numbers for you to solve and extend.

REVIEW

Stop and think about what you have learned.

Congratulations! You have finished the lessons for units 2–3. This means you have learned about the value of each place in a number and how it increases. You have practiced renaming, comparing, and rounding numbers through one million. You have noticed the difference between factors and multiples. You can even add and subtract numbers and regroup when necessary.

Now it is time to prove your skills. Solve the problems that follow. Use all of the methods you have learned.

Activity Section 1: Number Concepts

Compare the value of the underlined digits.

1. <u>5</u>,458 and 1,<u>5</u>19	**2.** 7<u>3</u>,792 and 2,1<u>3</u>1	**3.** <u>2</u>45,192 and 37<u>2</u>,806
The value of 5 in **<u>5</u>**,458 is ______ times the value of 5 in 1,**<u>5</u>**19.	The value of 3 in 7**<u>3</u>**,792 is ______ times the value of 3 in 2,1**<u>3</u>**1.	The value of 2 in **<u>2</u>**45,192 is ______ times the value of 2 in 37**<u>2</u>**,806.

Rename the number.

Sample: 73 tens = <u>730</u> (sample)	**4.** 125 thousands = ____________
5. 31 hundreds = ____________	**6.** 719 tens = ____________
7. 12 ten thousands = ____________	**8.** 92 hundreds = ____________

Write each number in two other forms.

9. one thousand, six hundred forty-one	**10.** 200,000 + 30,000 + 7,000 + 10	**11.** 467,028
Standard form ____________	Word form ____________	Expanded form ____________
Expanded form ____________	Standard form ____________	Word form ____________

Compare. Write >, <, or =.

12. 182,134 ◯ 182,130	13. 21,749 ◯ 21,794	14. 437,297 ◯ 437,297

Activity Section 2: Factor and Divisibility Concepts

Find all the factor pairs.

1. **35** has 4 factors. ___, ___, ___, ___	2. **8** has 4 factors. ___, ___, ___, ___
3. **12** has 6 factors. ___, ___, ___, ___, ___, ___	4. **28** has 6 factors. ___, ___, ___, ___, ___, ___

Is the given number divisible by each factor? Write *yes* or *no*.

Number	Is this divisible by?	Is this divisible by?	Is this divisible by?
5. 36	3: _____	5: _____	9: _____
6. 50	10: _____	2: _____	6: _____

Tell whether the number is prime or composite.

7. 43	8. 9	9. 56	10. 35
________	________	________	________

Activity Section 3: Addition and Subtraction

Solve. Remember to watch your signs!

1.	2.	3.	4.
383,429 + 152,748	111,243 + 628,127	21,896 – 20,734	502,701 – 41,526

Understand the meaning of what you have learned and apply your knowledge.

You will use place value understanding to round multi-digit whole numbers to any place.

Activity Section

Write at least 10 numbers that will round to 700,000. These numbers should NOT repeat any digits. Show your math thinking.

1. ______________	**2.** ______________
3. ______________	**4.** ______________
5. ______________	**6.** ______________
7. ______________	**8.** ______________
9. ______________	**10.** ______________
Without repeating a digit, what is the smallest number you can make that will round to 700,000? ______________	
Without repeating a digit, what is the largest number you can make that will round to 700,000? ______________	

DISCOVER

Discover how you can apply the information you have learned.

Some number patterns use more than one operation. These problems require you to find the rule and the pattern. This can also be done with multi-step word problems using any of the four operations.

Activity Section

Brian likes to collect stamps. He started his collection with only 4 stamps. Stamps come in packs of 5. If we let x represent the number of packs Brian purchases, you could use the rule $5x + 4$ to determine how many stamps he has, based on the number of stamp packages he might purchase.

Complete the table below by following the rule $5x + 4$.

Number of stamp packages	Rule: $5x + 4$
1	$(5 \times 1) + 4 = 9$
2	
3	
4	
5	
6	
7	
8	
9	
10	

What do you notice about the numbers in the table? ______________________________

____

____

UNIT 4

CORE Multiplication Concepts

Understanding Multiplication

UNPACK THE STANDARD
You will use multiplication to compare amounts.

LEARN IT: Multiplication can have different meanings in different problems. One way is to think of a multiplication problem as a comparison.

Example: 4 x 3 = 12

12 is 4 times as many as 3.

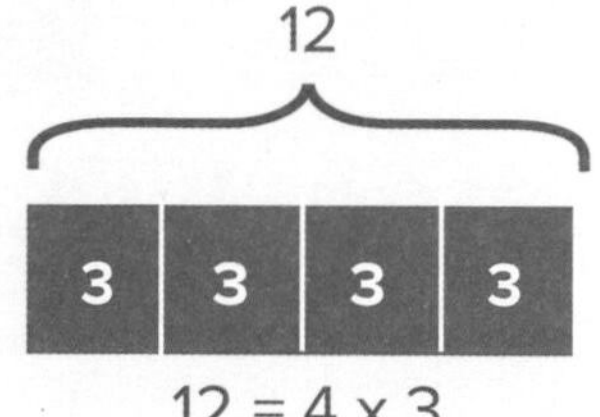

12 = 4 x 3

12 is 3 times as many as 4.

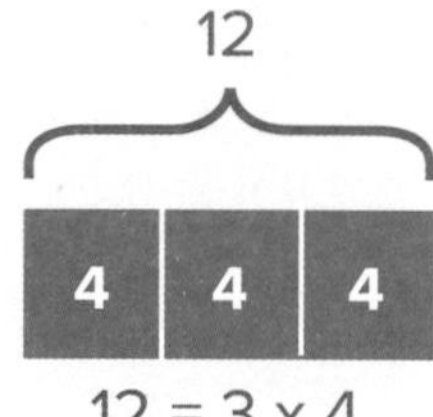

12 = 3 x 4

Drawing models is a helpful way to solve word problems involving comparisons.

Example: There are 10 students in the running club. There are 5 times as many students in the science club. How many students are in the science club?

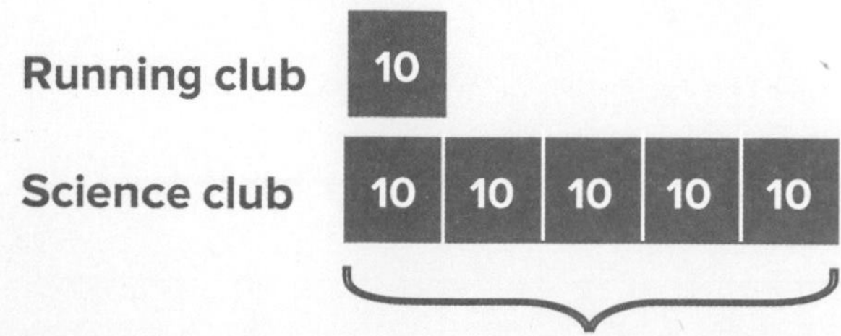

5 times as many as 10 = 50 students in the science club

5 x 10 = 50

think!
Remember the Commutative Property? How does it help you understand another way to compare this product?

PRACTICE: Now you try

Draw a model and write an equation to solve.

1. Jordan has 9 dimes. Leanne has 5 times as many dimes as Jordan. How many dimes does Leanne have?

Write an equation to match each statement.

2. 36 is 9 times as many as 4.
3. Six times as many as eight is 48.

Dylan and Dean went to the gym to lift weights. Dylan lifted twice as much weight as Dean. Together they lifted 51 pounds. How much did each boy lift? Show your work and explain your thinking on a piece of paper.

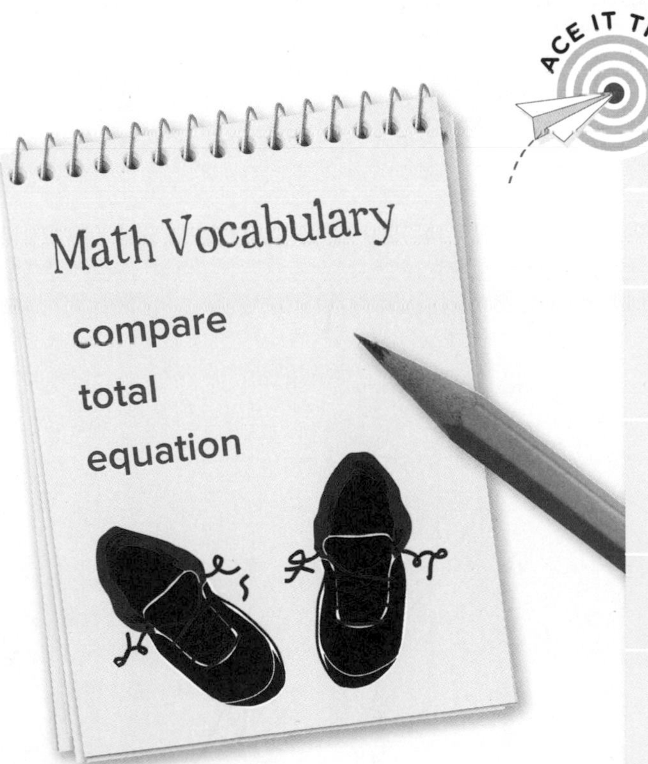

ACE IT TIME!

	yes	no
Did you underline the question in the word problem?		
Did you circle the numbers or number words?		
Did you box the supporting details or information needed to solve the problem?		
Did you draw a picture or a graphic organizer and write a math sentence to show your thinking?		
Did you label your numbers and your picture?		
Did you explain your thinking and use math vocabulary words in your explanation?		

MATH ON THE MOVE

Think of a multiplication fact and write a word problem for it. Write it more than one way by solving for the product, plus solving for a missing factor.

Multiplying with Tens, Hundreds, and Thousands

UNPACK THE STANDARD
You will use your understanding of place value to multiply by tens, hundreds, and thousands.

LEARN IT: There are several strategies you can use to multiply with multiples of 10, 100, or 1,000. You can use patterns, place value, or properties.

Using Patterns

When multiplying by 10, 100, or 1,000, there is a pattern: 2 x 10 = 20, 2 x 100 = 200, 2 x 1,000 = 2,000. As you can see from the pattern, when you multiply by tens, hundreds, and thousands, the place value of the product increases.

Example:

6 x 7 = 42
6 x 70 = 420
6 x 700 = 4,200
6 x 7,000 = 42,000

think! 6 x 7 = 42. Multiplying by a ten (420), by a hundred (4,200), and by a thousand (42,000) follows the pattern. Use the basic fact of 6 x 7 to help you see the pattern in multiplying by powers of 10.

Using Place Value

The number 50 has 5 tens and 0 ones, 500 has 5 hundreds and 0 ones, and 5,000 has 5 thousands and 0 ones. Use this to multiply.

90 x 5	5 x 700	4,000 x 8
= 9 (tens) x 5	= 5 × 7 (hundreds)	= 4 (thousands) x 8
= 45 (tens)	= 35 (hundreds)	= 32 (thousands)
= 450	= 3,500	= 32,000

think! Which properties are we using?

Using Properties

Remember your multiplication properties.

30 x 4 = 120
30 x 4 = (3 x 10) x 4
(3 x 10 x 4) = (3 x 4) x 10
(3 x 4) x 10 = 12 x 10 = 120

300 x 4 = 1,200
300 x 4 = (3 x 100) x 4
(3 x 100 x 4) = (3 x 4) x 100
(3 x 4) x 100 = 12 x 100 = 1,200

3,000 x 4 = 12,000
3,000 x 4 = (3 x 1,000) x 4
(3 x 1,000 x 4) = (3 x 4) x 1,000
(3 x 4) x 1,000 = 12 x 10 = 12,000

PRACTICE: Now you try

Complete the pattern. Find the product.

1. 3 x 9 = 27 30 x 9 = ______ 300 x 9 = ______ 3,000 x 9 = ______	**2.** 8,000 x 3 =	**3.** 9,000 x 5 =

The Sun Shack rents beach umbrellas. The Sun Shack rented 200 umbrellas each month in March and April. It rented 600 umbrellas each month from May through September. How many umbrellas did the Sun Shack rent during the 7 months? Show your work and explain your thinking on a piece of paper.

ACE IT TIME!

	yes	no
Did you underline the question in the word problem?		
Did you circle the numbers or number words?		
Did you box the supporting details or information needed to solve the problem?		
Did you draw a picture or a graphic organizer and write a math sentence to show your thinking?		
Did you label your numbers and your picture?		
Did you explain your thinking and use math vocabulary words in your explanation?		

Math Vocabulary

factor
product
hundreds
strategy
total

MATH ON THE MOVE

Take a multiplication fact and have fun multiplying it by tens, hundreds, and thousands. Challenge yourself to multiply it by even larger multiples, such as millions or billions.

Methods of Multiplication

UNPACK THE STANDARD
You can multiply multi-digit numbers using different methods.

LEARN IT: You can use four different strategies to multiply numbers. These strategies help you to regroup the factors (the numbers being multiplied) to make multiplication easier.

Break-Apart Strategy (The Distributive Property)

What two numbers will 15 break apart into that would be easy to multiply?

Multiply each number by the other factor to find **partial products.** Add the partial products together to find the total product.

15 x 7	**15 x 7**
(10 + 5) x 7	**(8 + 7) x 7**
(10 x 7) + (5 x 7)	**(8 x 7) + (7 x 7)**
70 + 35 = 105	**56 + 49 = 105**

think!
Could I solve it with a different sum?

Other Fractions

Write 524 in expanded form. Use the Distributive Property to multiply. Find each partial product, and then add the partial products to solve.

524 x 6 = ?

524	=	**500**	+	**20**	+	**4**
x 6		**x 6**		**x 6**		**x6**
?		**3,000**		**120**		**24**

500 x 6 = 3,000
20 x 6 = 120
4 x 6 = 24

```
  3,000
    120
+    24
-------
  3,144
```

(**3,144**)

Partial Products Strategy

Connect expanded form and the Distributive Property in a standard method format.

think!
How are these methods like the expanded form method? How are they different?

145 x 7 = ?

```
  145
×   7
-----
  700  → 7 x 1 hundred
  280  → 7 x 4 tens
+  35  → 7 x 5 ones
-----
1,015
```

(**1,015**)

Area Model Strategy

Draw a large rectangle and divide it into the number of sections needed for the expanded form of the largest factor. Multiply each section to find each partial product. Add the partial products to solve.

8,145 x 3 = ?

	8,000	**100**	**40**	**5**
	8,000 × 3	100 × 3	40 × 3	5 × 3
3 x	**24,000**	**300**	**120**	**15**

24,000 + 300 + 120 + 15 = 24,435

PRACTICE: Now you try

Find each product. Try different methods for each problem. Which method do you prefer?

1. 312 × 3	**2.** 4,852 × 5	**3.** 53 × 4	**4.** 473 × 9
I used the ________ method.	I used the ________ method.	I used the ________ method.	I used the ________ method.

Christa has 3 flash drives with 32 gigabytes of space each. She also has 2 other flash drives with 128 gigabytes of space each. Christa needs to back up 278 gigabytes of programs from her computer. How much memory will Christa have left on her flash drives after she backs up all the programs on her computer? Show your work and explain your thinking on a piece of paper.

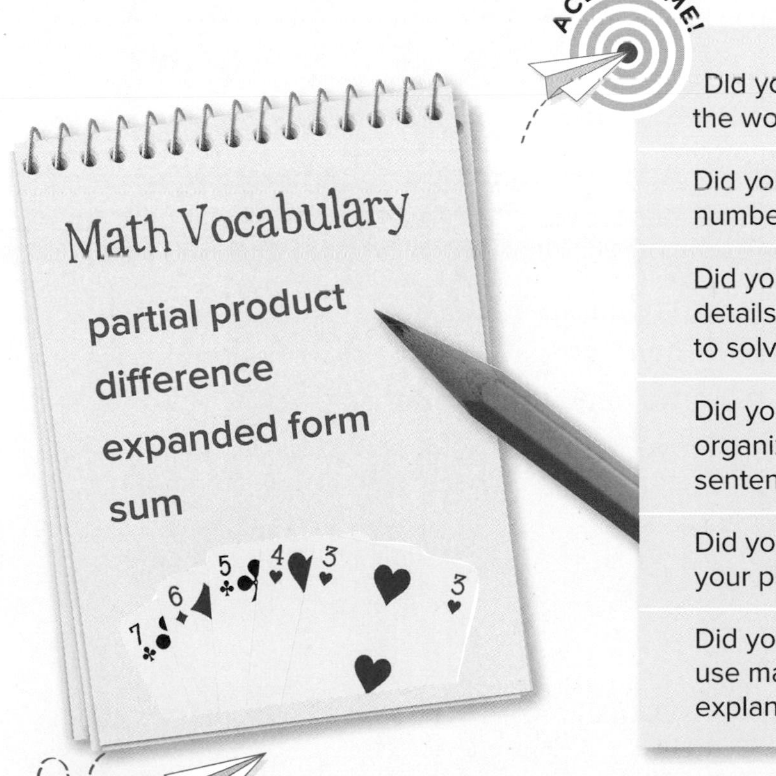

	yes	no
Did you underline the question in the word problem?	◯	◯
Did you circle the numbers or number words?	◯	◯
Did you box the supporting details or information needed to solve the problem?	◯	◯
Did you draw a picture or a graphic organizer and write a math sentence to show your thinking?	◯	◯
Did you label your numbers and your picture?	◯	◯
Did you explain your thinking and use math vocabulary words in your explanation?	◯	◯

MATH ON THE MOVE

Take a deck of playing cards. Remove the face cards. Place the deck face down. Each player should draw a card; the player who calls out the product of the two cards first wins the set. In the case of a tie, draw again. Play until you have used up all of the cards.

Multiply with Regrouping

UNPACK THE STANDARD

You will use regrouping to multiply up to four digits, by one digit.

LEARN IT: It is good practice to begin with an ***estimate*** to determine a reasonable answer. When you estimate, you are not trying to get the exact answer. You are finding a number that is ***close enough*** to the right answer.

Example: 3,254 x 3 = _____ Estimate: 3,000 x 3 = 9,000

Multiply.

Step 1. Multiply the ones.	**Step 2.** Multiply the tens.	**Step 3.** Multiply the hundreds.	**Step 4.** Multiply the thousands.
1 **3,254** **x 3** **2**	1 1 **3,254** **x 3** **62**	1 1 **3,254** **x 3** **762**	**3,254** **x 3** **9,762**
4 x 3 = 12 ones Regroup the 12 ones as 1 ten and 2 ones.	3 x 5 = 15 tens Add the regrouped tens. 15 tens + 1 ten = 16 tens. Regroup the 16 tens as 1 hundred and 6 tens.	3 x 2 = 6 hundreds Add the regrouped hundreds. 6 hundreds + 1 hundred = 7 hundreds. No need to regroup.	3 x 3 = 9 thousands **Answer: 9,762**

PRACTICE: Now you try

Estimate. Then find the product.

1. Estimate: _______	**2.** Estimate: _______	**3.** Estimate: _______	**4.** Estimate: _______
3,321 x 7	356 x 4	6,245 x 5	7,693 x 2

Estimate. Then find the product.

5. Estimate: ______	**6.** Estimate: ______	**7.** Estimate: ______	**8.** Estimate: ______
95 x 8	657 x 3	57 x 6	604 x 9

The Mitchell family is planning to take a cruise for their summer vacation this year. The price for each adult is $1,499 and the price for each child is $849. How much will the Mitchells pay for their summer cruise if 2 adults and 3 children go on the cruise? Show your work and explain your thinking on a piece of paper.

ACE IT TIME!

	yes	no
Did you underline the question in the word problem?		
Did you circle the numbers or number words?		
Did you box the supporting details or information needed to solve the problem?		
Did you draw a picture or a graphic organizer and write a math sentence to show your thinking?		
Did you label your numbers and your picture?		
Did you explain your thinking and use math vocabulary words in your explanation?		

Math Vocabulary

multiply

regroup

total

addition

MATH ON THE MOVE

Try to race the clock. Write a multiplication problem similar to the ones in this lesson. Ask your adult helper to time you. How fast did you solve it? Now solve it with a calculator. Ask your adult helper to time you again. Which strategy was faster? Were you faster than the calculator?

Multiply Two Two-Digit Numbers

UNPACK THE STANDARD
You will use regrouping to multiply up to two two-digit numbers.

LEARN IT: Remember, when you multiply whole numbers, the product, or answer, is always larger than the factors. It is good practice to begin with an estimate to determine what a reasonable answer would be. This is a good way to keep track of your work and to help you find any errors!

Example: 57 x 74 = _____ Estimate: 60 x 70 = 4,200

Multiply.

Step 1. Multiply the ones.	**Step 2.** Multiply the tens by the ones.	**Step 3.** Repeat steps 1 and 2 with the tens.	**Step 4.** Add the partial products.
2 **57** x **74** **8**	2 **57** x **74** **228**	4 2 **57** x **74** **228** 4 x 57 **3,990** 70 x 57	4 2 **57** x **74** **228** 4 x 57 **+ 3,990** 70 x 57 **4,218**
Think of 74 as 7 tens and 4 ones. Multiply 57 by 4. 4 ones x 7 ones = 28 ones Regroup the 28 as 2 tens and 8 ones.	4 x 5 tens = 20 tens Add the regrouped tens. 20 tens + 2 tens = 22 tens So, 57 x 4 = 228.	Write a "0" in the ones column below the first product. This shows that you are multiplying in the tens column. Multiply 57 by 7 tens: 70 x 7 ones = 490 ones. Regroup the 49. Multiply 70 x 5 tens = 350 tens. Add the regrouped 4 tens = 39 tens. So, 57 x 7 tens = 3,990.	228 + 3,990 = 4,218 The product of 4,218 is close to the estimate of 4,200 so the answer is reasonable.

think!
You carried the 2 when you regrouped 28. Now you must carry a 4 to regroup 49. What can you do to keep from confusing them? Cross off the 2 that you already regrouped!

PRACTICE: Now you try

Estimate. Then find the product.

1. Estimate: _______	2. Estimate: _______	3. Estimate: _______	4. Estimate: _______
$\begin{array}{r} 67 \\ \times\ 85 \\ \hline \end{array}$	$\begin{array}{r} 96 \\ \times\ 17 \\ \hline \end{array}$	$\begin{array}{r} 45 \\ \times\ 28 \\ \hline \end{array}$	$\begin{array}{r} 75 \\ \times\ 32 \\ \hline \end{array}$

The fourth-grade students at West Elementary are having a recycling contest. The 21 students in Mrs. Peters' class each collected an average of 25 cans. The 24 students in Ms. Hernandez's class each collected an average of 21 cans. The 22 students in Mr. Juarez's class collected an average of 24 cans each. Which class won the recycling contest? Show your work and explain your thinking on a piece of paper.

ACE IT TIME!

	yes	no
Did you underline the question in the word problem?	○	○
Did you circle the numbers or number words?	○	○
Did you box the supporting details or information needed to solve the problem?	○	○
Did you draw a picture or a graphic organizer and write a math sentence to show your thinking?	○	○
Did you label your numbers and your picture?	○	○
Did you explain your thinking and use math vocabulary words in your explanation?	○	○

Math Vocabulary

multiply

regroup

compare

MATH ON THE MOVE

You and a partner roll dice to create numbers to multiply. For example, if you roll a 3 and a 2, the first number is 32. Roll the dice again for the second number. Solve the problem. Have your partner check your work with a calculator. If you are correct, take 1 counter. If you are not correct, give a counter to the other player. The player with the most counters wins.

UNIT 5

CORE Concepts of Area and Perimeter

Area

UNPACK THE STANDARD
You will use a formula to find the area of a rectangle.

LEARN IT: ***Area*** is the number of square units needed to cover a flat surface. To find the area of a figure, you will use the formula ***Area = base x height***.

A = b x h
Area = base x height

Note: The base and height of the rectangle can also be described as the length (l) and width (w). The formula may also be written as:
A = l x w

Example: Use the area formula to find the area of a rectangle and a square.

Area of a rectangle:
A = b x h
A = 8 x 3
A = 24 square feet

Area of a square:
A = b x h
A = 2 x 2
A = 4 square inches

think!
How can you find the area of a square if you only know the length of one side?

PRACTICE: Now you try

Find the area of the rectangle or square.

1. Area = ________ square kilometers

2. Area = ________ square inches

3 in.
20 in.

3. Area = ________ square yards

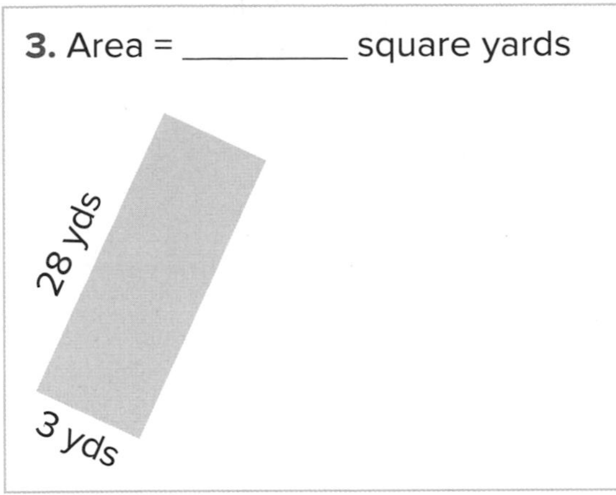

4. Area = ________ square feet

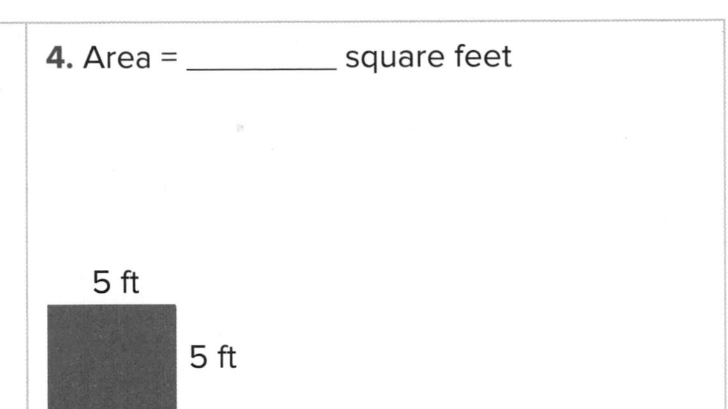

Lindsay and Catherine are making plans to build rectangular vegetable gardens. Lindsay wants her vegetable garden to be a 17-foot by 12-foot rectangle. Catherine wants her garden to be a 15-foot by 15-foot square. Which garden will have the greater area? How many more square feet will the bigger garden have? Show your work and explain your thinking on a piece of paper.

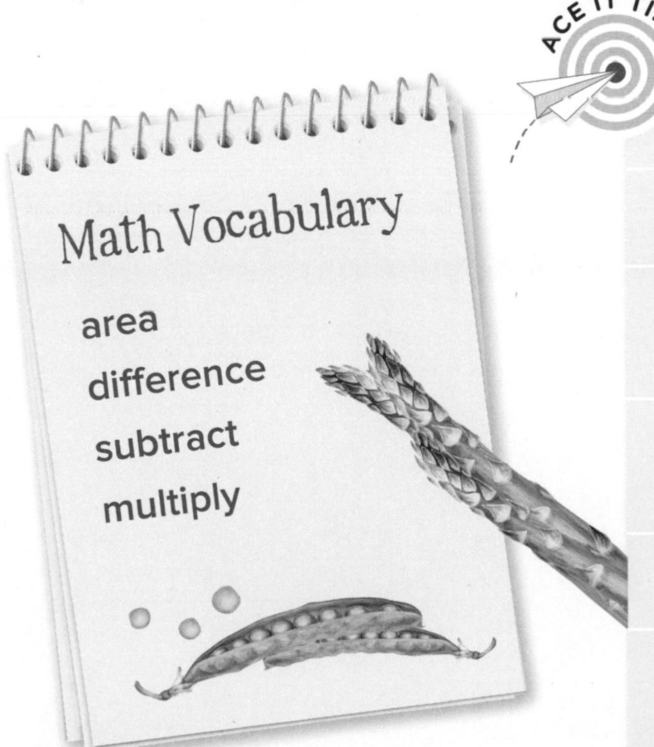

ACE IT TIME!

	yes	no
Did you underline the question in the word problem?		
Did you circle the numbers or number words?		
Did you box the supporting details or information needed to solve the problem?		
Did you draw a picture or a graphic organizer and write a math sentence to show your thinking?		
Did you label your numbers and your picture?		
Did you explain your thinking and use math vocabulary words in your explanation?		

MATH ON THE MOVE

Go on an exploration around your house to find area problems. Find the area of a window, a door, the front of your refrigerator, a wall, and a floor. If the surface is a square or rectangle, find out its area by measuring the base and the height and then multiplying. *Hint:* What tool should you use to measure larger objects?

Area Models and Partial Products

UNPACK THE STANDARD
You can multiply multi-digit numbers using area models and partial products.

LEARN IT: Two methods can help you multiply multi-digit numbers and regroup the factors, making multiplication easier. The two methods are the ***area model*** and ***partial products***.

Use the Area Model

Draw a large rectangle model and divide it into four sections. Break apart the factors into tens and ones to show partial products. Multiply each section to find each partial product. Then add the partial products to solve.

```
  45
× 17
 400
 280
  50
+ 35
 765
```

	40	5	
	40 x 10 = **400**	10 × 5 = **50**	10
	40 x 7 = **280**	7 × 5 = **35**	7

Use Partial Products

1. Multiply the tens by the tens.
2. Multiply the ones by the tens.
3. Multiply the tens by the ones.
4. Multiply the ones by the ones.
5. Add the partial products.

```
   65
 × 37
1,800  →  30 x 6 tens = 180 tens
  150  →  30 x 5 ones = 150 ones
  420  →  7 x 6 tens = 42 tens
+  35  →  7 x 5 ones = 35 ones
2,405
```

PRACTICE: Now you try

Use the model to represent each problem. Solve.

Sample

```
  23
× 25
 400
 100
  60
+ 15
 575
```

	20	3	
	20 x 20 = **400**	20 × 3 = **60**	20
	20 x 5 = **100**	3 × 5 = **15**	5

1.

```
  32
× 16
```


CCSS.Math.Content.4.MD.A.3; 4.OA.A.3

2.

$$\begin{array}{r} 35 \\ \times\ 27 \\ \hline \end{array}$$

3.

$$\begin{array}{r} 37 \\ \times\ 48 \\ \hline \end{array}$$

Samantha made the following model to find the product of 23 x 29. Is her model correct? Show your work and explain your thinking on a piece of paper.

	20	3
20	400	60
9	18	27

400 + 60 + 18 + 27 = 505

ACE IT TIME!

	yes	no
Did you underline the question in the word problem?		
Did you circle the numbers or number words?		
Did you box the supporting details or information needed to solve the problem?		
Did you draw a picture or a graphic organizer and write a math sentence to show your thinking?		
Did you label your numbers and your picture?		
Did you explain your thinking and use math vocabulary words in your explanation?		

Math Vocabulary

partial product
multiply
area model
sum

MATH ON THE MOVE

Use number cards 1–9. Flip four cards over to make any two two-digit numbers. Multiply the numbers by first using the area model of multiplication and then partial products. For example, you flip a 3, 4, 2, and 6. First, solve 34 x 26 using the area model. Then solve the same problem with partial products. What similarities do you notice in your work?

Area by Combining Rectangles

UNPACK THE STANDARD
You will find the area of combined rectangles.

LEARN IT: In a previous lesson, you learned the formula A = b x h to find the area of a square or rectangle. But what about other shapes that are not perfect squares or rectangles? Let's see how this formula applies.

Example: How would you find the area of a shape like the one below?

Make rectangles or squares (the fewest possible).

think!
Where could you divide the shape?

3 ft.
3 ft.
2 ft.
8 ft.

Calculate the area of each rectangle or square using the formula A = b x h.

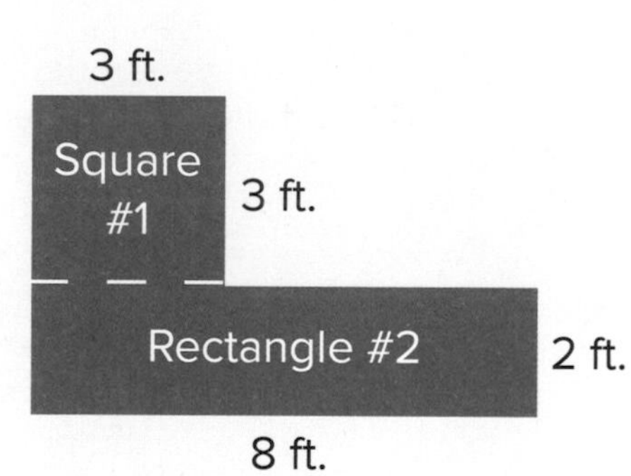

Square 1:
A = b x h
A = 3 ft. x 3 ft.
A = 9 sq. ft.

Rectangle 2:
A = b x h
A = 8 ft. x 2 ft.
A = 16 sq. ft.

Add the area of each rectangle or square to find the total area of the shape.

Square #1: 9 sq. ft.
Rectangle #2: + 16 sq. ft.
25 sq. ft.

PRACTICE: Now you try
Find the area of the combined rectangles.

1.

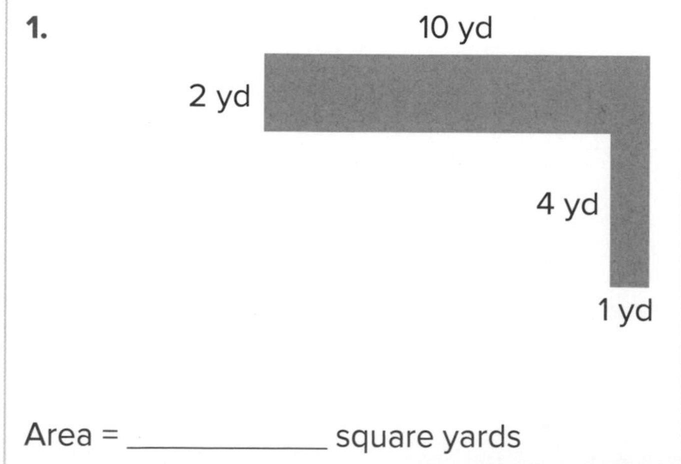

Area = ____________ square yards

2.

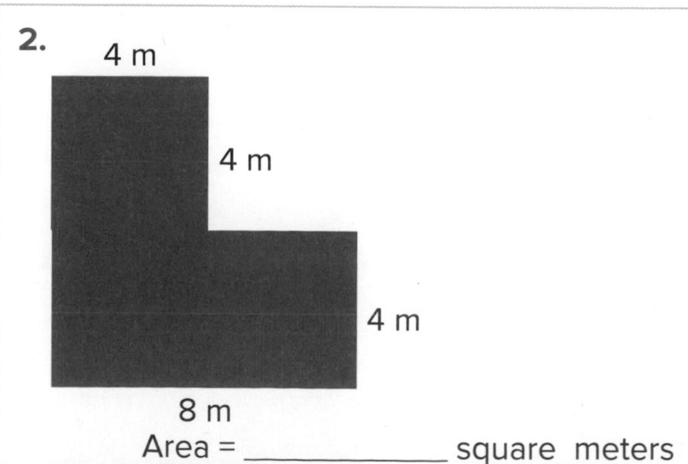

Area = ____________ square meters

3.

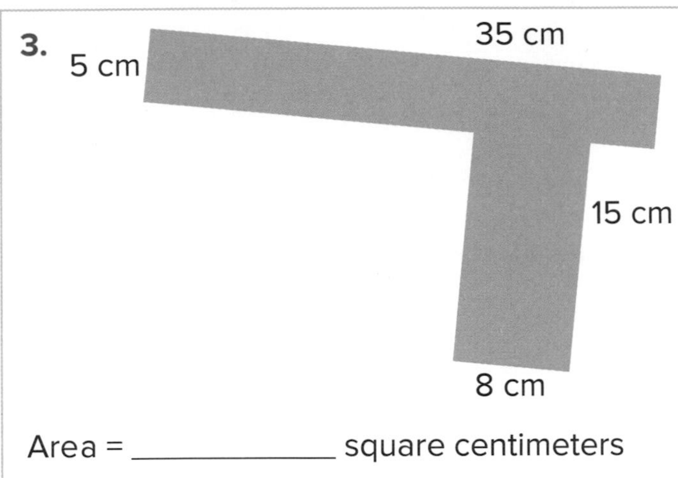

Area = ____________ square centimeters

4.

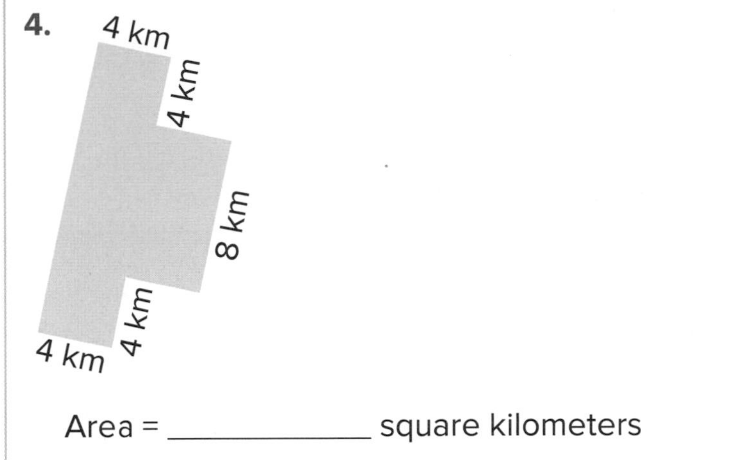

Area = ____________ square kilometers

Keira's horse needs a corral that has an area of 45 square yards. Which of these corral plans would be perfect for Keira's horse? Show your work and explain your thinking on a piece of paper.

6 yd
3 yd
3 yd
Corral A
5 yd
9 yd

6 yd
6 yd
3 yd
Corral B
3 yd
9 yd

ACE IT TIME!

	yes	no
Did you underline the question in the word problem?		
Did you circle the numbers or number words?		
Did you box the supporting details or information needed to solve the problem?		
Did you draw a picture or a graphic organizer and write a math sentence to show your thinking?		
Did you label your numbers and your picture?		
Did you explain your thinking and use math vocabulary words in your explanation?		

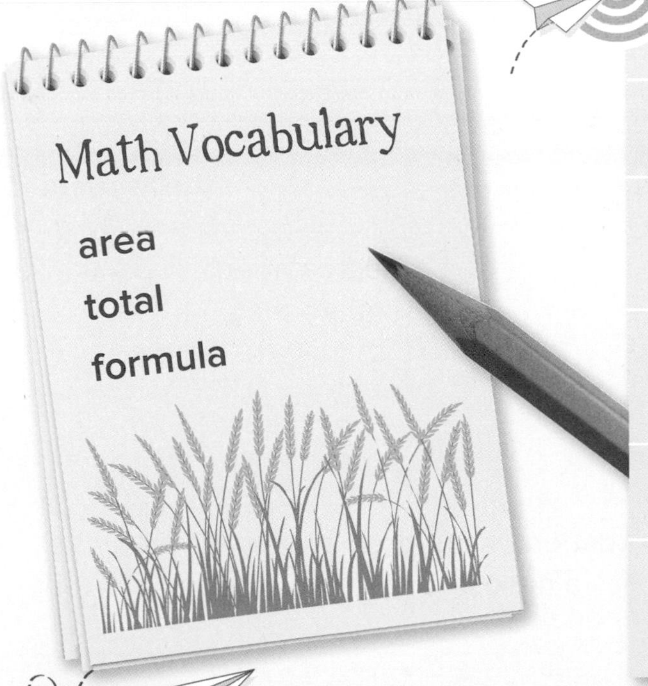

MATH ON THE MOVE

Take a piece of gridded graph paper and cut out a shape similar to the ones in this lesson. Now cut it apart, making two or more rectangles or squares. Calculate the areas of the smaller shapes. See how the smaller areas added together equal the area of the original shape.

Area by Excluding Rectangles

UNPACK THE STANDARD
You will find the area of rectangles.

LEARN IT: In the previous lesson, you added the area of smaller rectangles and squares together to find the total area of a shape. In this lesson, you will see that in some situations you may need to subtract or remove the area of a rectangle or square to find the total area.

Example: Saritha wants to paint a wall in her bedroom that has a window. The wall has a base of 25 feet and a height of 12 feet. The window has a base of 4 feet and a height of 5 feet. What is the area in square feet of Saritha's wall?

Saritha wants to paint the wall, NOT the window. How can she find the area of the wall and NOT include the area of the window? 	Calculate the area of the wall AND the window using the formula A = b x h. **Wall:** A = b x h A = 25 ft. x 12 ft. A = 300 square ft. **Window:** A = b x h A = 4 ft. x 5 ft. A = 20 square ft.	Subtract the area of window from the area of the wall to find the total area of wall Saritha needs to paint. Wall: 300 ft. Window – 20 ft. 280 square ft. Saritha needs to paint 280 square feet.

PRACTICE: Now you try
Find the total area for each problem.

1. Mrs. Jenson wants to wallpaper one wall in her daughter's bedroom. She will cover the whole wall except for the doorway. The door has a base of 3 feet and a height of 7 feet.

Area = ____________ square feet

2. Franco helps his father tile a patio with square tiles. Tiles will cover the whole patio except for a rectangular grilling space in the center of the patio. The grilling space has a length of 2 meters and a width of 3 meters.

9 m

Area = __________ square meters

A rectangular dining room floor is 15 feet long and 12 feet wide. Part of the floor is covered by a rectangular rug that is 5 feet long and 7 feet wide. How many square feet of the floor are NOT covered by the rug? Show your work and explain your thinking on a piece of paper.

	yes	no
Did you underline the question in the word problem?		
Did you circle the numbers or number words?		
Did you box the supporting details or information needed to solve the problem?		
Did you draw a picture or a graphic organizer and write a math sentence to show your thinking?		
Did you label your numbers and your picture?		
Did you explain your thinking and use math vocabulary words in your explanation?		

MATH ON THE MOVE

Ask your adult helper for a measuring tape to practice this skill. Pick a wall in your home that has a door or window. Measure the base of the wall and then measure the height of the wall to find the area of the wall. Now measure the base and height of the door or window and find its area. Subtract the area of the door or window from the area of the wall. Think about why this is helpful to know.

Perimeter

UNPACK THE STANDARD
You will use a formula to find the perimeter of a rectangle or square.

LEARN IT: There are three formulas you can use to find the ***perimeter*** or distance around a rectangle or square. You can use addition, multiplication for rectangles, and multiplication for squares.

Example:

15 cm

6 cm | 6 cm

15 cm

think!
How are perimeter and area alike? How are they different?

Use addition:	**Use multiplication:**	**Use multiplication:**
Perimeter = length + width + length + width	Perimeter of rectangles = (2 x length) + (2 x width)	Perimeter of a square = P = 4 x one side
Perimeter = 15 + 6 + 15 + 6 15 6 15 + 6 Perimeter = 42 cm	P = (2 x 15) + (2 x 6) P = 30 + 12 P = 42 cm	8 mm 8 mm 8 mm 8 mm Perimeter: 4 x 8 = 32 mm

PRACTICE: Now you try

Find the perimeter of the rectangle or square.

1. 23 m 65 m Perimeter = ____________ meters	**2.** 12 cm 12 cm Perimeter = ____________ centimeters

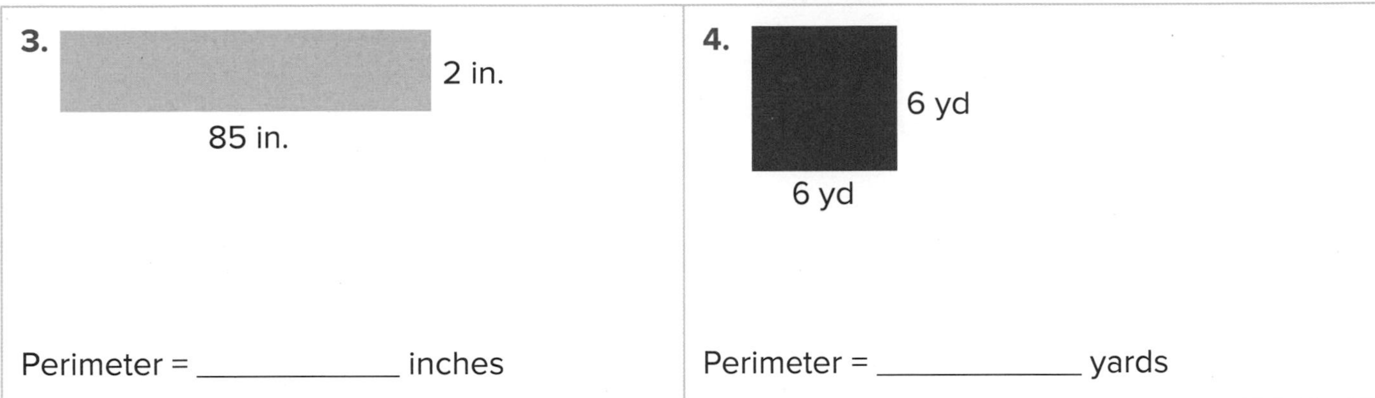

Heather wants to add fringe around the edge of a blanket she is making for her grandmother. The blanket is rectangular in shape and has a length of 60 inches. The width of the blanket is one half the length. How much fringe will Heather need? If 10 inches of fringe costs $1.00, how much money will Heather spend on buying fringe for this blanket? Show your work and explain your thinking on a piece of paper.

ACE IT TIME!

	yes	no
Did you underline the question in the word problem?		
Did you circle the numbers or number words?		
Did you box the supporting details or information needed to solve the problem?		
Did you draw a picture or a graphic organizer and write a math sentence to show your thinking?		
Did you label your numbers and your picture?		
Did you explain your thinking and use math vocabulary words in your explanation?		

Math Vocabulary

perimeter
divide
formula
multiply

MATH ON THE MOVE

Practice measuring objects inside and outside of the house. You can use a ruler or other tools to measure. Practice adding up all the sides of an object to find its perimeter.

Apply Area and Perimeter Formulas

UNPACK THE STANDARD
You will find an unknown measure of a rectangle when given its area or perimeter.

LEARN IT: Sometimes we aren't given all of the measurements of an area. Understanding the ***formulas*** for ***area*** and ***perimeter*** will help you determine an unknown measure.

Look at the following examples.

The **area** of a rug is 35 square feet. The length of the rug is 7 feet. What is its width?

W = ? | Area = 35 sq. ft. | 7 ft.

I know the formula for area is:

Area = length x width

I can label what I know in the formula:

Area (35) square feet = length (7) x width (?)

35 = 7 x w

I don't know what the width is, but I can figure it out by asking:

7 x ______ = 35   7 x 5 = 35

So the missing width is **5 feet**.

The **perimeter** of a rectangular rug is 24 feet. The rug is 3 feet wide. What is its length?

3 ft. | Perimeter = 24 ft. | L = ?

I know the formula for perimeter is:

Perimeter = (2 x length) + (2 x width)

I can label what I know in the formula:

Perimeter (24) feet = (2 x length) + (2 x 3 (width))

24 = (2 x L) + (2 x 3)

24 = (2 x L) + 6

I don't know what the length is, but I can figure it out by first subtracting the known width from the total perimeter:

24 – 6 = 18

Now I need to figure out the length by asking:

2 x _____ = 18   2 x 9 = 18

So the missing length is **9 feet**.

PRACTICE: Now you try

Find the unknown measure.

Lindsay wants to make matching cages for her 2 guinea pigs. She has the wooden parts of each cage built, but needs to buy enough wire mesh to fit around each cage. Each cage measures 4 feet by 5 feet. How much wire mesh will Lindsay need to surround the 2 matching cages? Show your work and explain your thinking on a piece of paper.

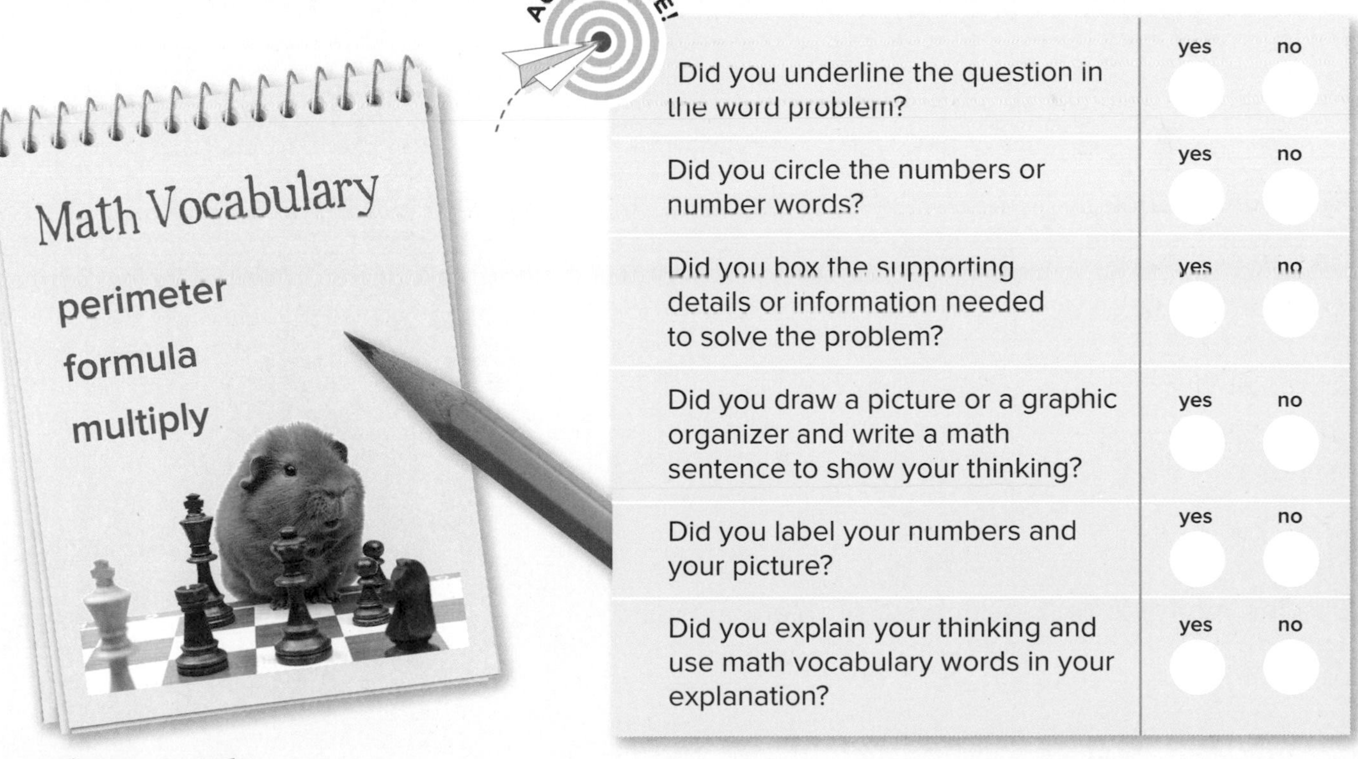

MATH ON THE MOVE

Be a zoo designer! Using a piece of graph paper, design a zoo by assigning rectangles for each animal's habitat. Bigger animals will require larger habitats. The habitats can be any shape, but each rectangle must be complete and follow the grid. Multi-part habitats can also be made by attaching rectangles or squares to each other. Once your map is done, measure the area and perimeter of each habitat and the totals for your entire map.

REVIEW

Stop and think about what you have learned.

Congratulations! You have finished the lessons for this unit. This means you have learned how to multiply numbers using different methods. You have practiced multiplying numbers and can regroup when necessary. You have noticed the difference between area and perimeter. You can even find the area of rectangles by combining or subtracting squares or rectangles.

Now it is time to prove your multiplication skills. Solve the problems that follow using all of the methods you have learned.

Activity Section 1: Multiplication Concepts

Write an equation to match each statement.

1. 72 is 9 times as many as 8.	**2.** 88 is 11 times as many as 8.	**3.** 50 is 10 times as many as 5.

Find the product.

Estimate. Then find the product.

4.	**5.**	**6.** Estimate: _______	**7.** Estimate: _______
$\begin{array}{r} 5{,}000 \\ \times\ 4 \\ \hline \end{array}$	$\begin{array}{r} 300 \\ \times\ 7 \\ \hline \end{array}$	$\begin{array}{r} 6{,}212 \\ \times\ 8 \\ \hline \end{array}$	$\begin{array}{r} 356 \\ \times\ 4 \\ \hline \end{array}$

Use the model to represent each problem. Solve.

8. 42 x 21 = _________	**9.** 24 x 18 = _________	**10.** 33 x 29 = _________

CCSS.Math.Content.4.NBT.B6; CCSS.Math.Practice.MP1; MP2; MP3; MP4; MP6; MP7; MP8

Estimate. Then find the product.

11. Estimate: ______	**12.** Estimate: ______	**13.** Estimate: ______
$\begin{array}{r} 93 \\ \times\ 86 \\ \hline \end{array}$	$\begin{array}{r} 77 \\ \times\ 21 \\ \hline \end{array}$	$\begin{array}{r} 44 \\ \times\ 32 \\ \hline \end{array}$

Activity Section 2: Area and Perimeter

Find the area and perimeter of the rectangle or square.

1.

4 yd

24 yd

Area = ______ Perimeter = ______

2.

35 cm

22 cm

Area = ______ Perimeter = ______

Find the total area.

3.

3 cm

45 cm

19 cm

5 cm

Area = ______ square centimeters

Find area by excluding rectangle.

4. You want to paint one wall in your room. You will cover the whole wall except for the doorway. The door has a base of 3 feet and a height of 7 feet.

9 ft.

18 ft.

Area = ______ square feet

UNDERSTAND

Understand the meaning of what you have learned and apply your knowledge.

You will use place value understanding and properties of operations to multiply two two-digit numbers.

Activity Section

Four students were each given a different problem to multiply. Their teacher noticed an error in one student's work. Identify which student made the error and explain what the student did incorrectly.

Jared's Problem: 53 x 68 = __________

	50	3	
60	3,000	180	
	40	24	8

3,040 + 204 = 3,244

Josh's Problem: 98 x 75 = __________

```
   5
   4
  98
×  75
 490
+ 6,860
 7,350
```

Jenn's Problem: 87 x 45 = __________

```
    87
  × 45
 3,200
+  280
   400
    35
 3,915
```

Jillian's Problem: 58 x 74 = __________

	50	8	
	3,500	560	70
4	200	32	

3,700 + 592 = 4,292

Who has the wrong answer? ______________________________

The mistake the student made was ______________________________

The correct answer is ______________________________

DISCOVER

Discover how you can apply the information you have learned.

You will apply area and perimeter formulas. You will find all factor pairs for a whole number. You will solve multi-step word problems using the four operations.

Activity Section

In the first two columns list the factor pairs of 36. Draw each of the rectangles that have the area of 36 square units (see below). In the last column calculate the perimeter of each. Then answer the questions below.

Area = L x W Square units	Length L units	Width W units	Rectangle	Perimeter (2 x L) + (2 x W) units
36 (sample)	1	36	1 cm, 36 cm	(2 x 1) + (2 x 36) 2 + 72 = 74
36				
36				
36				
36				

1. Which rectangle has the largest perimeter?
2. Which has the smallest perimeter?

CORE Division Concepts

Understanding Division—Estimate a Quotient

UNPACK THE STANDARD
You will use what you know about multiples and rounding to estimate answers (quotients) in a division problem.

LEARN IT: ***Compatible numbers*** **is a strategy you can use to estimate a quotient. Compatible numbers divide easily.**

6x
6 × 1 = 6
6 × 2 = 12
6 × 3 = 18
6 × 4 = 24
6 × 5 = 30
6 × 6 = 36
6 × 7 = 42
6 × 8 = 48
6 × 9 = 54
6 × 10 = 60

Dividend Divisor

To **estimate** the quotient in the problem 52 ÷ 6 ask yourself, "*What* multiplied by 6 is about 52?" ← Think of the multiples of the divisor, 6.

What x 6 = 9? 9 x 6 = 54.

The quotient of 52 ÷ 6 is **about** 9 because 54 is close to 52, so it is a reasonable estimate.

think!
When dividends have 4 digits, wouldn't it be quicker to find multiples in powers of 100?

think!
In problems with 3-digit dividends, think of the divisor and multiples of 10.

PRACTICE: Now you try
Estimate the quotient of the following problems. List the multiples like the example shown.

Problem	Multiples	Quotient Estimate
Sample: 33 ÷ 7	7, 14, 21, 28, 35, 42 1 2 3 4 5 6	5
48 ÷ 9		
138 ÷ 5		
710 ÷ 9		
2,417 ÷ 4		

Hint:
5 x 10
5 x 20
5 x 30...

Hint:
4 x 100
4 x 200
4 x 300...

A school serves lunch to 246 students each day. Each table in the cafeteria seats 8 students. Molly says the school needs at least 25 tables. Eric says the school needs at least 30 tables. Who has the better estimate of the number of tables needed to serve all the students? Show your work and explain your thinking on a piece of paper.

ACE IT TIME!

	yes	no
Did you underline the question in the word problem?		
Did you circle the numbers or number words?		
Did you box the supporting details or information needed to solve the problem?		
Did you draw a picture or a graphic organizer and write a math sentence to show your thinking?		
Did you label your numbers and your picture?		
Did you explain your thinking and use math vocabulary words in your explanation?		

Math Vocabulary

- estimate
- quotient
- divisor
- dividend
- multiples

Practice your estimation skills at the grocery store. Select a box of cereal, a bag of cookies or chips, and another item you could share with 3 friends. Think about the cost of your chosen items and estimate how much it would cost you and your 3 friends to buy the food, if each of you paid a fair share. *Hint:* Round the cost of the food to the nearest dollar for easier estimating!

Division with Partial Quotients

UNPACK THE STANDARD
You will divide numbers by finding partial quotients.

LEARN IT: Using your knowledge of place value and multiples of 10 and 100, practice the ***partial quotients*** strategy. Find partial quotients by performing division in steps. At each step you will get partial answers. Add the partial answers together to find the quotient.

Example: Solve 84 ÷ 4. 4) 84 (Divisor: 4; Dividend: 84)

Step 1: Identify the highest place value in the dividend 84. There are 8 tens (80).

Step 2: Ask yourself what multiple of 10 can be multiplied by the divisor (4) to get close to but not exceed the 8 tens (80) in 84.

4 x ___ = 80
4 x 10 = 40
4 x 20 = 80

think!
Which multiple of 4 comes close to 80?

Step 3: 20 is the first partial quotient. Now subtract 80 from 84 to see if there is another partial quotient.

```
   2  ← Note, 2 is placed in tens place.
4 ) 84
  – 80       4 x 20      20  ← Partial Quotient
     4
```

Step 4: Move to the next lowest place value (ones) and repeat. But this time, since we only have 4 left, we can't take out multiples of 10. Let's take out a smaller part, or a smaller multiple!

```
4 ) 4      4 x ___ = 4
           4 x 1          1  ← Partial Quotient
```

Step 5: Add the partial quotients (20 and 1) to find the total quotient.

```
   21
4 ) 84
  – 80       4 x 20      20  ← Partial Quotients
     4       4 x 1        1
   – 4
     0       So, 84 ÷ 4 = 21
```

PRACTICE: Now you try

Use partial quotients to solve the problems.

1. 69 ÷ 3 =	2. 555 ÷ 5 =	3. A bag contains 2,152 beads. The beads are 4 different colors. If the bag contains the same number of beads of each color, how many beads are in each color?

Mikal solved this problem using the partial quotients method of division. But he made a few errors! Find where he made the errors, correct his mistakes, and then complete the problem. Show your work and explain your thinking on a piece of paper.

6) 9,426

9,426		
− 6,000	6 × 1,000	6,000
3,426		
− 3,000	6 × 500	500
426		
− 420	6 × 60	60
6		

ACE IT TIME!

	yes	no
Did you underline the question in the word problem?		
Did you circle the numbers or number words?		
Did you box the supporting details or information needed to solve the problem?		
Did you draw a picture or a graphic organizer and write a math sentence to show your thinking?		
Did you label your numbers and your picture?		
Did you explain your thinking and use math vocabulary words in your explanation?		

MATH ON THE MOVE

As you travel in a car, look at license plates for numbers. Using the divisor of 7, 8, or 9, try to find a partial quotient.

Repeated Subtraction Strategy

UNPACK THE STANDARD
You will use repeated subtraction and multiples to find quotients in a division problem.

LEARN IT: To use *repeated subtraction* when solving a division problem, you subtract the divisor from the dividend until you reach zero or cannot subtract any more. Let's see how it is done in the example shown.

Example: Akinosho baked 72 cookies. She wants to bag them up in sets of 6 for her friends. How many bags will she have made to give to her friends? 72 ÷ 6

72	60	48	36	24	12
− 6 1 time	− 6 3 times	− 6 5 times	− 6 7 times	− 6 9 times	− 6 11 times
66	54	42	30	18	6
− 6 2 times	− 6 4 times	− 6 6 times	− 6 8 times	− 6 10 times	− 6 12 times
60	48	36	24	12	0

6 was subtracted a total of 12 times, so 72 ÷ 6 = 12

This takes a long time to do, and there are many chances to make a mistake!

To make this easier, you can subtract in multiples of the divisor—in this problem, multiples of 6.

$$\begin{array}{r} 72 \\ -\ 60 \\ \hline 12 \\ -\ 12 \\ \hline 0 \end{array}$$

6 x 10 = 60 This is like subtracting 6 ten times.

6 x 2 = 12 This is like subtracting 6 two times. 72 ÷ 6 = 12

When these are put together, 6 has been subtracted 12 times!

PRACTICE: Now you try

Use repeated subtraction to find the quotients in the problems. Try to use multiples of the divisor to make this subtraction method easier.

1. 42 ÷ 3 =	**2.** 60 ÷ 4 =

On vacation, Lydia collected 294 pebbles. She wants to put the same number of pebbles in each of 7 jars. How many pebbles will Lydia put in each jar? Show your work and explain your thinking on a piece of paper.

ACE IT TIME!

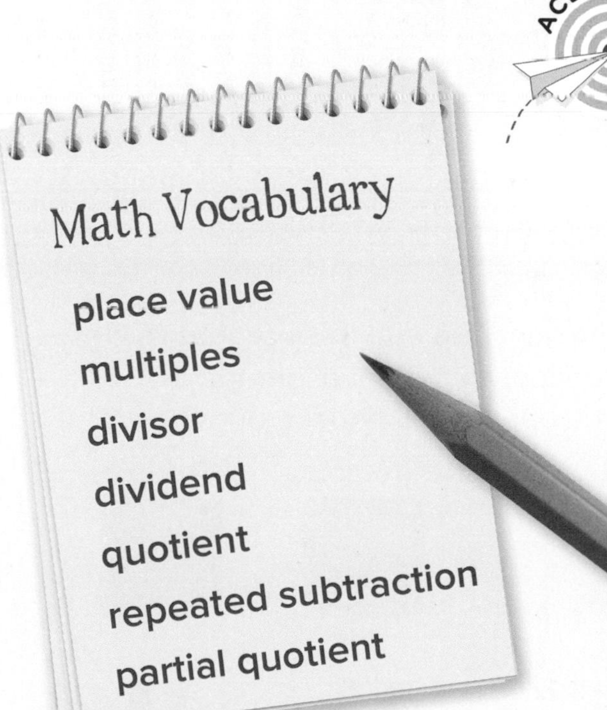

	yes	no
Did you underline the question in the word problem?		
Did you circle the numbers or number words?		
Did you box the supporting details or information needed to solve the problem?		
Did you draw a picture or a graphic organizer and write a math sentence to show your thinking?		
Did you label your numbers and your picture?		
Did you explain your thinking and use math vocabulary words in your explanation?		

Use a deck of cards and remove all the face cards. Have the aces count as 1. Pull 4 numbers from the deck and make a 4-digit number. Practice finding how many hundreds are in the number. Then see if you can find the multiples of that number.
Example: 4,573 = 45 hundreds
Multiples: 90 and 50; 900 and 5; 9 and 500; 50 and 90

Division with the Distributive Property

UNPACK THE STANDARD
You will use the Distributive Property or base-ten models to solve division problems.

LEARN IT: When you have to find the quotient in a division problem, it is helpful to use your knowledge of place value. You can represent the value of the dividend using the ***Distributive Property*** and base-ten blocks.

Distributive Property

Step 1. Break up the dividend into expanded form (thousands, hundreds, tens, and ones).

EXAMPLE: 369 ÷ 3

Show the dividend (369) in expanded form.

369 = 300 + 60 + 9 **OR** 360 + 9

Step 2. Use the divisor to solve the problem with the Distributive Property.

EXAMPLE: 369 ÷ 3

369 ÷ 3 = (300 + 60 + 9) ÷ 3

369 ÷ 3 = (300 ÷ 3) + (60 ÷ 3) + (9 ÷ 3)

= 100 + 20 + 3

= 123

So, 369 ÷ 3 = 123.

We can show the quotient in two ways:

$3\overline{)369}$ with quotient 123 OR 369 ÷ 3 = 123

NOTE: We ONLY break the dividend apart...the divisor stays the same!

Base Ten

Step 1. Use base-ten blocks to show the dividend in expanded form (thousands, hundreds, tens, and ones).

EXAMPLE: 369 ÷ 3

Show the dividend (369) in base-ten blocks.

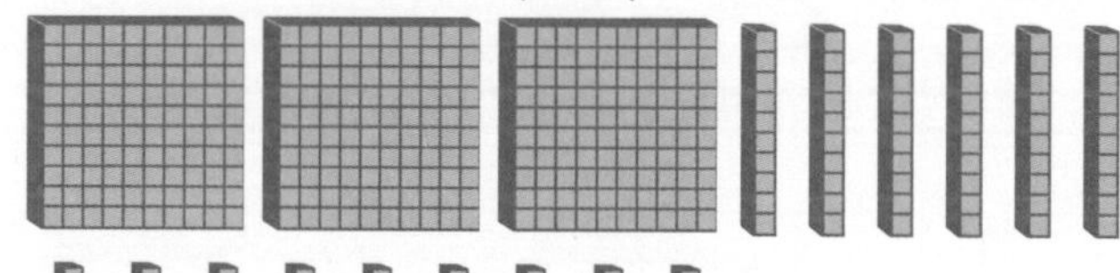

Step 2. Divide the base-ten blocks into equal groups (based on the divisor):

EXAMPLE: 369 ÷ 3

Divide the hundreds into 3 equal groups: 300 ÷ 3
Divide the tens into 3 equal groups: 60 ÷ 3
Divide the ones into 3 equal groups: 9 ÷ 3

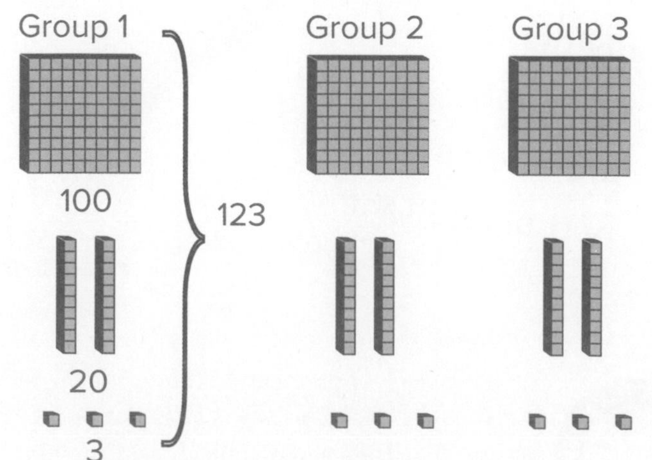

Since there are now 3 groups of 123, we see that 369 ÷ 3 = 123!

PRACTICE: Now you try

Use the Distributive Property to find the quotients.

think!
Look for multiples of 10,000 or 1,000 that 8 will divide into equally.

1. 84 ÷ 4 =	**2.** 2,416 ÷ 8 =

A cell phone store has 2,682 cell phones in stock. They only carry 2 different colors, black and white. If there is the same amount in each color, how many cell phones do they have in each color? *Hint:* You can draw base-ten blocks to show the distributive property to help you divide. Show your work and explain your thinking on a piece of paper.

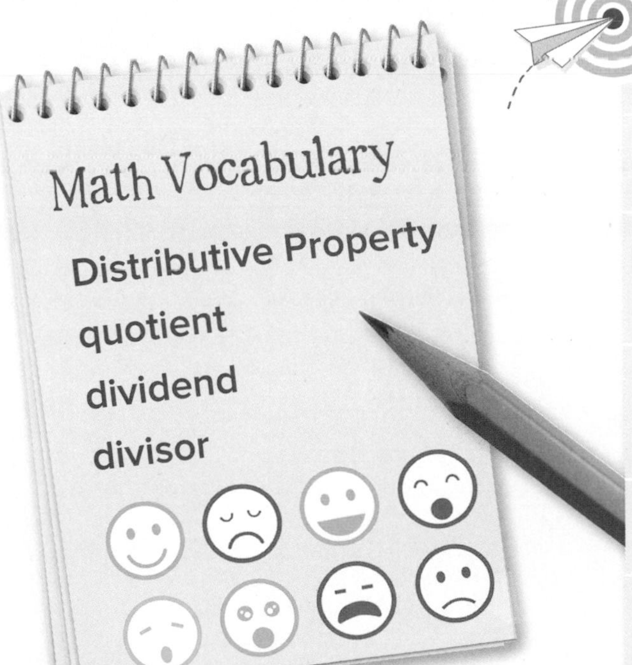

ACE IT TIME!

	yes	no
Did you underline the question in the word problem?		
Did you circle the numbers or number words?		
Did you box the supporting details or information needed to solve the problem?		
Did you draw a picture or a graphic organizer and write a math sentence to show your thinking?		
Did you label your numbers and your picture?		
Did you explain your thinking and use math vocabulary words in your explanation?		

Look around you for numbers with 4 digits. Use each number as a dividend. Roll a die to find a number to use as the divisor. Find the quotient using the Distributive Property. Draw a picture using base-ten blocks and explain how you would use the Distributive Property using that model.

Remainders

UNPACK THE STANDARD
You will be able to represent the remainder, or what is left over, when a dividend cannot be divided by the divisor evenly.

LEARN IT: You can use a model to help you divide and determine the *remainder*.

Example: Look at the problem 10 ÷ 3 or $3\overline{)10}$

Step 1: Draw 3 boxes to represent the divisor, or the number of groups. Evenly distribute X's to represent the dividend, 10.

XXX XXX XXX X

Step 2: There is 1 X left over. 10 cannot be divided evenly by 3. The X left over is called the remainder. It is represented like this:

$$\begin{array}{r} 3 \text{ R1} \\ 3\overline{)10} \end{array}$$

think!
How can you write this another way to make it easier?

think!
It is difficult to break large numbers into groups. Which problems might be better solved using a different strategy?

PRACTICE: Now you try

Use any method that you have learned so far to solve these division problems. If there is a remainder, use R in the answer.

1. 29 ÷ 6	**2.** $3\overline{)124}$

3. $6\overline{)3{,}940}$ =	**4.** 768 ÷ 9 =

Mabel loves to read. She collects books every chance she gets. By the time she is 12, she has collected 467 books. She wants to organize them equally into her 5-shelf bookshelf. Estimate how many books she can place on each shelf. Will she have any left over? If so, how many? Show your work and explain your thinking on a piece of paper.

ACE IT TIME!

	yes	no
Did you underline the question in the word problem?	◯	◯
Did you circle the numbers or number words?	◯	◯
Did you box the supporting details or information needed to solve the problem?	◯	◯
Did you draw a picture or a graphic organizer and write a math sentence to show your thinking?	◯	◯
Did you label your numbers and your picture?	◯	◯
Did you explain your thinking and use math vocabulary words in your explanation?	◯	◯

Divide a piece of paper in half. Label one side No Remainders and the other side Remainders. Roll 2 dice to get 3 numbers. Use 2 of these numbers to form a 2-digit dividend and use the other number as a divisor. Arrange the 3 numbers in different sequences to see how many division problems you can make where the quotient has no remainders and how many division problems you can make that have a remainder. Record the problems on the correct side of the paper. Roll the dice again and start over. *Challenge:* Use 4 dice to make the dividend 3 digits, or 5 dice to make a 4-digit dividend.

Understanding Remainders

UNPACK THE STANDARD
You will interpret the remainder, or understand what the remainder represents (means) in a division problem.

LEARN IT: The meaning of the *remainder* in a division problem depends on the question that you have to solve. You must *interpret* the remainder. See how the same problem with a different question will have a different answer because the remainder has a different meaning.

Example: Lori has 204 inches of material to make braided cloth bracelets. She needs 8 inches for each bracelet. Let's solve with the partial quotients strategy:

```
     25 R4
 8 ) 204
   - 160     (8 x 20 = 160)     20
      44
   -  40     (8 x 5 = 40)        5
       4
```

Partial Quotients

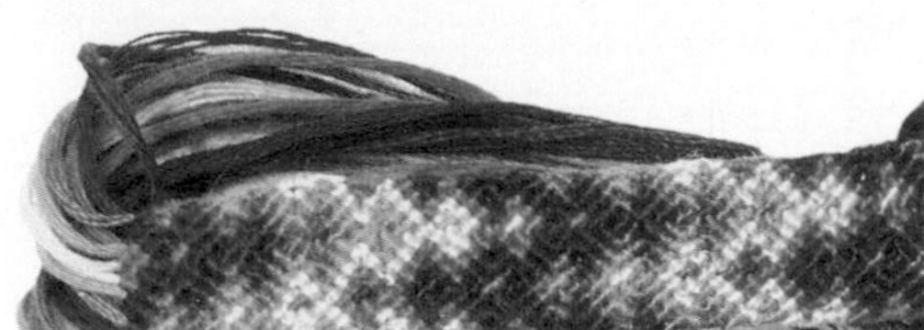

Now let's look closely at how the answer changes depending on the question:

Question	Answer
How many bracelets can she make?	**USE ONLY THE QUOTIENT** Even though she will have some material left over, *Lori will make 25 bracelets that use 8 inches of material.*
How much material will Lori have left?	**USE ONLY THE REMAINDER:** Lori will make 25 bracelets that use 8 inches of material. *She will have 4 inches left.*
How much smaller will a bracelet be if she makes a bracelet out of the leftover material?	**WRITE THE REMAINDER AS A FRACTION:** Lori will have $\frac{4}{8}$ of material left over. $\frac{4}{8}$ is the same as $\frac{1}{2}$. *The bracelet will be one-half the size of the others.*
How many bracelets will Lori make if she uses all the material?	**ADD 1 TO THE QUOTIENT:** Lori will make 25 bracelets that use 8 inches of material. She has 4 inches left over. She can make one extra bracelet using the 4 inches. *The answer is Lori can make 26 bracelets.*

PRACTICE: Now you try

There are 39 students that want to volunteer to work at the school fall carnival. Each booth needs 4 volunteers.

1. How many booths can 39 students cover at the carnival?

2. How many booths will have an extra volunteer?

Kennedy's mom bought 24 feet of ribbon. She is going to make bows for 8 packages. If each bow is the same length, how long is each piece? If Kennedy's mom plans to put a bow on 9 packages, how much ribbon will she use for each package? Show your work and explain your thinking on a piece of paper.

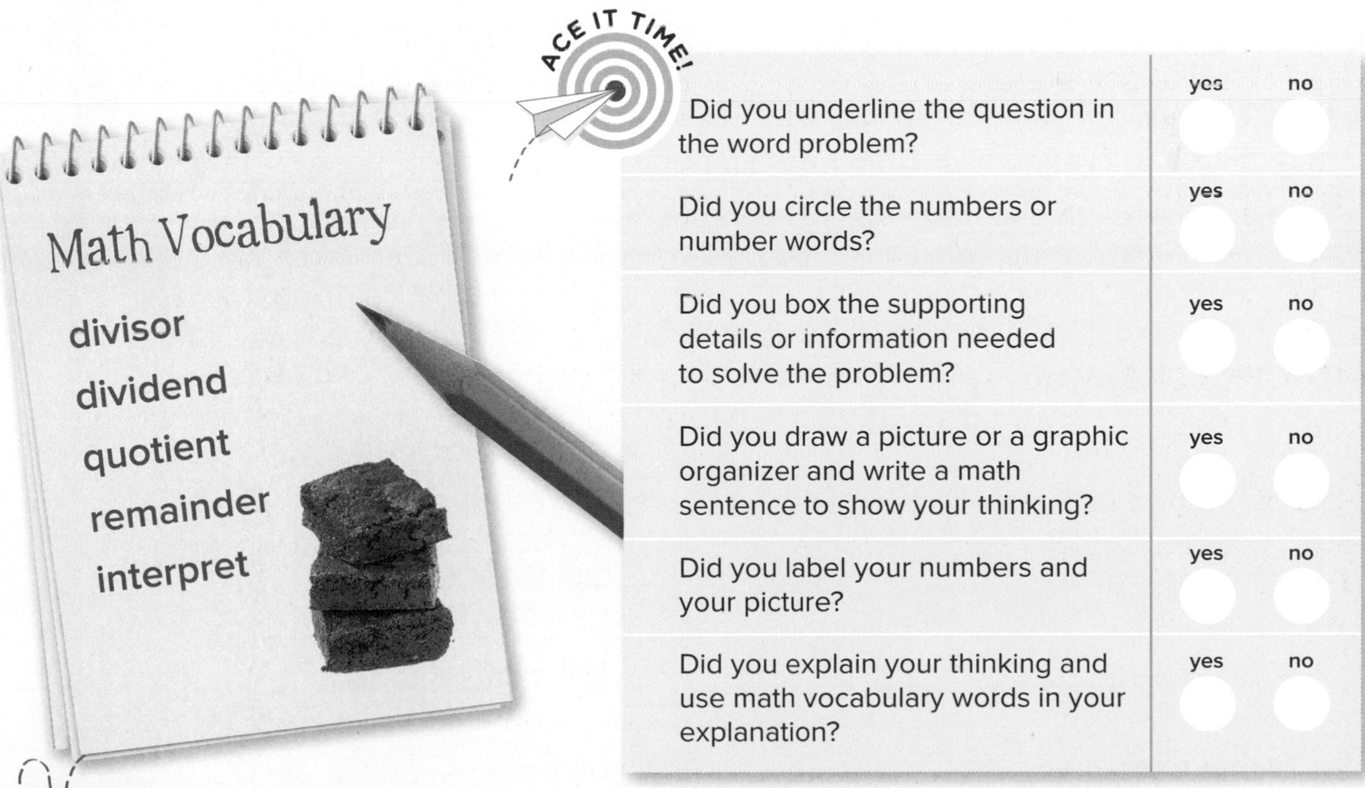

	yes	no
Did you underline the question in the word problem?		
Did you circle the numbers or number words?		
Did you box the supporting details or information needed to solve the problem?		
Did you draw a picture or a graphic organizer and write a math sentence to show your thinking?		
Did you label your numbers and your picture?		
Did you explain your thinking and use math vocabulary words in your explanation?		

MATH ON THE MOVE

Look for ways in your daily life that you see remainders! For example, you and your friend want to share 3 brownies. You each get one brownie, but what do you do with the remaining brownie?

Divide by 10, 100, or 1,000

UNPACK THE STANDARD
You will divide numbers by using basic division facts and multiples of 10, 100, and 1,000.

LEARN IT: You can divide using basic fact knowledge and what you know about place value.

Example A

think!
If 16 ÷ 8 = 2, then
16 tens ÷ 8 = 2 tens

Step 1: 160 ÷ 8 Identify the basic fact 16 ÷ 8
Step 2: Think—160 is the same as 16 tens
Step 3: Divide—16 tens ÷ 8 = 2 tens
160 ÷ 8 = 20

Example B

think!
If 16 ÷ 8 = 2, then
16 hundreds ÷ 8 =
2 hundreds

Step 1: 1,600 ÷ 8 Identify the basic fact 16 ÷ 8
Step 2: Think—1,600 is the same as 16 hundreds
Step 3: Divide—16 hundreds ÷ 8 = 2 hundreds
1,600 ÷ 8 = 200

PRACTICE: Now you try

1. 2,700 ÷ 9	**2.** 240 ÷ 6
Name the basic fact: ______	Name the basic fact: ______
2,700 = 27 ______	240 = 24 ______
27 hundreds ÷ 9 = ______	24 tens ÷ 6 = ______
2,700 ÷ 9 = ______	240 ÷ 6 = ______

3. 3,500 ÷ 7	**4.** 640 ÷ 8
Name the basic fact: ________________	Name the basic fact: ________________
3,500 = 35 ________________	640 = 64 ________________
35 hundreds ÷ 7 = ________________	64 tens ÷ 8 = ________________
3,500 ÷ 7 = ________________	640 ÷ 8 = ________________

Sherri collects 420 shells from the beach. She makes six trips in one year. Each time she goes to the beach, she takes a different bucket. Sherri wants to be sure that she places the same number of shells in each bucket. She is thinking about placing 50 shells in each bucket. Is this good thinking? How would you help her solve this problem? Show your work and explain your thinking on a piece of paper.

ACE IT TIME!

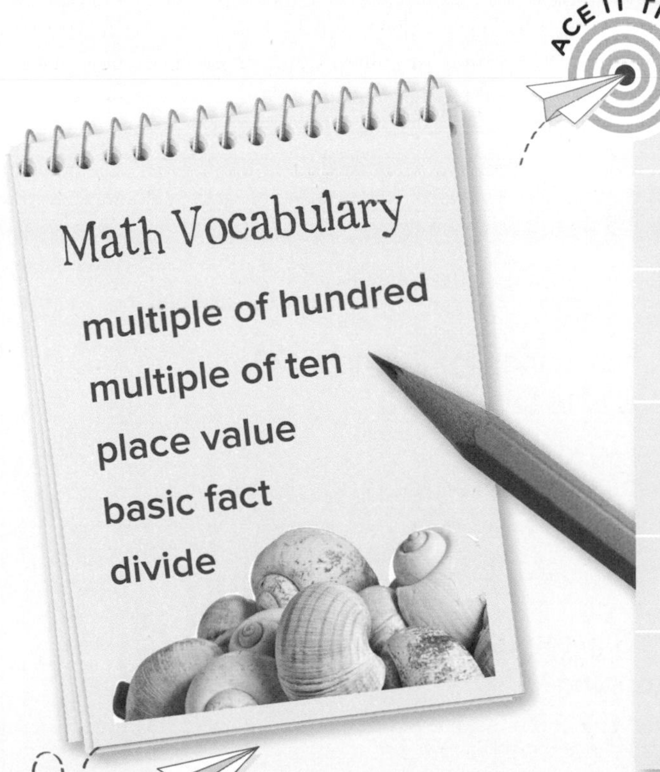

	yes	no
Did you underline the question in the word problem?	○	○
Did you circle the numbers or number words?	○	○
Did you box the supporting details or information needed to solve the problem?	○	○
Did you draw a picture or a graphic organizer and write a math sentence to show your thinking?	○	○
Did you label your numbers and your picture?	○	○
Did you explain your thinking and use math vocabulary words in your explanation?	○	○

Write down the basic fact family of 3, 4, and 12. Remember, you will have two multiplication sentences and two division sentences in this family. Then try to write the basic fact family of 30, 4, and 120. Do you see the pattern? Try 300, 4, and 1,200. Can you think of any other fact families using this pattern?

Divide by One Digit

UNPACK THE STANDARD
You will divide numbers by one digit using the standard algorithm.

LEARN IT: You now have an understanding of the place value meaning of division. All the previous lessons have prepared you to use the standard way to divide by a one-digit divisor! Let's see how to use the ***standard algorithm*** to solve the problem below. Remember, an algorithm is a way to solve a problem.

Example: 894 ÷ 7

Step 1:
Divide the hundreds. Look at the hundreds in 894. Ask, can 800 be shared among 7 groups without regrouping? Yes, the first digit in the quotient will be 1.

```
   1
7)894
```

Step 2:
Multiply the 1 (which has a value of 100 since it is in the 1 hundreds place) with 7.
You get 700, so put the 7 in the hundreds column.
Subtract 7 from the 8 in the dividend.
This leaves 1 group of one hundred.
Check. Can the 1 hundred be shared among 7 groups without regrouping? No.

```
   1
7)894
 -7
 ---
  1
```

Step 3:
Divide the tens. There are 9 tens in 894.
Bring down the 9 in the tens place next to the 1 in the hundreds place.
Can 19 tens be shared in 7 groups without regrouping?
Yes, the second digit in the quotient will be 2 (which stands for 2 tens or 20).
Multiply the 2 in the tens place with 7. 7 x 2 tens is 14 tens or 140.
Subtract the 14 tens from the 19 tens.
Check. Can the 5 tens be shared among 7 groups without regrouping? No.

```
   12
7)894
 -7
 ---
  19
 -14
 ---
   5
```

Step 4:
Divide the ones. There are 4 ones in 894.
Bring down the 4 in the ones place next to the 5 in the tens place.
Can 54 tens be shared in 7 groups without regrouping?
Yes, the third digit in the quotient will be 7 because 7 x 7 = 49.
Multiply the 7 in the ones place with the divisor.
Subtract 49 from the 54 ones.
Nothing more can be divided.

There will be a remainder of 5.

```
   127 R5
7)894
 -7
 ---
  19
 -14
 ---
   54
 - 49
 ----
    5
```

PRACTICE: Now you try

Use the standard way of dividing with one digit.

1. 369 ÷ 3 =

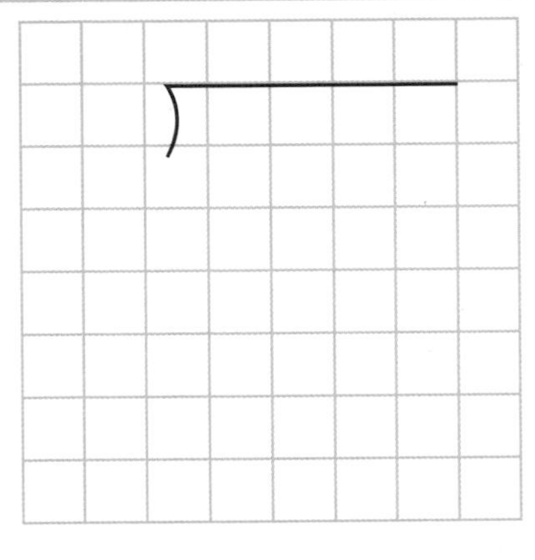

2. 4,584 ÷ 6 =

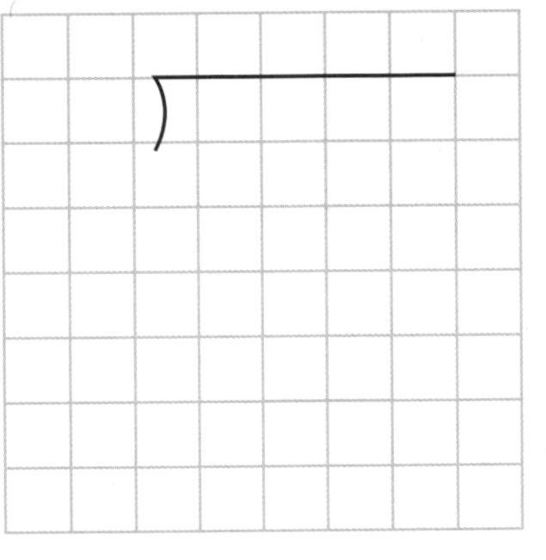

Miguel's physical education teacher has 145 students that signed up for the relay race. Each relay team includes 4 students. How many relay teams can the PE teacher form? Show your work and explain your thinking on a piece of paper.

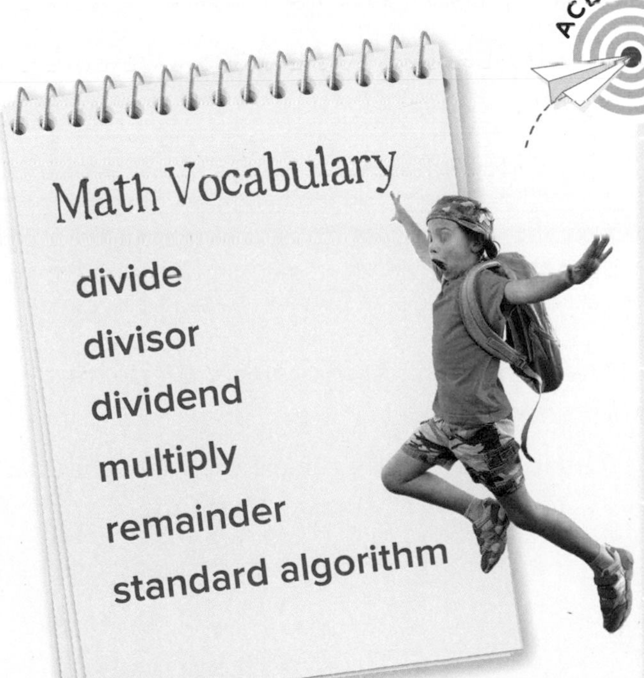

ACE IT TIME!

	yes	no
Did you underline the question in the word problem?		
Did you circle the numbers or number words?		
Did you box the supporting details or information needed to solve the problem?		
Did you draw a picture or a graphic organizer and write a math sentence to show your thinking?		
Did you label your numbers and your picture?		
Did you explain your thinking and use math vocabulary words in your explanation?		

Make a list of the number of times you can use division in a day. See if you can increase the list every day for a week. Talk to your friends and family to get ideas. Set a goal of 84 for the week. How many times would you have to use division each day to reach that goal?

REVIEW

Stop and think about what you have learned.

Congratulations! You have finished the lessons for this unit. This means that you have learned the principles of division and understand how your knowledge of multiples and multiplication can provide meaning to the process.

Now it's time to prove your skills with division. Solve the problems below! Use all of the methods you have learned.

Activity Section 1: Estimate the following quotients (answers).

1. 230 ÷ 8 =	**2.** 4,505 ÷ 9 =

Find the quotient using the partial quotients method.

3. 408 ÷ 8 =	**4.** 291 ÷ 3 =

Use multiples and the repeated subtraction to solve.

5. 2,049 ÷ 5 =	**6.** 3,062 ÷ 3 =

Use the Distributive Property to solve.

7. 255 ÷ 5 =	**8.** 424 ÷ 7 =

Use the following problem and questions to interpret the remainder. *Mary bought 68 ounces of cat food. Each of her three cats eats 4 ounces of food a day.*

9. How many days can she feed her cats?	**10.** How much extra cat food will be left, if any?	**11.** How could she divide the last amount to feed her cats one extra day?

Use the standard algorithm to solve.

12. $5\overline{)4,526}$	**13.** $6\overline{)8,259}$

CCSS.Math.Content.4.NBT.B6; CCSS.Math.Practice.MP1; MP2; MP3; MP6; MP7; MP8

UNDERSTAND

Understand the meaning of what you have learned and apply your knowledge.

You will demonstrate that you know how to read and understand a multi-step word problem that requires you to use the relationship between multiplication and division.

Activity Section 2

Luke saved $280 to pay for many summer activities during a two-week period in July. He figured he wanted to spend about $10 a day for 14 days. Does he have enough money for his plan? How much money does he have left over? If he wanted to, how much more money could he spend on each of the 14 days to use all his money?

CCSS.Math.Content.4.NBT.B6; CCSS.Math.Practice.MP1; MP2; MP3; MP6; MP7; MP8

DISCOVER

Discover how you can apply the information you have learned.

You will demonstrate that you understand how to apply what you know about the division process to a real-world situation by using a divisor with two digits instead of one digit.

Activity Section 3

Pretend you are a teacher! Look at the work that one of your students did below to answer this math problem. Explain to her what she did correctly and then where she made her mistake.

Karen and Dennis wanted to travel from Florida to California and then back again. It is 3,561 miles, one way. They planned to travel an average of 50 miles an hour and 7 hours a day each way. While there, they wanted to spend 10 days visiting family and friends. How much vacation time must they request in order to be able to take the trip?

Florida — California

3,561 miles

50 miles per hour for 7 hours....350 miles per day   50 × 7 = 350 miles in one day.

How many days will it take if they travel 350 miles a day to go 3,561 miles?

3,561 ÷ 350 = ??

Student Work

3,500 61	350 × **10** = 3,500 partial quotient 10 days Extra 61 miles...about 1 hour.
	If it takes 10 days for Karen and Dennis to travel across the country one way, they need to request 20 vacation days.

CORE Fractions Concepts

Equivalent Fractions

UNPACK THE STANDARD
You will be able to use fraction models to recognize and create equivalent fractions. You will also be able to explain why a fraction is equivalent.

LEARN IT: Fractions that have different names but have the same value are called *equivalent* fractions. Fractions can be written many different ways by changing the number of equal parts in the whole.

How Can You Use Models to Show Equivalent Fractions?

Example: Is $\frac{1}{4}$ of a turkey sandwich equivalent to $\frac{2}{8}$ of the same-sized turkey sandwich?

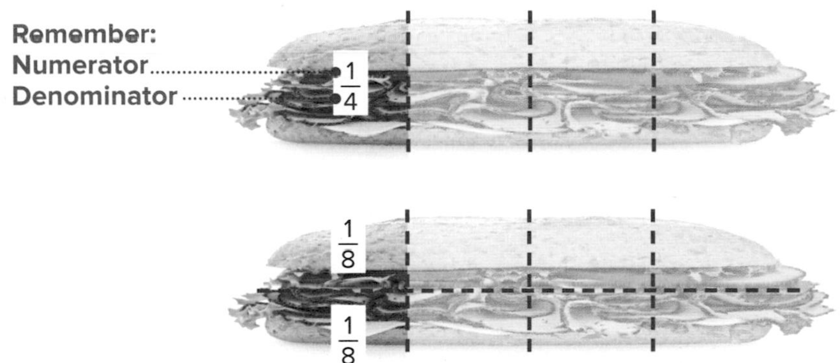

think!
Combine unit fractions to name the shaded area $\frac{2}{8}$.

Step 1: Compare the shaded areas. Both subs have the same shaded area of equal-sized rectangles, so you can rename $\frac{1}{4}$ as $\frac{2}{8}$. They are equivalent fractions. Look at the two fractions. What do you notice about the numerators and how are they are related? What do you notice about the denominators and how are they related? **There are 2 times as many total parts (denominators) and 2 times as many shaded parts (numerators).**

Step 2: You can find equivalent fractions by multiplying the numerator and the denominator by the same number.

$$\frac{1 \times 2}{4 \times 2} = \frac{2}{8}$$

Example: Let's use the same rectangle to write another equivalent fraction. Model $\frac{2}{4}$ using 16th-sized parts. Find an equivalent fraction with a denominator of 16 using multiplication.

think!
When a fraction has a denominator of 16, the whole needs to be divided into 16 equal parts.

8 out of 16 pieces is equivalent to 2 out of 4 pieces of the same-sized rectangle.

Step 1: $\frac{2}{4} = \frac{?}{4\times4} = \frac{\ }{16}$

Since 16 = 4 × 4, the equivalent fraction has 4 times the total number of equal parts.

Step 2: There are $\frac{4}{16}$ for each fourth. **There are 4 times as many total parts and 4 times as many parts shaded.** Multiply the number of fourths (2 shaded parts) by 4 to find the number of 16ths in the equivalent fraction.

$$\frac{2}{4} = \frac{2\times4}{4\times4} = \frac{\ }{16}$$

Since 8 = 2 × 4, the equivalent fraction is $\frac{8}{16}$.

Step 3: Both rectangles have the same shaded area, so you can rename $\frac{2}{4}$ as $\frac{8}{16}$. They are equivalent fractions.

Step 4: You can find equivalent fractions by multiplying the numerator and the denominator by the same number.

$$\frac{2}{4} \times \frac{4}{4} = \frac{8}{16}$$

You can also divide to find equivalent fractions:

$$\frac{8}{16} = \frac{8\div4}{16\div4} = \frac{2}{4}$$

think!
Division is the opposite operation of multiplication.

You can divide a numerator and a denominator by the same number to find equivalent fractions.

PRACTICE: Now you try

Draw on the model and fill in the blanks. Use the given denominator to make an equivalent fraction.

1. 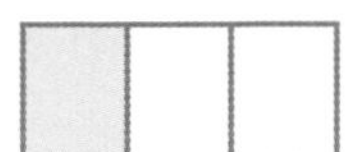 $\frac{1}{3} = \frac{1}{3} \times \frac{\square}{\times} = \frac{\square}{9}$

think!
What times 3 is equal to 9? Now multiply the numerator by that same number.

2. 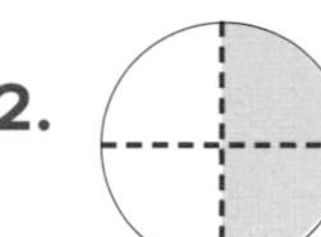 $\frac{2}{4} = \frac{2}{4} \times \frac{\square}{\times} = \frac{\square}{8}$

Write Equivalent Fractions

3. $\frac{1}{2} = \frac{1}{2} \times \frac{\square}{\times} = \frac{\square}{8}$

4. $\frac{3}{5} =$ ________ $= \frac{\square}{10}$

5. $\frac{3}{4} =$ ________ $= \frac{\square}{12}$

Circle all equivalent fractions. Show your work.

6. $\frac{1}{2}, \frac{2}{3}, \frac{3}{6}, \frac{5}{12}, \frac{5}{10}$

7. $\frac{1}{2}, \frac{1}{3}, \frac{2}{3}, \frac{4}{12}, \frac{2}{5}, \frac{2}{6}$

Kali wants to make a stir fry. She needs $\frac{4}{6}$ of a cup of onions. She can only find $\frac{1}{3}$ and $\frac{1}{8}$ measuring cups. Which one can she use? Show your work and explain your thinking on a piece of paper.

ACE IT TIME!

	yes	no
Did you underline the question in the word problem?	○	○
Did you circle the numbers or number words?	○	○
Did you box the supporting details or information needed to solve the problem?	○	○
Did you draw a picture or a graphic organizer and write a math sentence to show your thinking?	○	○
Did you label your numbers and your picture?	○	○
Did you explain your thinking and use math vocabulary words in your explanation?	○	○

Volunteer to help in the kitchen. You can practice finding equivalent fractions using measuring cups and measuring spoons. Ask yourself: “How many $\frac{1}{2}$ cups does it take to fill 1 cup?” or “How many $\frac{1}{4}$ cups fill $\frac{1}{2}$?” The kitchen is where fractions come alive.

Fractions in Simplest Form

UNPACK THE STANDARD
You will be able to recognize, find, and write fractions in their simplest form.

LEARN IT: You can use common factors to write fractions in their *simplest* form. Use what you know about equivalent fractions.

Example: Write $\frac{9}{12}$ in its simplest form.

To write a fraction in its simplest form, you must find the common factors of the numerator and the denominator.

Step 1: List the factors of the numerator and the denominator. Find the factors they both have in common. In this case, both the numerator and the denominator have the common factor of **3**.

9	factors of 9:	1, 3, 9
12	factors of 12:	1, 2, 3, 4, 6, 12

Step 2: Divide the numerator and denominator by the largest common factor, if it is greater than 1.

$9 \div 3 = 3$ $\qquad$ $12 \div 3 = 4$

So, $\frac{9}{12} = \frac{3}{4}$

Wait, what if a fraction is already written in simplest form? Let's look at the fraction $\frac{3}{7}$. In this case, the ONLY common factor of the numerator and denominator is 1. Because 1 is the only factor that 3 and 7 have in common, it is already in its simplest form!

PRACTICE: Now you try

Find the common factors of the numerator and the denominator. Write each fraction in its simplest form.

1. $\frac{6}{10}$ = ____________ **2.** $\frac{2}{4}$ = ____________ **3.** $\frac{8}{12}$ = ____________

4. $\frac{4}{8}$ = ____________ **5.** = ____________ **6.** $\frac{40}{100}$ = ____________

Is the fraction in its simplest form? Circle yes or no.

7. $\frac{3}{5}$ yes no **8.** $\frac{8}{10}$ yes no **9.** $\frac{5}{15}$ yes no **10.** $\frac{7}{11}$ yes no

Write each fraction in its simplest form.

11. $\frac{12}{16} = \frac{\_}{4}$	**12.** $\frac{3}{9} = \frac{\_}{3}$	**13.** $\frac{10}{15} = \frac{\_}{3}$
14. $\frac{18}{20} = \frac{\_}{10}$	**15.** $\frac{2}{6} = \frac{\_}{3}$	**16.** $\frac{14}{16} = \frac{\_}{8}$

Trevon is making banana bread. The recipe says that he needs $\frac{6}{8}$ of a cup of nuts. He can only find a $\frac{1}{4}$-cup measuring cup. How many $\frac{1}{4}$-cups of nuts does Trevon need?

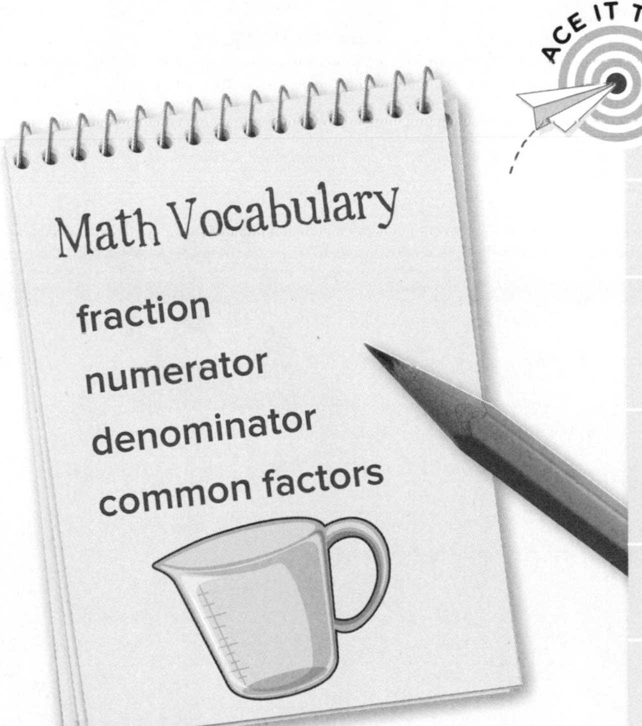

ACE IT TIME!

	yes	no
Did you underline the question in the word problem?		
Did you circle the numbers or number words?		
Did you box the supporting details or information needed to solve the problem?		
Did you draw a picture or a graphic organizer and write a math sentence to show your thinking?		
Did you label your numbers and your picture?		
Did you explain your thinking and use math vocabulary words in your explanation?		

MATH ON THE MOVE

Ask an adult to name a fraction. Use what you learned in this lesson to determine whether or not the fraction is in its simplest form. If it is not, find its simplest form. Make sure you explain how you know. Don't stop there; ask her or him to name another and another!

Common Denominators

UNPACK THE STANDARD
You will be able to recognize, find, and calculate fractions to have the same denominator, or bottom number.

LEARN IT: Common denominators can be found by finding common multiples of the denominators of two or more fractions. Fractions with ***common denominators*** have wholes divided into the same number of equal pieces. This makes it easier to add or subtract fractions.

Use a Model to Find Common Denominator

Example: Find a common denominator for $\frac{1}{3}$ and $\frac{1}{9}$.

$\frac{1}{3}$

$\frac{1}{9}$

think!
Step 1: I can divide both of these wholes into the same amount of equal parts so that they both have the same or ***common denominator***.

think!
Step 2: Once I draw lines to divide the whole into ninths, I realize that $\frac{1}{3}$ is equivalent to $\frac{3}{9}$.

Step 1: Draw lines to divide the whole into ninths.

You can see how $\frac{1}{3} = \frac{3}{9}$. 9 becomes your new **common denominator.**

Step 2: Rename your fractions if necessary.

$$\frac{1 \times 3 = \boxed{3}}{3 \times 3 = \mathbf{9}}$$

$$\frac{1 \times 1 = \mathbf{1}}{9 \times 1 = \mathbf{9}}$$

$\frac{1}{3}$ can be renamed $\frac{3}{9}$, but $\frac{1}{9}$ does not have to be renamed.

Both fractions now have a common denominator of 9.

Use Common Multiples to Find Common Denominator

Example: Find a common denominator for $\frac{3}{4}$ and $\frac{2}{5}$.

Step 1: Find the multiples of the denominators 4 and 5. See which multiples they have in common.

Multiples of 4: 4, 8, 12, 16, 20, 24
Multiples of 5: 5, 10, 15, 20, 25

20 is the common multiple of 4 and 5, so it becomes your new common **denominator**.

Step 2: Write the equivalent fractions with the common denominator of 20

$$\frac{3 \times 5}{4 \times (5)} = \frac{\mathbf{15}}{\mathbf{20}}$$

think!

4 times what is equal to the common denominator of 20? I know that 4 times 5 is equal to 20. Whatever I do to the bottom, I do to the top, so I will multiply my numerator by 5 also.

Let's follow the same steps for fraction $\frac{2}{5}$.

$$\frac{2 \times 4}{5 \times 4} = \frac{\mathbf{8}}{\mathbf{20}}$$

$$\frac{2}{5} = \frac{8}{20}$$

think!

5 times what is equal to the common denominator of 20? I know that 5 times 4 is equal to 20. Whatever I do to the bottom, I do to the top, so I will multiply my numerator by 4 also.

$\frac{3}{4}$ can be renamed $\frac{15}{20}$, and $\frac{2}{5}$ can be renamed $\frac{8}{20}$. Both fractions now have a common denominator of 20.

PRACTICE: Now you try

Use models and draw lines to make common denominators. Rename fractions.

1. $\frac{1}{4}$ $\frac{3}{8}$

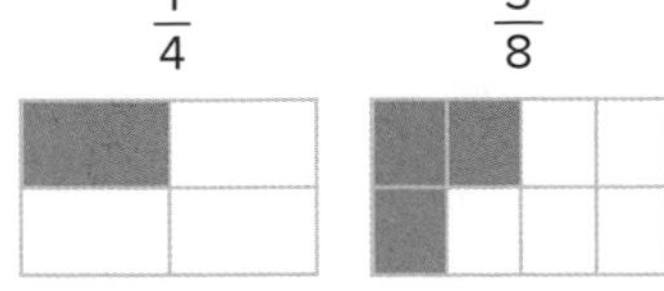

Common denominator ________

$\frac{1}{4}$ = ________

$\frac{3}{8}$ = ________

2. $\frac{2}{3}$ $\frac{4}{12}$

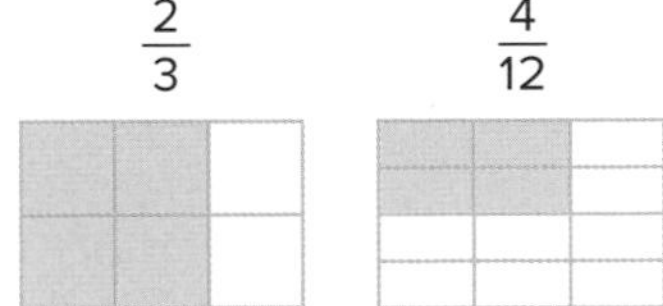

Common denominator ________

$\frac{2}{3}$ = ________

$\frac{4}{12}$ = ________

3. $\frac{1}{4}$ $\frac{6}{16}$

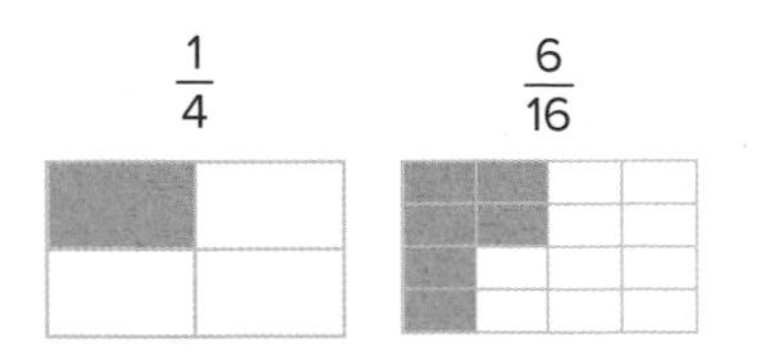

Common denominator ________

$\frac{1}{4}$ = ________

$\frac{6}{16}$ = ________

Use models and draw lines to make common denominators. Rename fractions.

4. $\frac{1}{3}$ and $\frac{1}{4}$	**5.** $\frac{3}{12}$ and $\frac{7}{8}$
Multiples of 3 : ____, ____, ____, ____, ____, ____	Multiples of 12: ____, ____, ____
Multiples of 4: ____, ____, ____, ____, ____, ____	Multiples of 8: ____, ____, ____, ____
Common denominator ________	Common denominator ________
$\frac{1}{3} \times \frac{\square}{\square} = \frac{\square}{\square}$	$\frac{3}{12} \times \frac{\square}{\square} = \frac{\square}{\square}$
$\frac{1}{4} \times \frac{\square}{\square} = \frac{\square}{\square}$	$\frac{7}{8} \times \frac{\square}{\square} = \frac{\square}{\square}$

Nigel is working on a math problem with one of his friends in class. He says that the common denominator for $\frac{4}{5}$ and $\frac{2}{3}$ is 8. Is he correct? If he is, explain. If not, what did he do wrong? Show your work and explain your thinking on a piece of paper.

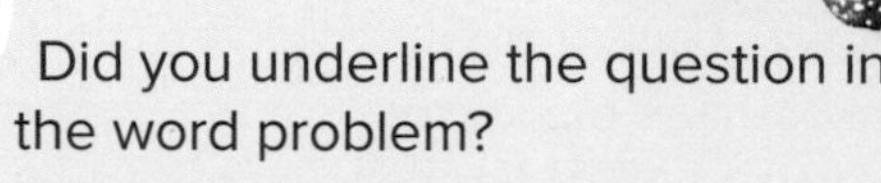

ACE IT TIME!

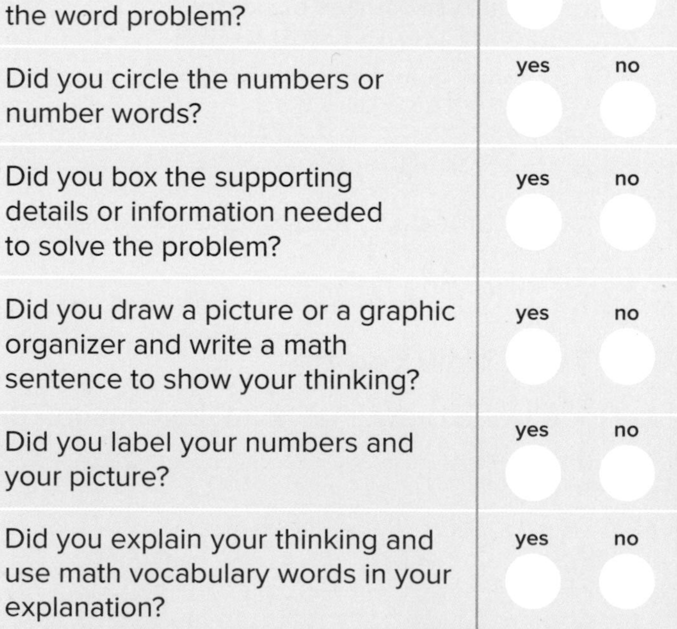

	yes	no
Did you underline the question in the word problem?	○	○
Did you circle the numbers or number words?	○	○
Did you box the supporting details or information needed to solve the problem?	○	○
Did you draw a picture or a graphic organizer and write a math sentence to show your thinking?	○	○
Did you label your numbers and your picture?	○	○
Did you explain your thinking and use math vocabulary words in your explanation?	○	○

Math Vocabulary

fraction
numerator
denominator
common denominator
multiples
equivalent

In order to find common denominators, it is important that you know your multiples. Practice makes perfect! So start by picking a number and practice saying its multiples. Remember you can find a number's multiples by skip-counting by that number. Now pick another number and say its multiples. You could even share all of this fun with an adult!

Compare Fractions

UNPACK THE STANDARD
You will compare fractions with different numerators and different denominators.

LEARN IT: You can compare fractions by drawing models and using *benchmark* numbers. You can also use what you have learned about equivalent fractions and finding a common denominator to help you compare fractions.

Using Benchmarks to Compare Fractions

A **benchmark** is a known amount that you can use to compare or estimate other amounts.

Example: Compare fractions $\frac{3}{8}$ and $\frac{9}{10}$ using the $\frac{1}{2}$ benchmark.

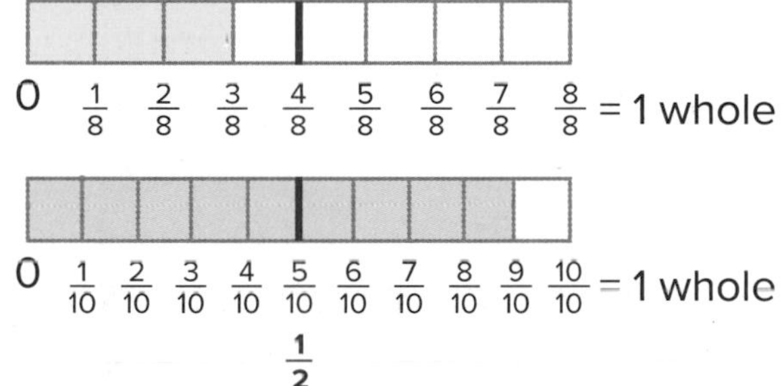

think!
$\frac{3}{8}$ is less than $\frac{4}{8}$, which is $\frac{1}{2}$.
$\frac{9}{10}$ is greater than $\frac{5}{10}$, which is $\frac{1}{2}$

Draw models. Make sure the wholes are equal. Look at the models. Compare them to the benchmark fraction $\frac{1}{2}$. So $\frac{9}{10}$ is greater than $\frac{3}{8}$.

You can also use the benchmark of 1 whole to compare the fractions above. Look at the models. Notice $\frac{9}{10}$ is closer to 1 whole than $\frac{3}{8}$ is.

Using Equivalent Fractions to Help Compare Fractions

Example: Find the common denominator to help you compare fractions. Compare $\frac{2}{3}$ and $\frac{3}{4}$.

Multiples of 3: 3, 6, 9, 12
Multiples of 4: 4, 8, 12, 16

Common denominator: **12**

Now write equivalent fractions using the common denominator.

$\frac{2}{3}$ is renamed as $\frac{8}{12}$. $\frac{3}{4}$ is renamed as $\frac{9}{12}$.

Since $\frac{8}{12}$ is less than $\frac{9}{12}$, then $\frac{2}{3}$ is less than $\frac{3}{4}$.

So $\mathbf{\frac{2}{3}} < \mathbf{\frac{3}{4}}$.

$$\frac{2 \times 4}{3 \times 4} = \frac{\mathbf{8}}{\mathbf{12}} \qquad \frac{3 \times 3}{4 \times 3} = \frac{\mathbf{9}}{\mathbf{12}}$$

think!
3 times what number is equal to the common denominator of 12? 3 times 4 is equal to 12. Whatever you do to the bottom, you do to the top, so multiply the numerator by 4 also.

Cross Multiplying to Compare Fractions

8 9

$\frac{2}{3} \times \frac{3}{4}$

Since 9 is greater than 8, $\frac{3}{4}$ is greater than $\frac{2}{3}$.

think!
Multiply the opposite numerators by the opposite denominators.
4 × 2 = 8 and 3 × 3 = 9

PRACTICE: Now you try

Draw models and use benchmark numbers to compare fractions. Write > or <.

1. $\frac{8}{10}$ ◯ $\frac{4}{8}$	**2.** $\frac{1}{3}$ ◯ $\frac{4}{5}$	**3.** $\frac{1}{4}$ ◯ $\frac{3}{6}$

Use equivalent fractions to compare fractions. Write > , <, or =.

4. $\frac{2}{10}$ ◯ $\frac{1}{4}$	**5.** $\frac{4}{5}$ ◯ $\frac{8}{10}$	**6.** $\frac{5}{12}$ ◯ $\frac{2}{6}$

Tatiana vacuumed $\frac{4}{10}$ of her bedroom. Troy has exactly the same-sized bedroom as Tatiana. He vacuumed $\frac{2}{3}$ of his bedroom. Who did the most vacuuming? Show your work and explain your thinking on a piece of paper.

ACE IT TIME!

	yes	no
Did you underline the question in the word problem?	◯	◯
Did you circle the numbers or number words?	◯	◯
Did you box the supporting details or information needed to solve the problem?	◯	◯
Did you draw a picture or a graphic organizer and write a math sentence to show your thinking?	◯	◯
Did you label your numbers and your picture?	◯	◯
Did you explain your thinking and use math vocabulary words in your explanation?	◯	◯

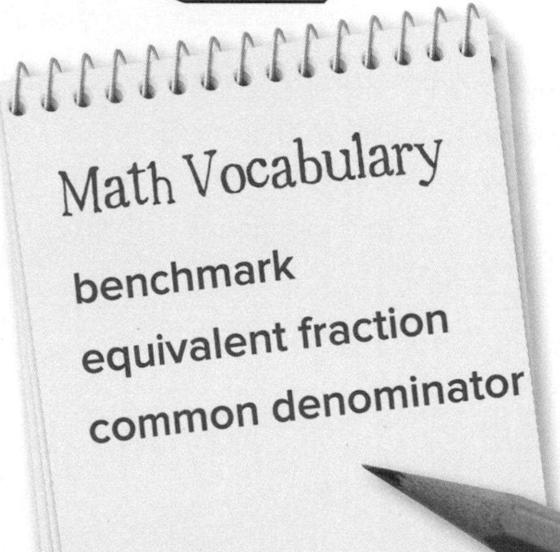

Measuring cups and measuring spoons are great tools that you can find in your own kitchen to practice comparing fractions. Ask yourself: "What is larger, $\frac{1}{2}$ of a teaspoon or $\frac{1}{4}$ of a teaspoon? Or ask yourself: "Would you rather have $\frac{1}{2}$ of a cup of orange juice or $\frac{1}{8}$ of a cup?"

Order Fractions

UNPACK THE STANDARD
You will compare and order fractions with different numerators and different denominators.

LEARN IT: Remember, fractions can only be compared when working with the same-sized whole. You can use benchmark numbers to help you compare and order fractions or you can use what you know about equivalent fractions to help you compare and order fractions. Remember, a benchmark is a known amount that you can use to compare or estimate other amounts.

Using Benchmarks to Compare and Order Fractions

Example: Order the fractions $\frac{5}{8}$, $\frac{7}{10}$, $\frac{1}{4}$ from least to greatest using the $\frac{1}{2}$ benchmark.

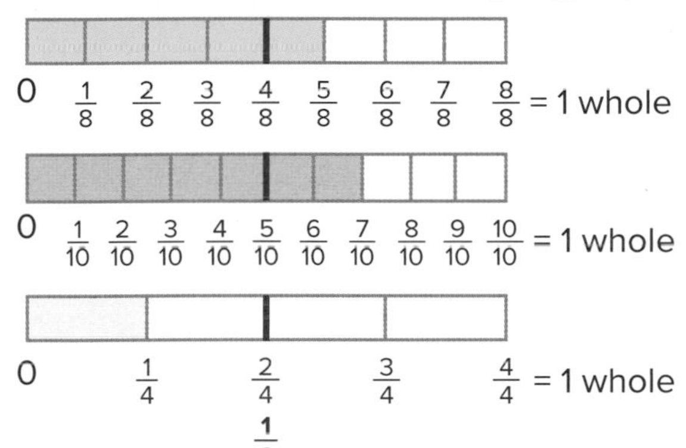

think!
$\frac{5}{8}$ is greater than $\frac{4}{8}$, which is $\frac{1}{2}$ and . . .
$\frac{1}{4}$ is less than $\frac{2}{4}$, which is $\frac{1}{2}$.

Draw models. Make sure the wholes are equal. Look at the models. Compare them to the benchmark fraction $\frac{1}{2}$. Notice $\frac{1}{4}$ is less than $\frac{1}{2}$ and both $\frac{5}{8}$ and $\frac{7}{10}$ are greater than $\frac{1}{2}$. Also notice $\frac{7}{10}$ is greater than $\frac{5}{8}$.

You can also use the benchmark of 1 whole to compare the fractions. Look at the models. Notice $\frac{7}{10}$ is closer to 1 whole than $\frac{5}{8}$ is and $\frac{5}{8}$ is closer to 1 whole than $\frac{1}{4}$ is.

So these fractions ordered from least to greatest are: $\frac{1}{4}$, $\frac{5}{8}$, $\frac{7}{10}$.

Using Equivalent Fractions to Help Compare and Order Fractions

Example: Order the fractions $\frac{2}{3}$, $\frac{1}{4}$, $\frac{3}{6}$ from greatest to least using a common denominator to make equivalent fractions.

Find Multiples of 3: 3, 6, 9, 12
Find Multiples of 4: 4, 8, 12, 16
Find Multiples of 6: 6, 12, 18

Common denominator: **12**

Now write equivalent fractions using the common denominator.

$\frac{2 \times 4}{3 \times 4} = \frac{\mathbf{8}}{\mathbf{12}}$ $\frac{1 \times 3}{4 \times 3} = \frac{\mathbf{3}}{\mathbf{12}}$ $\frac{3 \times 2}{6 \times 2} = \frac{\mathbf{6}}{\mathbf{12}}$

$\frac{2}{3}$ is renamed as $\frac{8}{12}$, $\frac{1}{4}$ is renamed as $\frac{3}{12}$, and $\frac{3}{6}$ is renamed as $\frac{6}{12}$.

So these fractions ordered from greatest to least are: $\frac{2}{3}$, $\frac{3}{6}$, $\frac{1}{4}$.

think!
3 times what number is equal to the common denominator of 12? 3 times 4 is equal to 12. Whatever you do to the bottom, you do to the top, so multiply the numerator by 4 also.

PRACTICE: Now you try

Write the fractions in order from **least to greatest**. Show your work.	Write the fractions in order from **greatest to least**. Show your work.	Compare fractions. Write >, <, or =. Show your work.
1. $\frac{2}{3}, \frac{5}{6}, \frac{1}{2}$ ___, ___, ___	**3.** $\frac{5}{8}, \frac{1}{4}, \frac{1}{2}$ ___, ___, ___	**5.** $\frac{4}{8}$ ◯ $\frac{2}{4}$
2. $\frac{5}{8}, \frac{2}{8}, \frac{2}{4}$ ___, ___, ___	**4.** $\frac{2}{10}, \frac{4}{5}, \frac{6}{10}$ ___, ___, ___	**6.** $\frac{3}{4}$ ◯ $\frac{2}{6}$

Majella decided that she would hike the trail behind her house a little bit each day for 3 days. On Monday, she walked $\frac{2}{3}$ of a mile. On Tuesday, she walked $\frac{3}{6}$ of a mile. On Wednesday, she walked $\frac{5}{12}$ of a mile. Put the fractions in order from least to greatest. Which day did she walk the most? Show your work and explain your thinking on a piece of paper.

ACE IT TIME!

	yes	no
Did you underline the question in the word problem?	◯	◯
Did you circle the numbers or number words?	◯	◯
Did you box the supporting details or information needed to solve the problem?	◯	◯
Did you draw a picture or a graphic organizer and write a math sentence to show your thinking?	◯	◯
Did you label your numbers and your picture?	◯	◯
Did you explain your thinking and use math vocabulary words in your explanation?	◯	◯

Practice ordering fractions. You can ask an adult to write fractions on index cards. You can use what you learned in this lesson to put them in order from least to greatest and from greatest to least.

Break Apart Fractions

UNPACK THE STANDARD

You will break apart fractions into a sum of fractions with the same denominator. You will do this in different ways and keep track of each by writing an equation.

LEARN IT: You can *decompose,* or break apart, a fraction into the sum of other fractions with the same denominator.

Decompose Fractions Using Unit Fractions

Example: Decompose the fraction $\frac{5}{10}$ using unit fractions.

$\frac{1}{10}$	$\frac{1}{10}$	$\frac{1}{10}$	$\frac{1}{10}$	$\frac{1}{10}$					

$\frac{5}{10} = \frac{1}{10} + \frac{1}{10} + \frac{1}{10} + \frac{1}{10} + \frac{1}{10}$

You can also think of it this way:

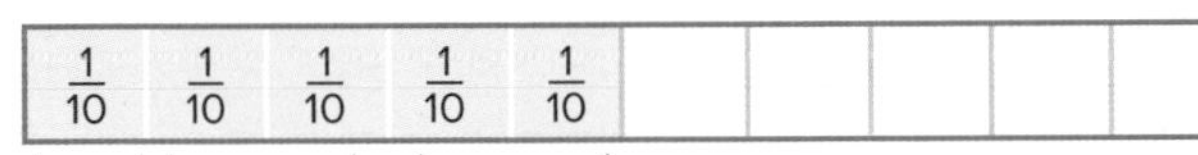

$\frac{5}{10} = \frac{1}{10} + \frac{2}{10} + \frac{2}{10}$

think!
The sum of the numerators must add up to 5.

Decompose Fractions Using Other Fractions

Example: Decompose the fraction $\frac{5}{10}$ using unit fractions.

$\frac{1}{10}$	$\frac{1}{10}$	$\frac{1}{10}$	$\frac{1}{10}$	$\frac{1}{10}$					

$\frac{5}{10} = \frac{2}{10} + \frac{3}{10}$ So, $\frac{5}{10} = \frac{2}{10} + \frac{3}{10}$

PRACTICE: Now you try

Write each fraction as a sum of unit fractions.

1. $\frac{5}{6}$	**2.** $\frac{3}{4}$	**3.** $\frac{7}{8}$

Write each fraction as a sum of other fractions.

4. $\frac{5}{6}$	**5.** $\frac{3}{4}$	**6.** $\frac{7}{8}$

Write each fraction as a sum of unit fractions.

7. $\frac{6}{10}$	**8.** $\frac{3}{5}$	**9.** $\frac{9}{6}$

Write each fraction as a sum of other fractions.

10. $\frac{6}{10}$	**11.** $\frac{3}{5}$	**12.** $\frac{9}{6}$

Nakeesha says that you can break apart a fraction, with a numerator of 3, four different ways. Is she right? Explain. Show your work and explain your thinking on a piece of paper.

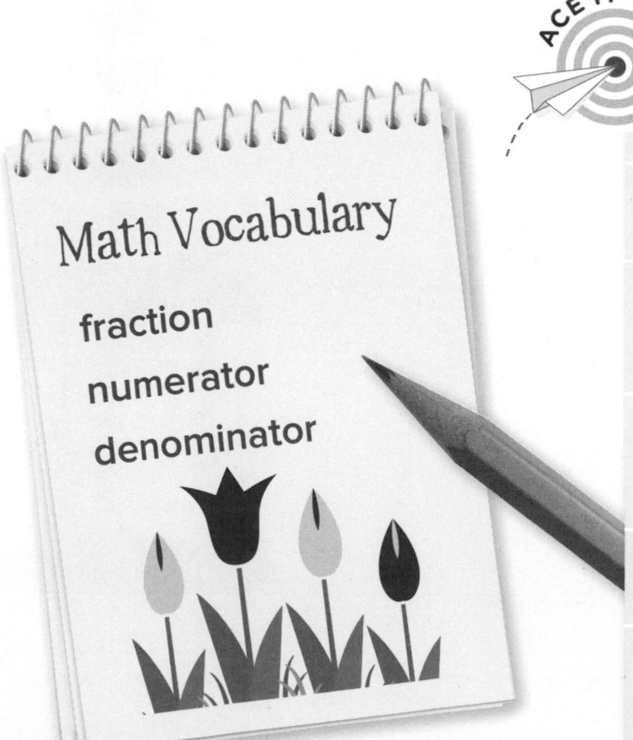

ACE IT TIME!

	yes	no
Did you underline the question in the word problem?	○	○
Did you circle the numbers or number words?	○	○
Did you box the supporting details or information needed to solve the problem?	○	○
Did you draw a picture or a graphic organizer and write a math sentence to show your thinking?	○	○
Did you label your numbers and your picture?	○	○
Did you explain your thinking and use math vocabulary words in your explanation?	○	○

Practice decomposing fractions. When you are out and about, look for fractions out in the world. Practice decomposing the fractions that you may find.

Rename Fractions and Mixed Numbers

UNPACK THE STANDARD
You will break apart fractions into a sum of fractions with the same denominator.

LEARN IT: In the last lesson you learned how to decompose fractions in different ways. You can use what you have learned to help you rename fractions and mixed numbers. A ***mixed number*** is a fraction greater than 1. It shows a whole number plus a fractional part.

Rename a Fraction Greater than 1 as a Mixed Number

Example: Rename the fraction $\frac{8}{3}$ as a mixed number. *Hint:* $\frac{8}{3}$ is a fraction greater than 1 because the numerator (8) is greater than the denominator (3).

Step 1: Model $\frac{8}{3}$.

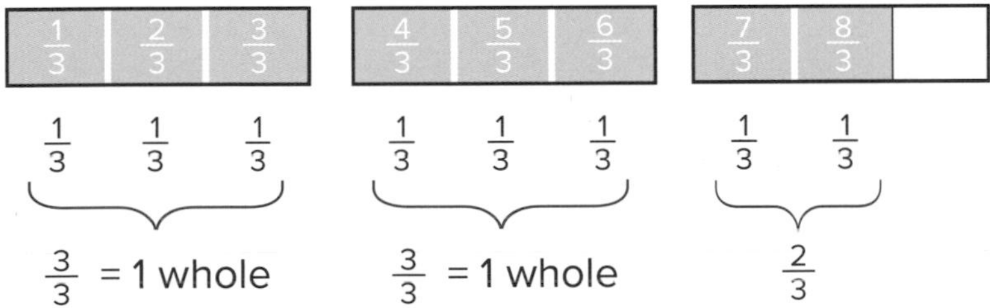

Step 2: There are 2 wholes and $\frac{2}{3}$ left over. So $\frac{8}{3}$ can be renamed $2\frac{2}{3}$.

$2\frac{2}{3}$ is a mixed number. Notice how it shows the sum of a whole number and a fraction.

Rename a Mixed Number as a Fraction Greater than 1

Example: Rename the mixed number $2\frac{2}{3}$.

Step 1: Model $2\frac{2}{3}$. This equals 2 wholes and $\frac{2}{3}$.

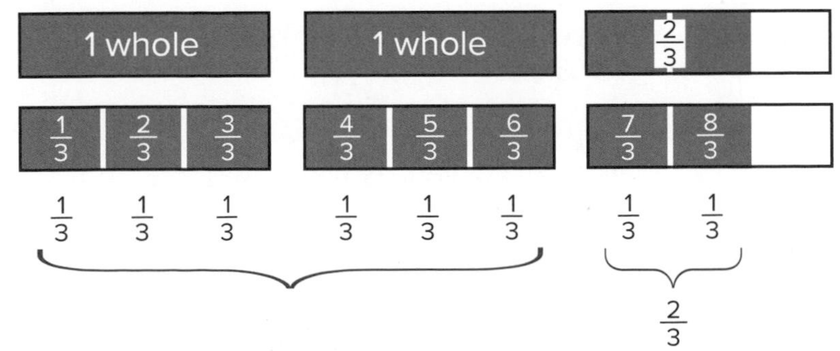

think!
Because the denominator is 3, the wholes must be divided into 3 equal parts. So we must find how many third-sized pieces are in 2 wholes. Then count the third-sized pieces in $\frac{2}{3}$ and combine to find the mixed number.

There are 6 third-sized pieces in 2 wholes and 2 third-sized pieces in $\frac{2}{3}$, so if I add them together I see that there are 8 third-sized pieces in $2\frac{2}{3}$.

So $2\frac{2}{3}$ can be renamed $\frac{8}{3}$.

PRACTICE: Now you try

Write the fraction greater than 1 as a mixed number. Show your work.

1. $\frac{6}{5}$ **2.** $\frac{10}{4}$ **3.** $\frac{9}{2}$

Write the mixed number as a fraction greater than 1. Show your work.

4. $4\frac{3}{5}$ **5.** $2\frac{4}{6}$ **6.** $1\frac{3}{8}$

Gabriel is doing his math homework. He comes across a problem that asks him to rename the mixed number $3\frac{1}{5}$ as a fraction greater than one. How can Gabriel solve this problem? Show your work and explain your thinking on a piece of paper.

ACE IT TIME!

Math Vocabulary

- fraction
- numerator
- denominator
- decompose
- mixed number
- unit fractions
- fraction greater than one

	yes	no
Did you underline the question in the word problem?		
Did you circle the numbers or number words?		
Did you box the supporting details or information needed to solve the problem?		
Did you draw a picture or a graphic organizer and write a math sentence to show your thinking?		
Did you label your numbers and your picture?		
Did you explain your thinking and use math vocabulary words in your explanation?		

Ask an adult if you could use a cookbook or any recipe around the house. Use the fraction measurements in the recipe to practice renaming mixed numbers as fractions greater than 1 and fractions greater than 1 as mixed numbers. Ask the adult to check to see if you are correct.

REVIEW

Stop and think about what you have learned.

Congratulations! You've finished the lessons for this unit. This means you used fraction models to recognize and create equivalent fractions, and you compared fractions with different numerators and denominators. You even practiced breaking apart fractions into a sum of fractions with the same denominator.

Now it's time to prove your skills with fractions! Solve the problems below. Use all of the methods you have learned.

Activity Section 1: Equivalent Fractions

Write equivalent fractions.

1. $\frac{1}{2} = \frac{1}{2}\ \frac{\times}{\times}$ ______ $= \frac{\square}{10}$	**2.** $\frac{2}{6} = \frac{2}{6}\ \frac{\times}{\times}$ ______ $= \frac{\square}{12}$	**3.** $\frac{3}{4} = \frac{3}{4}\ \frac{\times}{\times}$ ______ $= \frac{\square}{16}$
4. $\frac{6}{9} = \frac{6}{9}\ \frac{\div}{\div}$ ______ $= \frac{\square}{3}$	**5.** $\frac{4}{20} = \frac{4}{20}\ \frac{\div}{\div}$ ______ $= \frac{\square}{5}$	**6.** $\frac{8}{12} = \frac{8}{12}\ \frac{\div}{\div}$ ______ $= \frac{\square}{6}$

Circle all equivalent fractions. Show your work.

7. $\frac{1}{2}, \frac{2}{3}, \frac{2}{8}, \frac{3}{6}, \frac{6}{12}, \frac{5}{9}$	**8.** $\frac{1}{2}, \frac{1}{3}, \frac{2}{3}, \frac{4}{12}, \frac{2}{5}, \frac{5}{15}$

Activity Section 2: Fractions in Simplest Form

Find the common factors of the numerator and the denominator. Write each fraction in its simplest form.

1. $\frac{6}{9} =$ ___	**2.** $\frac{3}{6} =$ ___	**3.** $\frac{8}{20} =$ ___	**4.** $\frac{3}{12} =$ ___

Is the fraction in its simplest form? Circle yes or no.

5. $\frac{4}{5}$ yes no	**6.** $\frac{6}{8}$ yes no	**7.** $\frac{9}{11}$ yes no	**8.** $\frac{5}{25}$ yes no

Activity Section 3: Common Denominators

Use the common multiples to find the common denominator. Rename fractions.

1. $\frac{1}{3}$ and $\frac{1}{5}$	2. $\frac{3}{12}$ and $\frac{6}{8}$
Multiples of 3: ___, ___, ___, ___, ___, ___	Multiples of 12: ___, ___, ___, ___, ___, ___
Multiples of 5: ___, ___, ___, ___, ___, ___	Multiples of 8: ___, ___, ___, ___, ___, ___
Common denominator ________	Common denominator ________
$\frac{1 \times \square}{3 \times \square} = \frac{\square}{\square}$ $\frac{1 \times \square}{5 \times \square} = \frac{\square}{\square}$	$\frac{3 \times \square}{12 \times \square} = \frac{\square}{\square}$ $\frac{6 \times \square}{8 \times \square} = \frac{\square}{\square}$

Activity Section 4: Compare Fractions and Order Fractions

Use equivalent fractions to compare the fractions. Write >, <, or =.

1. $\frac{2}{10}$ ◯ $\frac{2}{4}$

Write the fractions in order **greatest to least**. Show your work.

2. $\frac{2}{3}$, $\frac{5}{6}$, $\frac{1}{2}$, ___, ___, ___

Activity Section 5: Break Apart Fractions

Write the fraction as a sum of unit fractions.

1. $\frac{5}{8}$

Write the fraction as a sum of other fractions.

2. $\frac{3}{5}$

Activity Section 6: Rename Fractions and Mixed Numbers

Write the fraction greater than 1 as a mixed number. Show your work.

1. $\frac{7}{5}$

Write the mixed number as a fraction greater than 1. Show your work.

2. $3\frac{4}{5}$

UNDERSTAND

Understand the meaning of what you have learned and apply your knowledge.

You can use fraction models to recognize and create equivalent fractions. Situations such as finding equal shares or finding out who has the bigger piece are ways we use equivalent fractions in real life.

Activity Section

Mike and Carla each had the same-sized pizza for dinner. Mike cut his pizza into 5 equal pieces and he ate 2 of them. Carla cut her pizza into 6 equal pieces and she ate 4 of them. Did they eat the same amount of pizza? If not, who ate more? Explain your answer and show your work.

DISCOVER

Discover how you can apply the information you have learned.

You can compare fractions, including fractions greater than 1, with different numerators and different denominators. This is a helpful skill in real life, because not all fractions will always have the same denominator!

Activity Section

A few of the children in Mrs. Popell's class ran in a race. It took Melissa $3\frac{1}{2}$ minutes to finish the race. It took Lisa $3\frac{2}{3}$ minutes to finish the race. It took Terry $3\frac{5}{6}$ minutes to finish the race, and it took Brian $3\frac{1}{4}$ minutes to finish the race. Who came in first place? Who came in last place? Show your work and explain your answer.

CCSS.Math.Content.4.NF.C.5, CCSS.Math.Practice.MP2; MP3; MP4; MP5; MP7

CORE Operations with Fractions

Add and Subtract Fractions with Like Denominators

UNPACK THE STANDARD
You will add and subtract fractions with the same denominator by using visual fraction models and equations.

LEARN IT: You can use models to help you add and subtract fractions with like denominators.

Adding Fractions with Like Denominators

Example: Kelly baked a casserole and cut it into 8 equal parts. She gave her brother 1 piece. She gave her dad 2 pieces, and she took 1 piece for herself. What fraction of the casserole has been eaten?

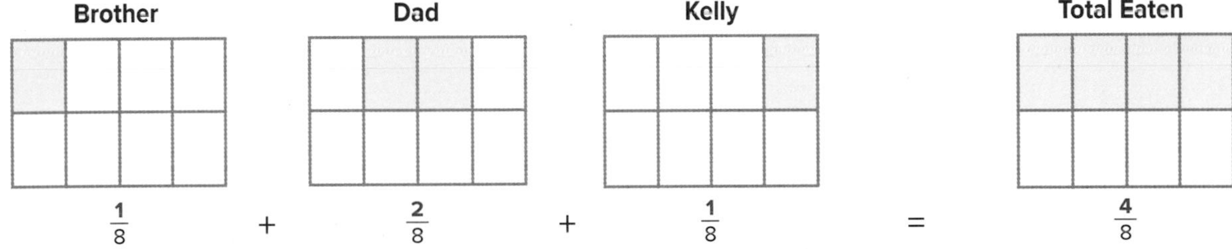

$\frac{1}{8} + \frac{2}{8} + \frac{1}{8} = \frac{4}{8}$

$\frac{4}{8}$ of the casserole has been eaten.

When the denominators of the addends are alike or the same, you add the numerators to find the sum. **The denominator stays the same.**

Subtracting Fractions with Like Denominators

Example: Lisa baked a casserole and cut it into 8 equal parts. She and her family ate 5 pieces. How many pieces were left?

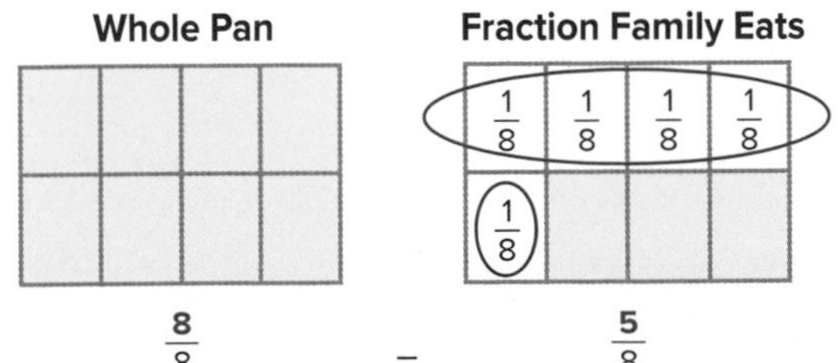

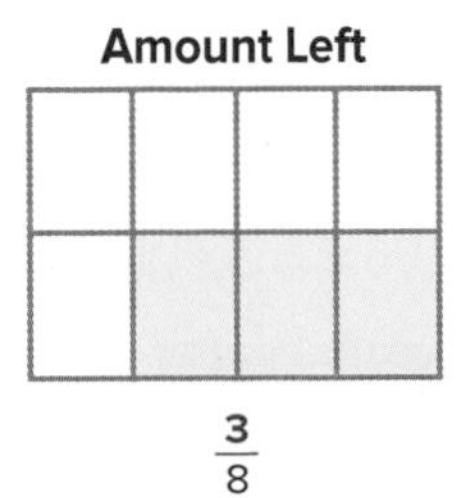

Amount Left

$\frac{8}{8} - \frac{5}{8} = \frac{3}{8}$

think!
Remember that 1 whole can be rewritten as a fraction that has the same digit in the numerator and the denominator. So, in this case, because the whole is cut into 8 equal parts, the whole is 8/8.

Just like in addition, when fractions have denominators that are the same, you subtract the numerators to find the difference. The denominator stays the same.

PRACTICE: Now you try

Find the sum. Draw a model to represent the problem.

1. $\frac{4}{12} + \frac{5}{12} =$	**2.** $\frac{1}{6} + \frac{3}{6} =$	**3.** $\frac{4}{10} + \frac{5}{10} =$

Horace needs 2 pieces of rope to tie up some newspaper for the recycling bin. He needs one piece that is $\frac{4}{8}$ of a yard long and one that is $\frac{5}{8}$ of a yard long. He found a piece of rope that is exactly 1 yard in length. Will that be enough so he can cut it and use it to tie up the newspaper? Show your work and explain your thinking on a piece of paper.

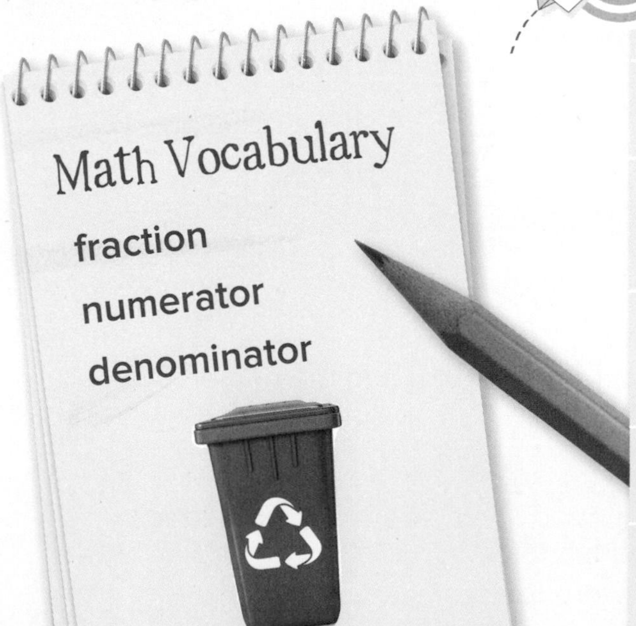

ACE IT TIME!

	yes	no
Did you underline the question in the word problem?	○	○
Did you circle the numbers or number words?	○	○
Did you box the supporting details or information needed to solve the problem?	○	○
Did you draw a picture or a graphic organizer and write a math sentence to show your thinking?	○	○
Did you label your numbers and your picture?	○	○
Did you explain your thinking and use math vocabulary words in your explanation?	○	○

MATH ON THE MOVE

You have learned how to draw a number line when working with fractions. Draw a number line and divide it into 6 equal parts. Starting with 0, label each part with a fraction (0, $\frac{1}{6}$, $\frac{2}{6}$, $\frac{3}{6}$ . . .). Use this number line to practice adding fractions. Try adding $\frac{2}{6} + \frac{2}{6}$. Put your finger at $\frac{2}{6}$ and make 2 hops. You should end up at $\frac{4}{6}$. Try practicing this with other fractions on the $\frac{1}{6}$ number line. When you are done, try making another number line. This time you get to decide how many equal parts you are going to divide it into! Label it and start hopping!

Add and Subtract Mixed Numbers

UNPACK THE STANDARD

You will add and subtract mixed numbers with like denominators.

LEARN IT: You can add and subtract Mixed Numbers with like denominators, the same way you would add whole numbers. Whenever you add fractions, you always get them to have the same denominator first, and then add.

Adding Mixed Numbers with Like Denominators

Example: Mrs. Chen baked 4 mini meat loaves. She served her family 2 on Monday night and saved the other 2 for Tuesday night. On Monday they ate $1\frac{4}{5}$, and on Tuesday they ate $1\frac{3}{5}$. How much meat loaf did they eat all together over both days?

Step 1: Add the fractional parts of the mixed numbers: $\frac{4}{5} + \frac{3}{5} = \frac{7}{5}$

Make a model:

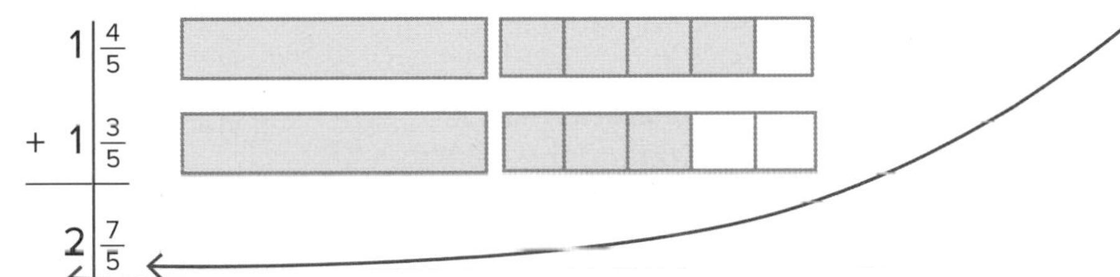

think!

I have to rename the fraction because $\frac{7}{5}$ is greater than 1. I know this because the numerator is greater than the denominator.

Step 2: Add the whole number parts of the mixed numbers: 1 + 1 = 2

Step 3: Rename the sum $2\frac{7}{5}$ to simplify: $2\frac{7}{5} = 2 + \frac{5}{5} + \frac{2}{5}$

$2 + 1 + \frac{2}{5}$

$3\frac{2}{5}$

The answer is $3\frac{2}{5}$.

think!

Use what you know about breaking apart fractions to show $\frac{7}{5}$ as $\frac{5}{5} + \frac{2}{5}$.

Subtracting Mixed Numbers with Like Denominators

Example: Dimitri baked 3 loaves of banana bread. His brother had some and left him with $2\frac{3}{4}$ loaves. He shared $1\frac{1}{4}$ of what he had left. How much banana bread did he have left?

Step 1: Make a model of $2\frac{3}{4}$ and cross out $1\frac{1}{4}$.

Step 2: Subtract the fractional parts of the mixed numbers: $\frac{3}{4} - \frac{1}{4} = \frac{2}{4}$ or $\frac{1}{2}$

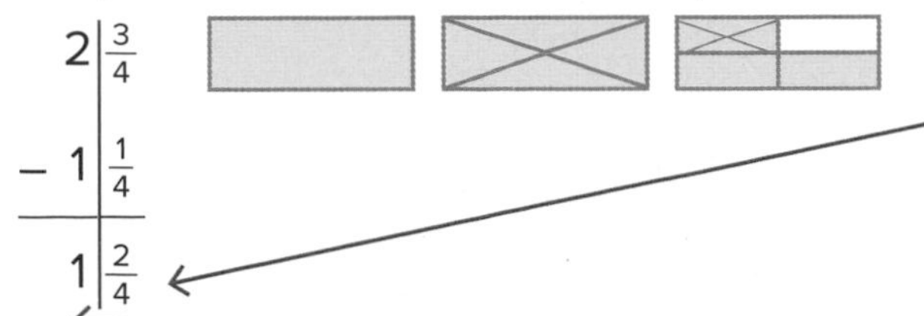

Step 3: Subtract the whole number parts of the mixed numbers: 2 – 1 = 1

The answer is $1\frac{1}{2}$.

PRACTICE: Now you try

Find the sum.
Draw a model to support your answer.

1. $\begin{array}{r} 1\frac{2}{4} \\ +\ 2\frac{1}{4} \\ \hline \end{array}$	**2.** $\begin{array}{r} 3\frac{3}{5} \\ +\ 3\frac{1}{5} \\ \hline \end{array}$

Find the difference.
Draw a model to support your answer.

3. $\begin{array}{r} 5\frac{7}{10} \\ -\ 2\frac{5}{10} \\ \hline \end{array}$	**4.** $\begin{array}{r} 9\frac{3}{5} \\ -\ 3\frac{1}{5} \\ \hline \end{array}$

Kirk decided he would participate in a race to raise money for his favorite charity. He ran for $1\frac{1}{6}$ miles and rode his bike for $2\frac{3}{6}$ miles. This only got him to the halfway point. He had to ride his bike and run back the same distance in order to get to the finish line. How many total miles did Kirk travel to raise money for his charity? Show your work and explain your thinking on a piece of paper.

ACE IT TIME!

	yes	no
Did you underline the question in the word problem?		
Did you circle the numbers or number words?		
Did you box the supporting details or information needed to solve the problem?		
Did you draw a picture or a graphic organizer and write a math sentence to show your thinking?		
Did you label your numbers and your picture?		
Did you explain your thinking and use math vocabulary words in your explanation?		

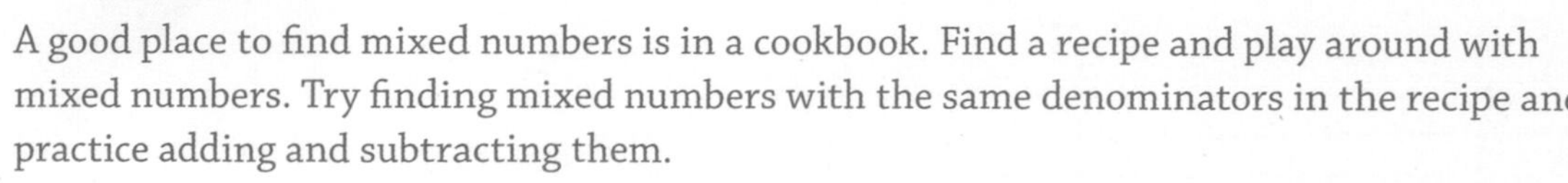

MATH ON THE MOVE

A good place to find mixed numbers is in a cookbook. Find a recipe and play around with mixed numbers. Try finding mixed numbers with the same denominators in the recipe and practice adding and subtracting them.

Subtract Mixed Numbers with Renaming

UNPACK THE STANDARD
You will add and subtract mixed numbers with like denominators.

LEARN IT: You can rename each mixed number as an equivalent fraction, or you can use properties of operations to help.

Rename the First Mixed Number

Example: Let's find the difference of $2\frac{1}{3} - 1\frac{2}{3} =$

think!
I cannot subtract $\frac{2}{3}$ from $\frac{1}{3}$, so I must regroup by renaming my mixed number.

Step 1: Rename the first mixed number as a mixed number with a fraction greater than 1.

$$2\frac{1}{3} = 1 + 1 + \frac{1}{3}$$
$$= 1 + \frac{3}{3} + \frac{1}{3}$$
$$1 + \frac{4}{3}$$

$$\begin{array}{r} 2\frac{1}{3} \\ -\ 1\frac{2}{3} \\ \hline \end{array} \longrightarrow \begin{array}{r} 1\frac{4}{3} \\ -\ 1\frac{2}{3} \\ \hline \frac{2}{3} \end{array}$$

Step 2: Subtract the fractional parts of the mixed numbers:
$\frac{4}{3} - \frac{2}{3} = \frac{2}{3}$

Step 3: Subtract the whole number parts of the mixed numbers: $1 - 1 = 0$

The answer is $\frac{2}{3}$.

Rename Both Mixed Numbers

Example: Let's find the difference of $2\frac{1}{3} - 1\frac{2}{3}$

Step 1: Rename both mixed numbers as a fraction greater than 1.

$$2\frac{1}{3} = 1 + 1 + \frac{1}{3}$$
$$= \frac{3}{3} + \frac{3}{3} + \frac{1}{3}$$
$$= \frac{7}{3}$$

$$1\frac{2}{3} = 1 + \frac{2}{3}$$
$$= \frac{3}{3} + \frac{2}{3}$$
$$= \frac{5}{3}$$

$$\begin{array}{r} 2\frac{1}{3} \\ -\ 1\frac{2}{3} \\ \hline \end{array} \longrightarrow \begin{array}{r} \frac{7}{3} \\ -\ \frac{5}{3} \\ \hline \frac{2}{3} \end{array}$$

Step 2: Subtract the fractions greater than 1:
$\frac{7}{3} - \frac{5}{3} = \frac{2}{3}$

The answer is $\frac{2}{3}$.

PRACTICE: Now you try

Find the difference. Draw a model to support your answer.

1. $6\frac{2}{6} - 3\frac{5}{6}$	2. $7\frac{3}{8} - 4\frac{5}{8}$	3. $4\frac{8}{12} - 2\frac{10}{12}$	4. $2\frac{4}{10} - \frac{6}{10}$

Carlene and Jazzy compare their pet snakes. When stretched out, Carlene's snake is $3\frac{1}{8}$ feet long and Jazzy's snake is $1\frac{4}{8}$ feet long. They discovered that Carlene's snake is longer. How much longer? Show your work and explain your thinking on a piece of paper.

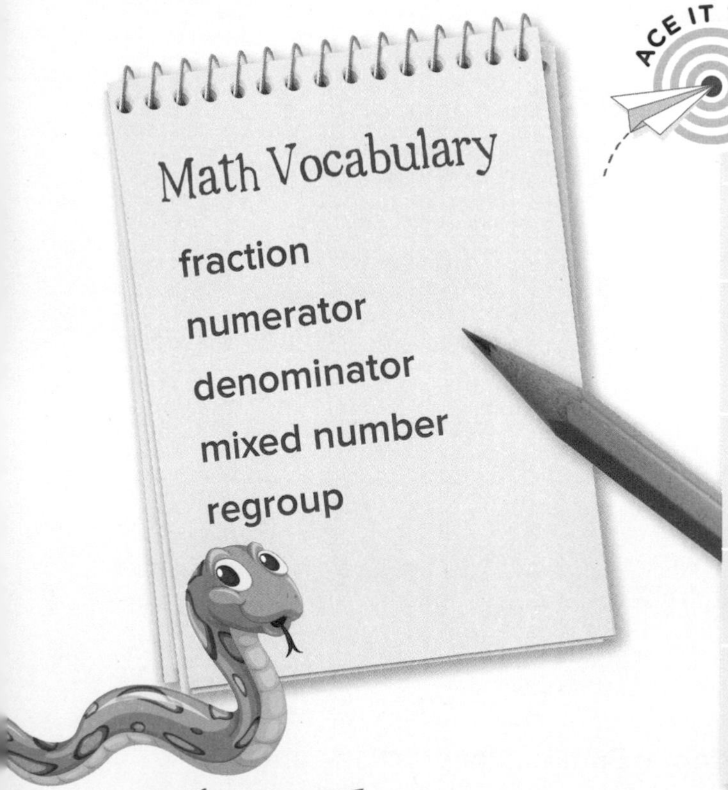

Math Vocabulary

- fraction
- numerator
- denominator
- mixed number
- regroup

ACE IT TIME!

	yes	no
Did you underline the question in the word problem?		
Did you circle the numbers or number words?		
Did you box the supporting details or information needed to solve the problem?		
Did you draw a picture or a graphic organizer and write a math sentence to show your thinking?		
Did you label your numbers and your picture?		
Did you explain your thinking and use math vocabulary words in your explanation?		

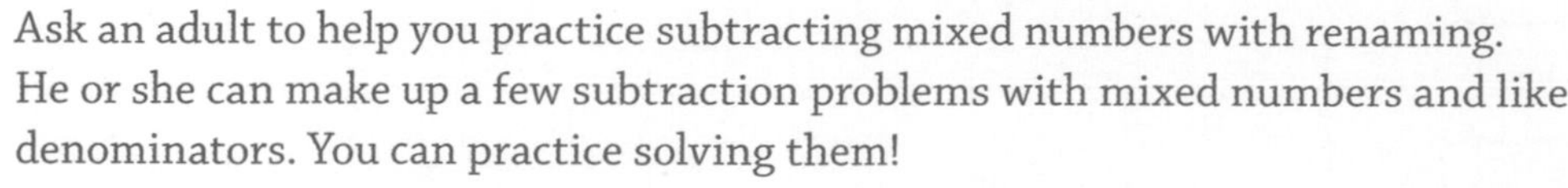

MATH ON THE MOVE

Ask an adult to help you practice subtracting mixed numbers with renaming. He or she can make up a few subtraction problems with mixed numbers and like denominators. You can practice solving them!

Multiply Unit Fractions by Whole Numbers

UNPACK THE STANDARD
You will understand a fraction as a multiple of a unit fraction.

LEARN IT: You can write a fraction as a product of a whole number and a *unit fraction*. You can use a number line and what you know about multiples to help. Remember, a unit fraction is a fraction that has 1 as the numerator.

Write a Fraction as a Product of a Whole Number and a Unit Fraction

Example: $\frac{3}{4}$

$\frac{1}{4}$	$\frac{1}{4}$
$\frac{1}{4}$	

You can use addition or multiplication.
Each shaded part is $\frac{1}{4}$ of a whole. There are 3 shaded parts.

$\frac{3}{4} = \frac{1}{4} + \frac{1}{4} + \frac{1}{4} = \frac{1+1+1}{4} = 3 \times \frac{1}{4}$

think!
$\frac{3}{4}$ can be decomposed into $\frac{1}{4} + \frac{1}{4} + \frac{1}{4}$.

Use a number line to find the multiples of the fraction $\frac{1}{4}$
Let's count by fourths.

think!
That is 3 hops on the number line. $\frac{3}{4}$ is $\frac{1}{4}$ three times.

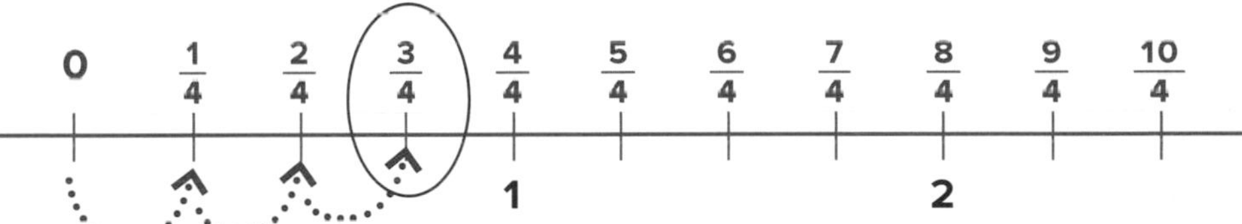

Write a Mixed Number or a Fraction Greater than 1 as a Product of a Whole Number and a Unit Fraction

Example: $1\frac{1}{3}$

Rewrite $1\frac{1}{3}$ as a fraction greater than 1.

$1 + \frac{1}{3}$

$\frac{3}{3} + \frac{1}{3} = \frac{4}{3}$

$\frac{1}{3}$	$\frac{1}{3}$	$\frac{1}{3}$

$\frac{1}{3}$		

Look at the relationship between addition and multiplication. Each shaded part is $\frac{1}{3}$ of a whole. There are 4 shaded parts.

$\frac{4}{3} = \frac{1}{3} + \frac{1}{3} + \frac{1}{3} + \frac{1}{3} = \frac{1+1+1+1}{3} = 4 \times \frac{1}{3}$

Use a number line to find the multiples of the fraction $\frac{1}{3}$
Let's count by thirds.

think!
That is 4 hops on the number line. $\frac{4}{3}$ is $\frac{1}{3}$ four times.

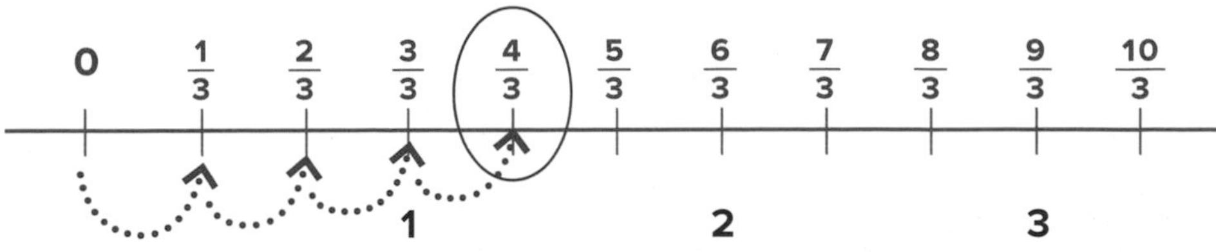

PRACTICE: Now you try

Complete the equation to find the product. Draw a model to show the product.

1. $2 \times \frac{1}{3} = \frac{1}{3} + \frac{1}{3} = \frac{\square}{3}$	2. $3 \times \frac{1}{5} = \frac{1}{5} + \frac{1}{5} + \frac{1}{5} = \frac{\square}{5}$

3. Write the missing fractions to count by fifths.

$\frac{1}{5}$, ______, $\frac{3}{5}$, ______, $\frac{5}{5}$, ______, $\frac{7}{5}$, ______, $\frac{9}{5}$, ______, $\frac{11}{5}$, ______

Write each fraction or mixed number as a product of a whole number and a unit fraction.

4. $\frac{2}{6} = 2 \times$	5. $\frac{7}{8} =$	6. $\frac{4}{10} =$

It takes Chris $\frac{1}{2}$ hour to walk a mile. If she walks 8 miles, how many hours did she walk? Show your work and explain your thinking on a piece of paper.

ACE IT TIME!

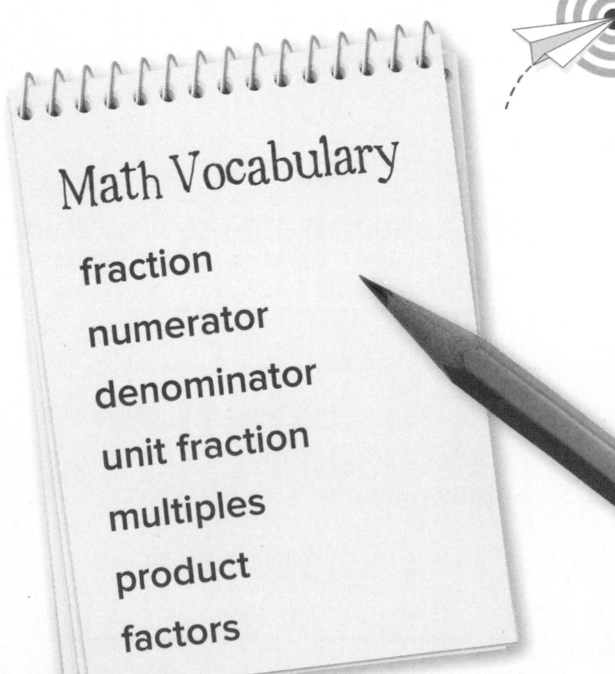

	yes	no
Did you underline the question in the word problem?	○	○
Did you circle the numbers or number words?	○	○
Did you box the supporting details or information needed to solve the problem?	○	○
Did you draw a picture or a graphic organizer and write a math sentence to show your thinking?	○	○
Did you label your numbers and your picture?	○	○
Did you explain your thinking and use math vocabulary words in your explanation?	○	○

You can practice finding the multiples of unit fractions. You can do this by skip-counting by the unit fraction. You could even make a number line to help you practice!

Multiply Fractions or Mixed Numbers by Whole Numbers

UNPACK THE STANDARD
You will understand how to multiply a fraction by a whole number.

LEARN IT: You can use various strategies to help you multiply a fraction or a mixed number by a whole number. Think of some of the strategies you use for multiplication such as repeated addition and the distributive property. Can *you* use those same strategies to multiply fractions by a whole number? Let's see!

Use **Repeated Addition** to Multiply

Example: $3 \times \frac{2}{4} =$

think!
Multiply the numerators. The denominator stays the same.

$\frac{1}{4}$	$\frac{1}{4}$		
$\frac{1}{4}$	$\frac{1}{4}$		
$\frac{1}{4}$	$\frac{1}{4}$		

$$3 \times \frac{2}{4} = \frac{2}{4} + \frac{2}{4} + \frac{2}{4}$$

$$= \frac{2 + 2 + 2}{4}$$

$$= \frac{3 \times 2}{4} = \frac{6}{4}$$

Write a Mixed Number as a Product of a Whole Number and a Unit Fraction

Example: $4 \times 1\frac{1}{3} =$

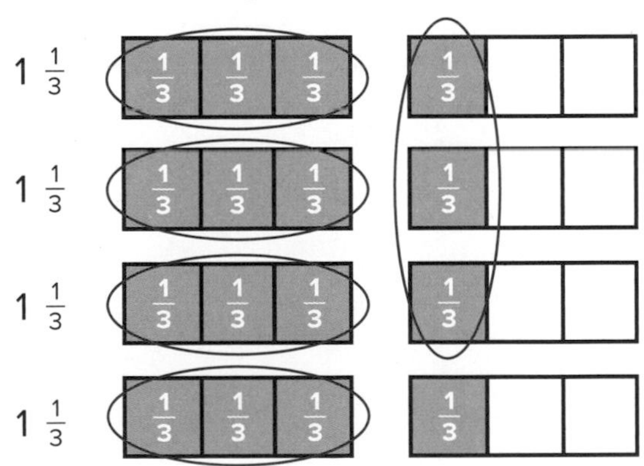

Rewrite $1\frac{1}{3}$ as a fraction greater than 1.

$1 + \frac{1}{3}$

$\frac{3}{3} + \frac{1}{3} = \frac{4}{3}$

So . . . $4 \times \frac{4}{3}$

$$4 \times \frac{4}{3} = \frac{4}{3} + \frac{4}{3} + \frac{4}{3} + \frac{4}{3}$$

$$= \frac{4 + 4 + 4 + 4}{3}$$

Rename $\frac{16}{3}$

think!
There are $\frac{3}{3}$ in 1 whole. The denominator tells us how many equal parts in the whole and the numerator tells us the number of equal parts that are counted.

How many wholes are in $\frac{16}{3}$ and how many thirds are left over?

There are 5 wholes, with $\frac{1}{3}$ left over. So $\frac{16}{3}$ can be renamed $5\frac{1}{3}$.

think!
How can we rename $\frac{4}{3}$? There is 1 whole ($\frac{3}{3}$) and $\frac{1}{3}$ left over. $\frac{4}{3}$ can be renamed as $1\frac{1}{3}$.

Or, use the distributive property:

$$4 \times 1\frac{1}{3} = (4 \times 1) + (4 \times \frac{1}{3})$$

$$4 + \frac{4}{3}$$

So . . . $4 + 1 + \frac{1}{3} = 5\frac{1}{3}$

PRACTICE: Now you try

Multiply. Use repeated addition to multiply. Draw a model to help solve.

1. $2 \times \frac{3}{8} =$	**2.** $5 \times \frac{3}{4} =$	**3.** $3 \times \frac{2}{3} =$

Multiply. Write the product as a mixed number.

4. $4 \times \frac{4}{5} =$	**5.** $5 \times \frac{2}{5} =$	**6.** $3 \times \frac{3}{8} =$

Mitch loves to read. He has been reading the past 5 nights for $2\frac{3}{4}$ hours each night. How many hours did Mitch read in the past 5 nights? Show your work and explain your thinking on a piece of paper.

ACE IT TIME!

	yes	no
Did you underline the question in the word problem?	○	○
Did you circle the numbers or number words?	○	○
Did you box the supporting details or information needed to solve the problem?	○	○
Did you draw a picture or a graphic organizer and write a math sentence to show your thinking?	○	○
Did you label your numbers and your picture?	○	○
Did you explain your thinking and use math vocabulary words in your explanation?	○	○

MATH ON THE MOVE

The next time you need a bag—how about making one yourself? With the help of an adult, you can either go online or to your local fabric store to get a sewing pattern. How much material will you need? Practice multiplying a whole number by a mixed number by doubling the instructions to make two or more bags! Have fun and let an adult check your figures!

CORE Decimals Concepts

UNIT 9

Tenths and Hundredths

UNPACK THE STANDARD
You will write a decimal to represent fractions with a denominator of 10 or 100.

LEARN IT: A number with 1 or more digits to the right of the decimal point is called a ***decimal***. Look at the place value chart below. The digits to the right of the decimal point represent a part of a whole, or a number less than 1 whole. You can use a fraction or a decimal to write the same number of ***tenths*** or ***hundredths***. In this lesson we will see the relationship between fractions and decimals.

Tenths

Fraction

think!
The model (or the whole) is divided into 10 equal parts. Each part is $\frac{1}{10}$. Because 4 parts are shaded, the model represents $\frac{4}{10}$.

Decimal

Decimal Point

Tens	Ones		Tenths	Hundredths
	0	.	4	

The decimal 0.4 also names 4 tenths. Look at the place value chart above. Notice that the 4 is in the tenths place. This is the place to the right of the **decimal point**.

So . . . 4 tenths can be written as a fraction ($\frac{4}{10}$) and as a decimal (0.4)
They are both read as "four tenths."

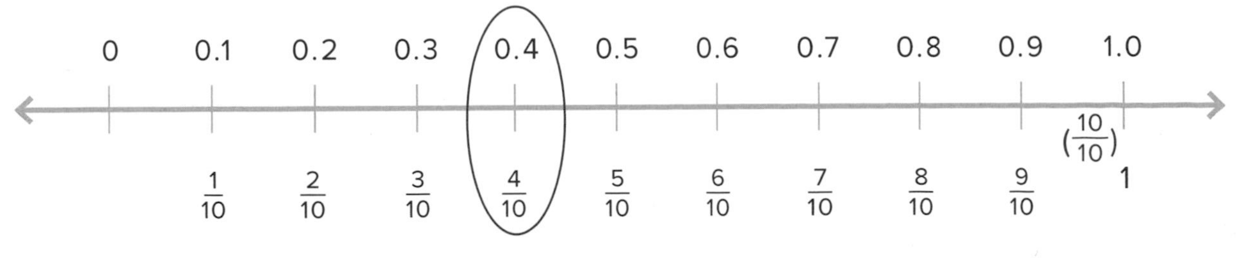

Hundredths

Fraction	Decimal

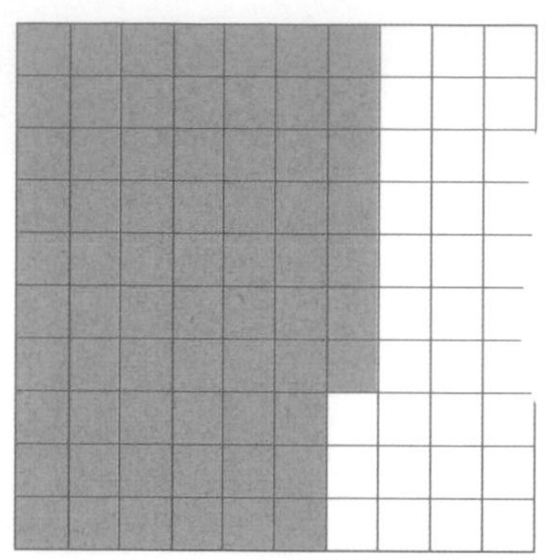

think!
The model (or the whole) is divided into 100 equal parts. Each part is $\frac{1}{100}$. Since 67 parts are shaded, the model represents $\frac{67}{100}$ or 67 hundredths.

Tens	Ones	.	Tenths	Hundredths
	0	.	6	7

The decimal 0.67 also names 67 hundredths. Look at the place value chart above. Notice that the 6 is in the tenths place. 6 tenths equals 0.60. The seven in the hundredths place equals 7 hundredths, or 0.07.
0.60 + 0.07 = 0.67, or 67 hundredths

So . . . 67 hundredths can be written as a fraction ($\frac{67}{100}$) and as a decimal (0.67).

Let's find 67 hundredths on the number line below.

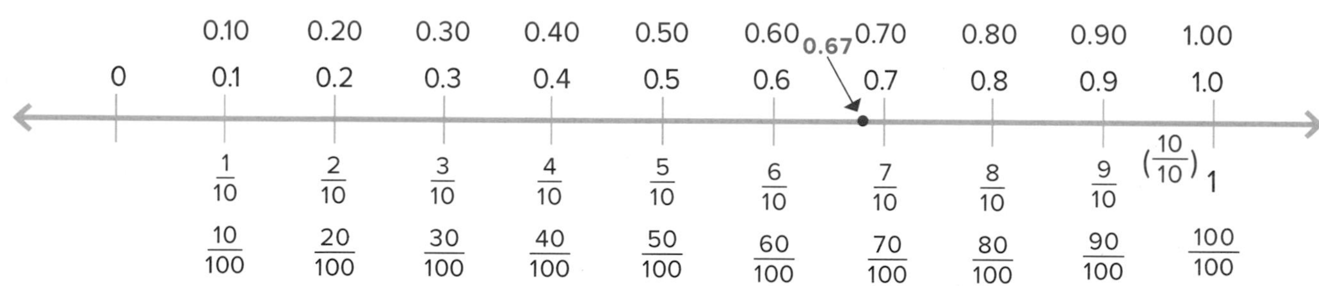

PRACTICE: Now you try

Shade in the model to show each amount. Write the amount as a fraction and as a decimal.

1. 4 tenths

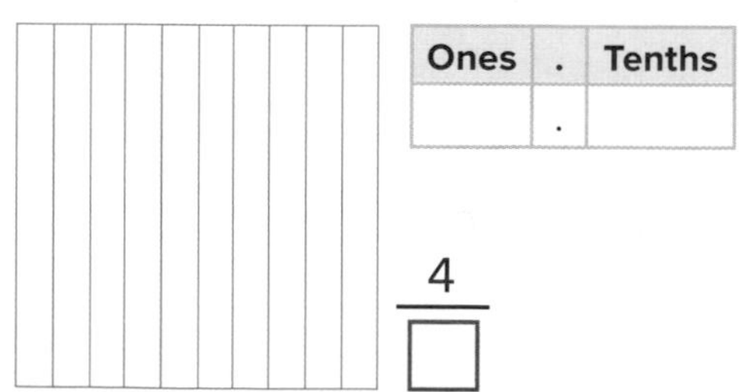

Ones	.	Tenths
	.	

$\frac{4}{\square}$

2. 25 hundredths

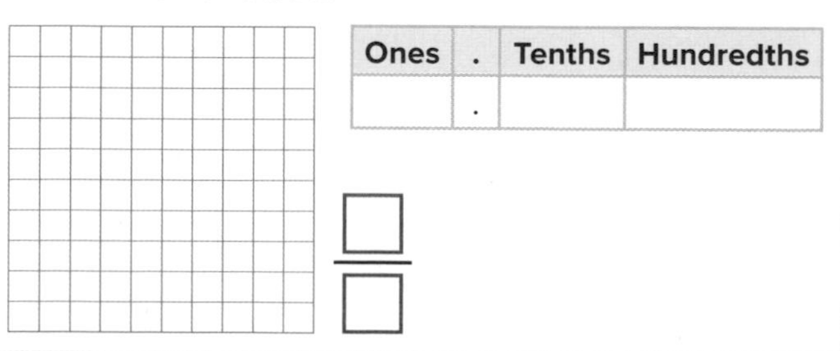

Ones	.	Tenths	Hundredths
	.		

$\frac{\square}{\square}$

Write each fraction or mixed number as a decimal.

3. $\frac{2}{10}$	**4.** $\frac{34}{100}$	**5.** $3\frac{1}{10}$

Draw points on the number line to represent the numbers. Write each amount as a fraction and as a decimal.

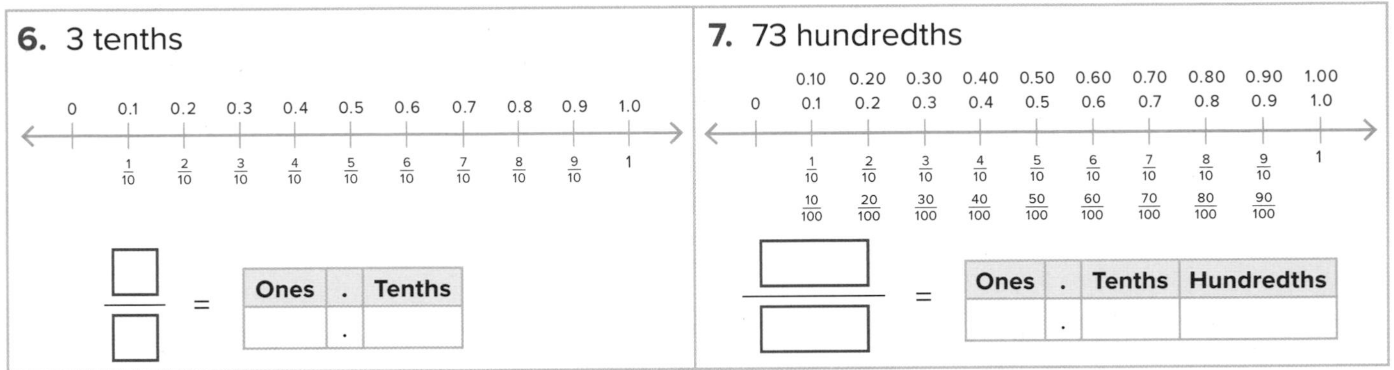

Roberto was excited about eating his turkey sandwich for lunch. He ate $\frac{7}{10}$ of his sandwich before he even sat at the lunch table. After he sat down, how much sandwich did Roberto have left to eat? Write your answer as a decimal. Show your work and explain your thinking on a piece of paper.

ACE IT TIME!

	yes	no
Did you underline the question in the word problem?		
Did you circle the numbers or number words?		
Did you box the supporting details or information needed to solve the problem?		
Did you draw a picture or a graphic organizer and write a math sentence to show your thinking?		
Did you label your numbers and your picture?		
Did you explain your thinking and use math vocabulary words in your explanation?		

Math Vocabulary

- decimal
- decimal point
- tenths
- hundredths
- fractions
- place value

Practice writing fractions with denominators of 10 or 100 as decimals. Have a friend or an adult give you a fraction with a denominator of 10 or 100. Write the decimals and also practice modeling and drawing them. Try making your own place value chart and fill in the digits after the decimal point. This will help to make sure that you truly understand the concept.

Equivalent Fractions and Decimals

UNPACK THE STANDARD
You will write a fraction with a denominator of 10 as an equivalent fraction with a denominator of 100.

LEARN IT: Remember that you learned in the last unit that ***equivalent fractions*** are fractions that name the same amount. Similarly, ***equivalent decimals*** are decimals that name the same amount. You can write numbers as tenths and hundredths in both decimal and fraction form.

4 tenths is equivalent to 40 hundredths

Let's show as a fraction:

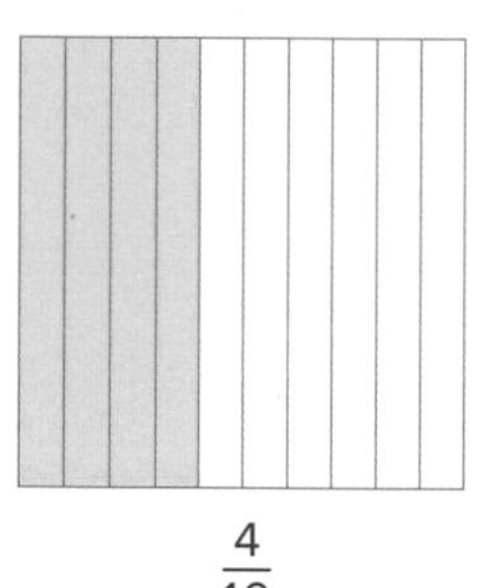

$\frac{4}{10}$

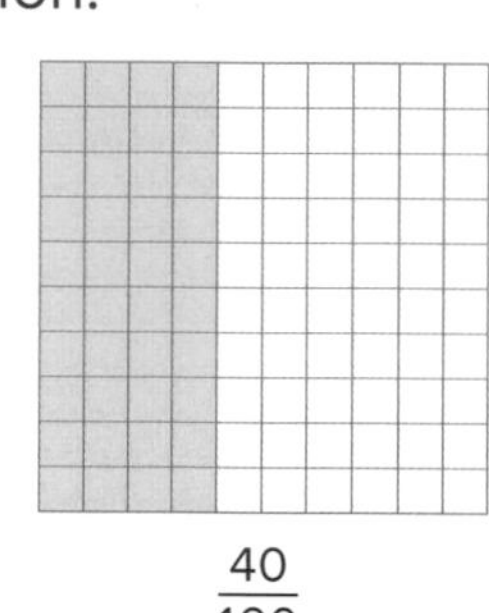

$\frac{40}{100}$

think!
4 tenths is the same as 4 tenths and 0 hundredths.

How can I record this?

$$\frac{4}{10} = \frac{4 \times 10}{10 \times 10} = \frac{40}{100}$$

Now show it as a decimal:

Tens	Ones	.	Tenths	Hundredths
	0	.	4	

or

Tens	Ones	.	Tenths	Hundredths
	0	.	4	0

0.4 = 0.40

PRACTICE: Now you try

Write the number as hundredths in both fraction form and decimal form.

Sample: $\frac{7}{10}$ $\frac{7}{10} = \frac{70}{100} = 0.70$	**1.** 3 tenths	**2.** 0.1

Write the number as tenths in fraction form.

Sample: $\frac{40}{100}$ $\frac{40}{100} = \frac{4}{10}$	**3.** 60 hundredths	**4.** 0.30

Write each mixed number as an equivalent decimal with hundredths.

Sample: $2\frac{7}{10} = 2.70$	**5.** $2\frac{3}{10}$	**6.** $1\frac{8}{10}$	**7.** $4\frac{6}{10}$

Write each number as an equivalent decimal with tenths.

Sample: $6\frac{20}{100} = 6.2$	**8.** $3\frac{40}{100}$	**9.** $5\frac{10}{100}$	**10.** $2\frac{50}{100}$

Shauntaey is measuring a piece of wood for an art project. The directions say that she needs a piece of wood 0.8 meters long. Shauntaey says that this is the same as $\frac{80}{100}$ meter. Is she correct? Show your work and explain your thinking on a piece of paper.

ACE IT TIME!

	yes	no
Did you underline the question in the word problem?		
Did you circle the numbers or number words?		
Did you box the supporting details or information needed to solve the problem?		
Did you draw a picture or a graphic organizer and write a math sentence to show your thinking?		
Did you label your numbers and your picture?		
Did you explain your thinking and use math vocabulary words in your explanation?		

Practice what you learned in this lesson by drawing a tenths decimal model and a hundredths decimal model. Shade in $\frac{2}{10}$ on the tenths model and $\frac{20}{100}$ on the hundredths model. Explain to a partner why these two numbers are equivalent. Now try it again. This time shade in $\frac{4}{10}$ and $\frac{40}{100}$. Keep challenging yourself to more decimals and fractions!

Fractions–Decimals–Money

UNPACK THE STANDARD
You will write a decimal to represent fractions with a denominator of 10 or 100.

LEARN IT: You can relate ***decimals*** to ***money***. You can think of dollars as ones or wholes. You can think of dimes as tenths and pennies as hundredths.

You can use money as a model for decimals

You can use dollars as your whole.

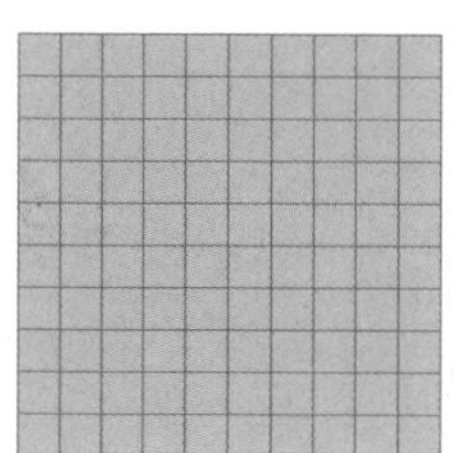

1 whole or $\frac{100}{100}$ or \$1.00 or 100 cents

You can use quarters.

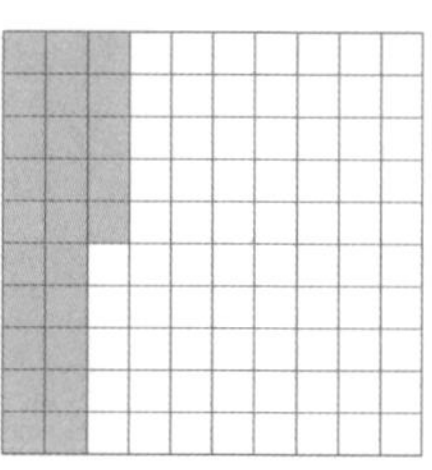

1 quarter or $\frac{25}{100}$ of a dollar or \$0.25 or 25 cents

You can use dimes.

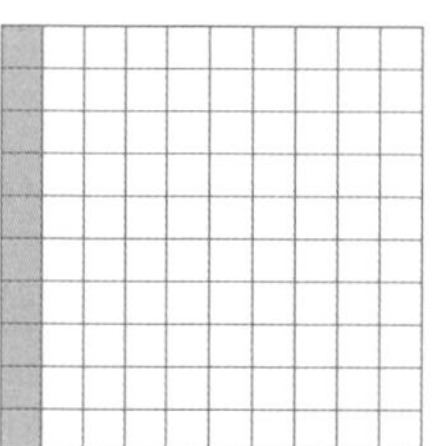

1 dime or $\frac{1}{10}$ of a dollar or $\frac{10}{100}$ or \$0.10 or 10 cents

You can use pennies.

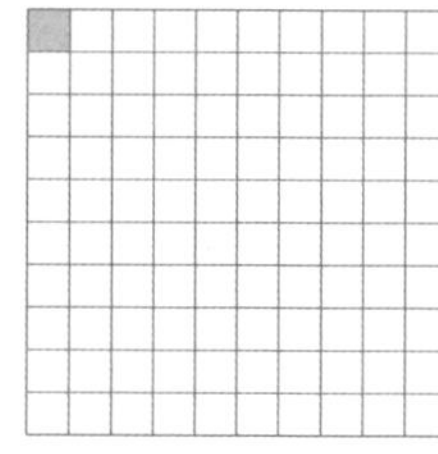

1 penny or $\frac{1}{100}$ of a dollar or \$0.01 or 1 cent

Think of money when working with decimals.
Here is how \$2.74 would look in a place value chart:

Dollars	.	Dimes	Pennies
Ones	.	**Tenths**	**Hundredths**
2	.	7	4

As a decimal it can be written as 2.74, and the word form is "two wholes and seventy-four hundredths."

PRACTICE: Now you try

Shade the model to show the money amount. Write the decimal.

1.

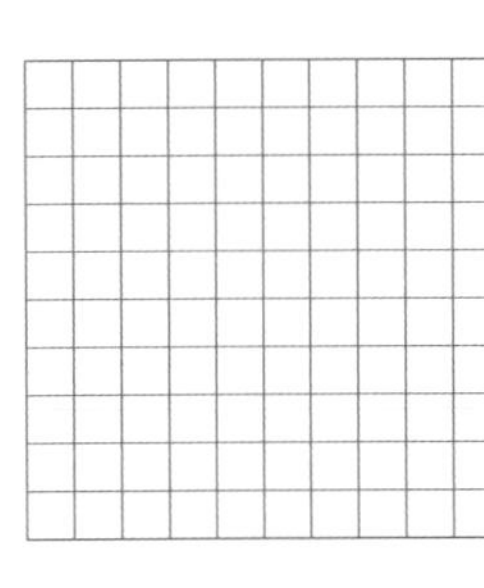

____.____ ____

2.

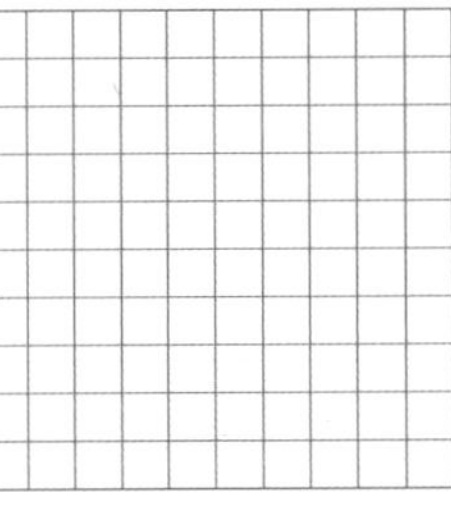

____.____ ____

3.

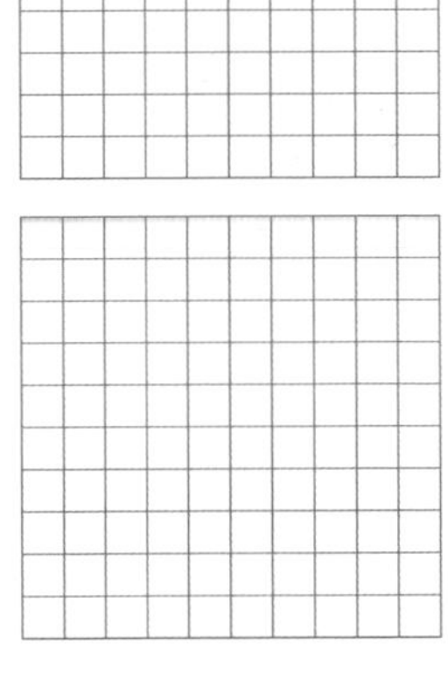

____.____ ____

Draw money to make the decimal amounts.

4. 0.41

5. 0.67

Draw money to make the decimal amounts.

6. 3.23	**7.** 2.83

Iyanna had $1.00. She spent $\frac{60}{100}$ of a dollar on a bag of chips. How much does she have left? Write the answer as a money amount. Show your work and explain your thinking on a piece of paper.

ACE IT TIME!

	yes	no
Did you underline the question in the word problem?	○	○
Did you circle the numbers or number words?	○	○
Did you box the supporting details or information needed to solve the problem?	○	○
Did you draw a picture or a graphic organizer and write a math sentence to show your thinking?	○	○
Did you label your numbers and your picture?	○	○
Did you explain your thinking and use math vocabulary words in your explanation?	○	○

Math Vocabulary

decimal
decimal point
tenths
hundredths
fractions
place value

MATH ON THE MOVE

You can use money to help you make sense out of decimals. Ask an adult if you can use change lying around the house to help you practice what you have learned in this lesson. Use different money amounts and practice writing a decimal for each amount.

Compare Decimals

UNPACK THE STANDARD
You will learn strategies to help you compare decimals up to hundredths.

LEARN IT: You can ***compare decimals*** using various strategies. You can compare by using models, number lines, and place value.

Compare using models: 0.23 ◯ 0.4

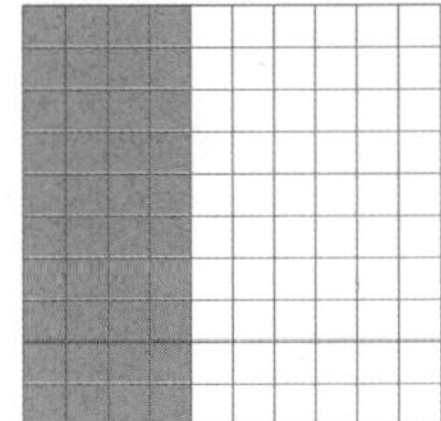

think!
0.4 or 4 tenths is the same as 4 tenths and 0 hundredths. This equals 40 hundredths. You will shade in 40 squares in the second hundredths model. According to both of my models, 23 squares is less than 40 squares.

So . . . 0.23 is less than 0.4 0.23 (<) 0.4

Compare using place value: 1.4 ◯ 1.08

Ones	.	Tenths	Hundredths
1	.	4	
1	.	0	8

You can line up your decimals by the decimal points and compare. The digits in the ones place are the same, so compare the digits in the tenths place. 4 tenths is greater than 0 tenths.

think!
The first decimal has 4 tenths and 0 hundredths. The second decimal has 0 tenths and 8 hundredths.

So . . . 1.4 is greater than 1.08 1.4 (>) 1.08

Compare using a number line: 0.32 ◯ 0.39

You can label points on a number line to show decimals.

Step 1: Estimate to label the points on the number line.

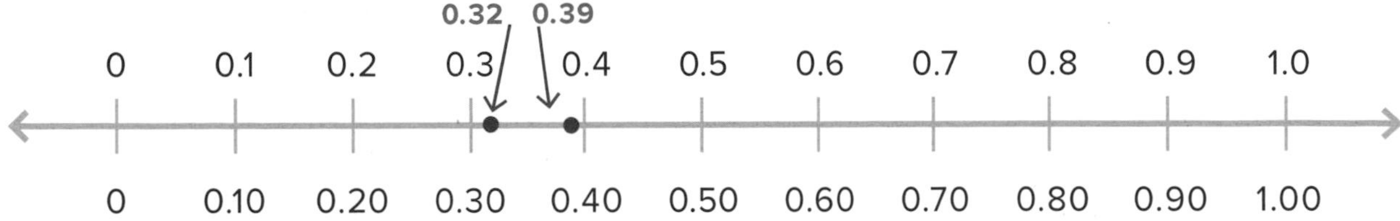

Step 2: Which point is closer to 0? The point closest to 0 is the least amount.
0.32 is closer to 0.

So . . . 0.32 is less than 0.39 0.32  0.39

PRACTICE: Now you try

Compare. Write >, <, =.

1. 0.7 ◯ 0.62

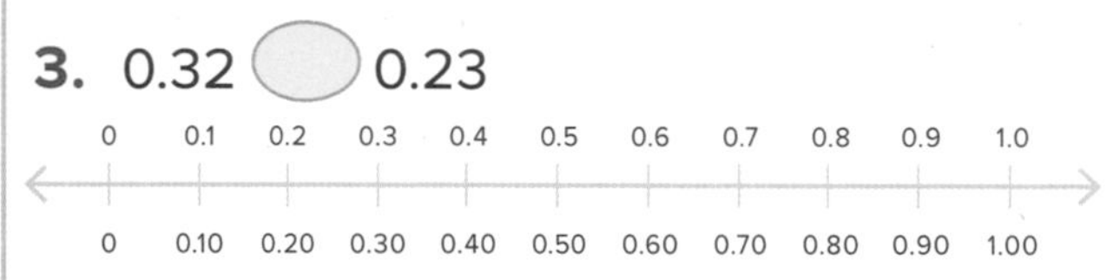

Ones	.	Tenths	Hundredths
	.		
	.		

2. 0.24 ◯ 2.45

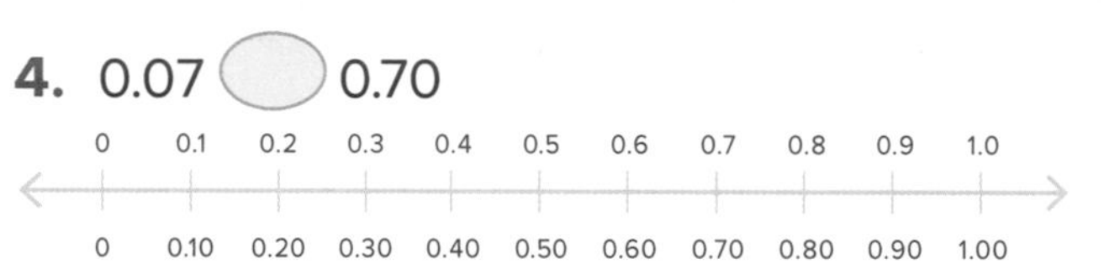

Ones	.	Tenths	Hundredths
	.		
	.		

Label points on number line. Compare. Write >, <, =.

3. 0.32 ◯ 0.23

0 0.1 0.2 0.3 0.4 0.5 0.6 0.7 0.8 0.9 1.0

0 0.10 0.20 0.30 0.40 0.50 0.60 0.70 0.80 0.90 1.00

4. 0.07 ◯ 0.70

0 0.1 0.2 0.3 0.4 0.5 0.6 0.7 0.8 0.9 1.0

0 0.10 0.20 0.30 0.40 0.50 0.60 0.70 0.80 0.90 1.00

Shane caught a worm that was 8.6 centimeters long. Nyla caught a worm that was 8.06 centimeters long. Nyla says that her worm is longer because when she wrote the lengths of the worms down as decimals, her worm had 2 digits to the right of the decimal point and Shane's worm only had 1 digit to the right of the decimal point. Is she right? Show your work and explain your thinking on a piece of paper.

ACE IT TIME!

	yes	no
Did you underline the question in the word problem?	◯	◯
Did you circle the numbers or number words?	◯	◯
Did you box the supporting details or information needed to solve the problem?	◯	◯
Did you draw a picture or a graphic organizer and write a math sentence to show your thinking?	◯	◯
Did you label your numbers and your picture?	◯	◯
Did you explain your thinking and use math vocabulary words in your explanation?	◯	◯

Math Vocabulary

tenths
hundredths
fractions
place value
compare
greater than
less than

MATH ON THE MOVE

You can practice what you learned in this lesson by making your own game. Ask an adult for a piece of paper. Cut up the sheet of paper and make playing cards. Write various decimals on the cards. Make sure you use tenths and hundredths on your cards. Ask a friend to play with you. Practice comparing the decimals that are on the cards you made. Use words like *greater than* or *less than* to help when you are comparing.

Add Fractions and Decimals with Tenths and Hundredths

UNPACK THE STANDARD
You will add decimals and fractions with denominators of tenths and hundredths.

LEARN IT: You already learned how to write equivalent fractions and decimals with denominators of ***tenths*** and ***hundredths***. You can use what you have learned to help you ***add fractions*** and ***decimals*** with these same denominators.

Example: Find the sum: $\frac{5}{100} + \frac{2}{10} =$

Step 1:
Rename $\frac{2}{10}$ so that the denominator is 100, just like the denominator in $\frac{5}{100}$.

$$\frac{2}{10} = \frac{2 \times 10}{10 \times 10} = \frac{20}{100}$$

So . . . $\frac{2}{10} = \frac{20}{100}$

Step 2:
Now that the denominators are the same, you can add.

$$\frac{5}{100} + \frac{20}{100} = \mathbf{\frac{25}{100}}$$

think!
In order to add fractions, my denominators must be the same. I can change the denominator to 100 by multiplying it by 10. Remember to multiply the numerator by 10 also.

Example: Let's try it with decimals. Find the sum: 0.6 + 0.35

Step 1:
Write your decimals as fractions.

$$\frac{6}{10} + \frac{35}{100} =$$

Step 2:
Rename $\frac{6}{10}$ so that the denominator is 100, just like the denominator in $\frac{35}{100}$.

$$\frac{6}{10} = \frac{6 \times 10}{10 \times 10} = \frac{60}{100}$$

So . . . $\frac{6}{10} = \frac{60}{100}$

Step 3: Add with like denominators. $\frac{60}{100} + \frac{35}{100} = \mathbf{\frac{95}{100}}$

Step 4: Now let's add as decimals.

Line the decimal points up and add.

$$\begin{array}{r} 0.60 \\ +\ 0.35 \\ \hline \end{array}$$

0.95 or 95 hundredths or $\frac{95}{100}$

think!
0.6 has 6 tenths and 0 hundredths. 0.6 is equal to 0.60.

PRACTICE: Now you try

Find the sum.

1. $\frac{4}{10} + \frac{21}{100} =$	**2.** $\frac{5}{100} + \frac{5}{10} =$	**3.** $\frac{7}{10} + \frac{16}{100} =$
4. 0.1 + 0.47 =	**5.** 0.15 + 0.3 =	**6.** 0.04 + 0.8 =

Landon took a math test at school. He got question number 3 marked wrong. He said that $\frac{2}{100} + \frac{6}{10} = \frac{8}{110}$. What is the correct answer? What was his error? Show your work and explain your thinking on a piece of paper.

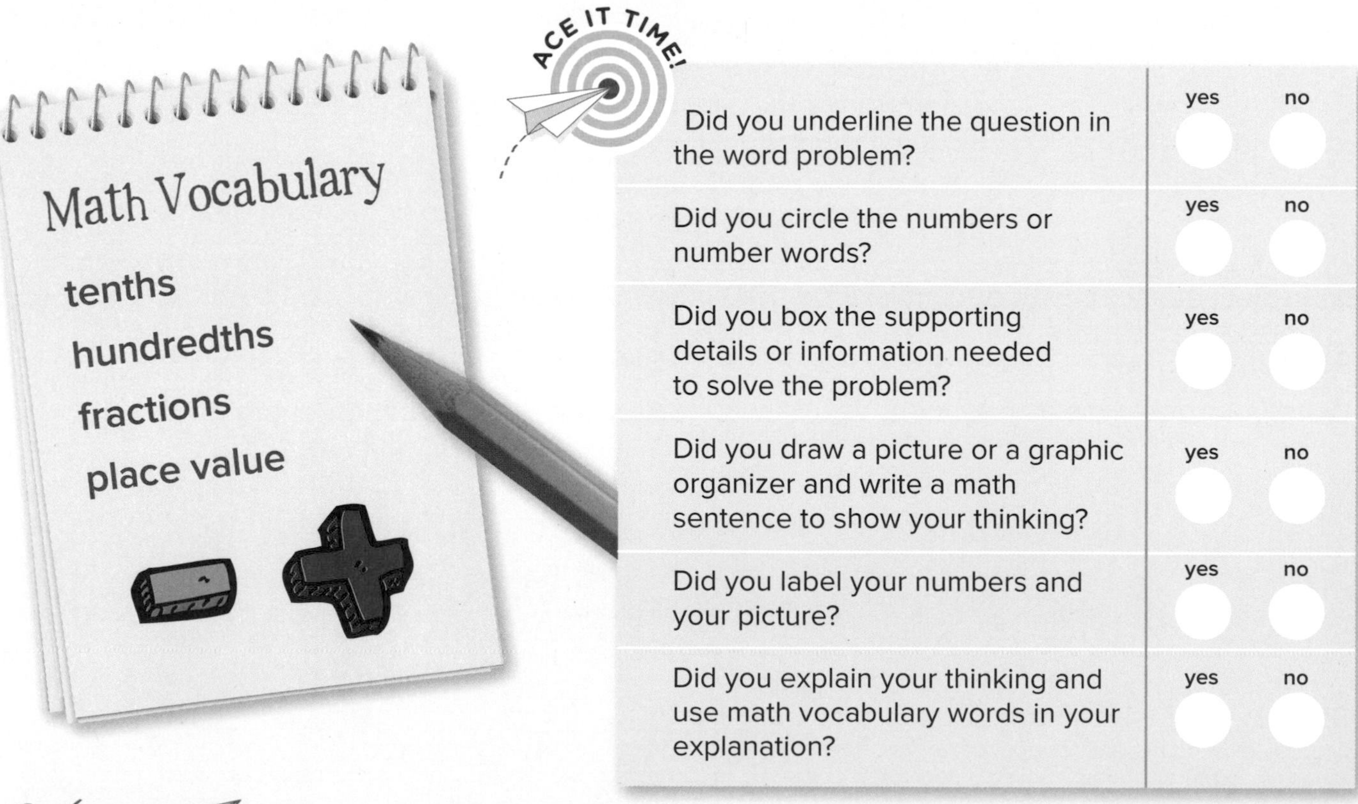

Practice adding fractions with denominators of tenths and hundredths. You can create your own addition problems. Renaming decimals and fractions is a very important part of this lesson. Try to explain renaming numbers to your friends or to an adult. If you need to, draw pictures or models to help you with your answers.

REVIEW

Stop and think about what you have learned.

Congratulations! You've finished the lessons for units 8–9. This means you understand a fraction as a multiple of a unit fraction and can add and subtract fractions and mixed numbers with like denominators. You have practiced multiplying a fraction by a whole number. You can add and subtract mixed numbers with like denominators and you can rename mixed numbers as equivalent fractions. You can write a fraction with a denominator of 10 as an equivalent fraction with a denominator of 100. You can write decimals to represent fractions with denominators of 10 or 100. You have even learned strategies to help you compare decimals up to hundredths.

Now it's time to prove your skills with fractions and decimals! Solve the problems below. Use all of the methods you have learned.

Activity Section 1: Add and Subtract Fractions with Like Denominators

Find the sum. Draw a model to represent the problem.

1. $\frac{6}{15} + \frac{5}{15} =$	**2.** $\frac{2}{6} \mid \frac{3}{6} -$

Find the difference. Draw a model to represent the problem.

3. $\frac{7}{8} - \frac{2}{8} =$	**4.** $\frac{7}{10} - \frac{3}{10} -$

Activity Section 2: Add and Subtract Mixed Numbers

Add and subtract mixed numbers. Draw a model to support your answer.

1. $\begin{array}{r} 4\frac{4}{8} \\ +\,2\frac{5}{8} \\ \hline \end{array}$	**2.** $\begin{array}{r} 9\frac{4}{6} \\ -\,4\frac{2}{6} \\ \hline \end{array}$

Activity Section 3: Subtract Mixed Numbers with Renaming

Find the difference. Draw a model to support your answer.

1. $\begin{array}{r} 4\frac{3}{10} \\ -\,\frac{6}{10} \\ \hline \end{array}$	**2.** $\begin{array}{r} 1\frac{3}{6} \\ -\,\frac{5}{6} \\ \hline \end{array}$

Activity Section 4: Multiply Unit Fractions by Whole Numbers

Write each fraction as a product of a whole number and a unit fraction.

1. $\frac{4}{6}$ =	**2.** $\frac{5}{8}$ =

Activity Section 5: Multiply Fractions or Mixed Numbers by Whole Numbers

Multiply. Write the product as a mixed number.

1. $3 \times \frac{3}{5}$ =	**2.** $5 \times \frac{2}{8}$ =

Activity Section 6: Tenths and Hundredths

Write each fraction or mixed number as a decimal.

1. $\frac{4}{10}$	**2.** $4\frac{66}{100}$	**3.** $6\frac{78}{100}$

Activity Section 7: Equivalent Fractions and Decimals

Write the number as hundredths in fraction form and decimal form.

1. $\frac{6}{10}$	**2.** 4 tenths	**3.** 0.9

Write the number as tenths in fraction form.

4. $\frac{20}{100}$	**5.** 70 hundredths	**6.** 0.50

Activity Section 8: Fractions—Decimals—Money

Draw money to make decimal amounts.

1. 0.76	**2.** 0.29

Activity Section 9: Compare Decimals

Compare. Write >, <, =.

1. 0.8 ◯ 0.52

Ones	.	Tenths	Hundredths
	.		
	.		

2. 0.37 ◯ 3.75

Ones	.	Tenths	Hundredths
	.		
	.		

Activity Section 10: Add Fractions and Decimals of Tenths and Hundredths

Find the sum.

1. $\frac{5}{10} + \frac{14}{100}$ =	**2.** $\frac{5}{10} + \frac{6}{100}$ =

UNDERSTAND

Understand the meaning of what you have learned and apply your knowledge.

Fractions and decimals are all around us! You can use what you know about operations with fractions to add, subtract, or multiply fractions in the real world.

Activity Section

The fifth graders at Shady Oaks Elementary School are going on a field trip. Mrs. Long's class takes up $\frac{3}{10}$ of the seats on the bus. Mrs. Rossi's class takes up $\frac{25}{100}$ of the seats on the bus, and Mrs. Quillan's students take up $\frac{4}{10}$ of the seats on the bus. How many seats will be left on the bus? Write your answer in fraction form with hundredths and in decimal form with hundredths. Explain your answer and show your work.

DISCOVER

Discover how you can apply the information you have learned.

Fractions are all around us, especially in the kitchen! We use a lot of fraction sense when we measure foods to cook. You can use your knowledge of adding and subtracting fractions with the same denominator, as well as your knowledge of equivalent fractions and mixed numbers.

Activity Section

1. Roy has $3\frac{3}{12}$ cups of chopped tomatoes. He needs $\frac{1}{4}$ cup of chopped tomatoes to make 1 serving of his famous salsa. How many servings of salsa can Roy make with all $3\frac{3}{12}$ cups of tomatoes? Draw a model, a number line, or use what you know about equivalent fractions. Show your work.

2. If $1\frac{6}{12}$ of Roy's tomatoes went bad and he had to use what he had left to make salsa, how many servings could he make now?

CORE Geometry Concepts

Lines and Relationships

UNPACK THE STANDARD
You will learn to identify and draw points, lines, line segments, rays, angles, and parallel lines.

LEARN IT: If you look all around you in the world, you will see examples of ***geometric figures,*** or things that have specific shapes. For example, you might see a dot over the letter "i" that models a ***point***. The horizon, where the sky meets the sea, models a ***line***. In this lesson, you will learn to identify these and other terms, how to draw them, and how to read and write them.

Term	Definition	Looks Like	Read It	Write It	Example
point	exact location in space	A	point A	point A	dot
line	path of points that continue *without end* in both directions	B C	line BC line CB	$\overleftrightarrow{BC}$ $\overleftrightarrow{CB}$	horizon
line segment	part of a line between 2 points	D E	line segment DE line segment ED	$\overline{DE}$ $\overline{ED}$	stop sign
ray	part of a line that has 1 **endpoint** and continues without end in 1 direction	F G	ray FG	$\overrightarrow{FG}$	arrow
angle	formed by 2 rays that have the same endpoint called the **vertex**	X Y Z vertex	angle X angle YXZ angle ZXY	< X <YXZ <ZXY	open door
parallel lines	2 lines that are always the same distance apart	R S T U	line RS is parallel to line TU	$RS \parallel TU$	stripes on something

PRACTICE: Now you try

Use the chart on the previous page to complete the following tasks.

1. Draw $\overline{EF}$ **2.** Draw $\overleftarrow{MN}$ **3.** Draw $\overleftrightarrow{XY}$

4. Draw 4 points that form a square when you connect them with line segments.

5. Where can you find parallel lines in the world?

6. What is the difference between a line and a line segment?

7. What is the difference between a line and a ray?

8. What is the difference between $\overrightarrow{AB}$ and $\overleftarrow{AB}$?

Try to draw a figure with the following criteria:

a. 1 set of parallel lines

b. 2 line segments that connect the parallel lines at points A, B, C, and D but do not cross each other.

c. When you add the line segments, they form 4 different angles.

d. Name any angles that you make.

Show your work and explain your thinking on a piece of paper.

ACE IT TIME!

	yes	no
Did you underline the question in the word problem?		
Did you circle the numbers or number words?		
Did you box the supporting details or information needed to solve the problem?		
Did you draw a picture or a graphic organizer and write a math sentence to show your thinking?		
Did you label your numbers and your picture?		
Did you explain your thinking and use math vocabulary words in your explanation?		

Math Vocabulary

point
line
line segment
parallel line
endpoint
vertex
angle
ray

Be a geometry detective. Start a geometry notebook. Look for examples of geometric figures in the real world. Keep a list of each figure that you find.

Angles

UNPACK THE STANDARD
You will learn to identify and draw different types of angles.

LEARN IT: In the last lesson, you learned how two rays with a common endpoint (vertex) form an angle. Angles have different names depending on their shapes. To determine what kind of angle it is, you have to compare it to a ***right angle***.

Term	Definition	Looks Like
angle	formed by 2 rays that have the same endpoint, called the **vertex**	X Y Z
right angle	forms a square corner; uses 2 rays that are **perpendicular** to each other	
straight angle	forms a line	
acute angle	forms an angle that is smaller than a right angle	
obtuse angle	forms an angle that is larger than a right angle	

think!
Think of a right angle as the corner of a piece of paper.

PRACTICE: Now you try Use the chart on the previous page and Figure 1 to help you complete the following problems and answer the questions.

1. Draw and label an example of right ∠ABC.
2. Draw 2 rays with a common vertex D to form an obtuse angle.
3. Draw a straight angle. *Hint:* Think of 2 right angles side by side, back to back.
4. Draw a set of perpendicular lines. Show the square corners.
5. Draw and label acute ∠RST
6. Name 3 line segments.
7. Name 3 obtuse angles.
8. Name 3 acute angles.

think!
Think of 2 right angles side by side, back to back.

Figure 1

J
H
K
L
M

Can 2 acute angles make a straight angle? Show your work and explain your thinking on a piece of paper.

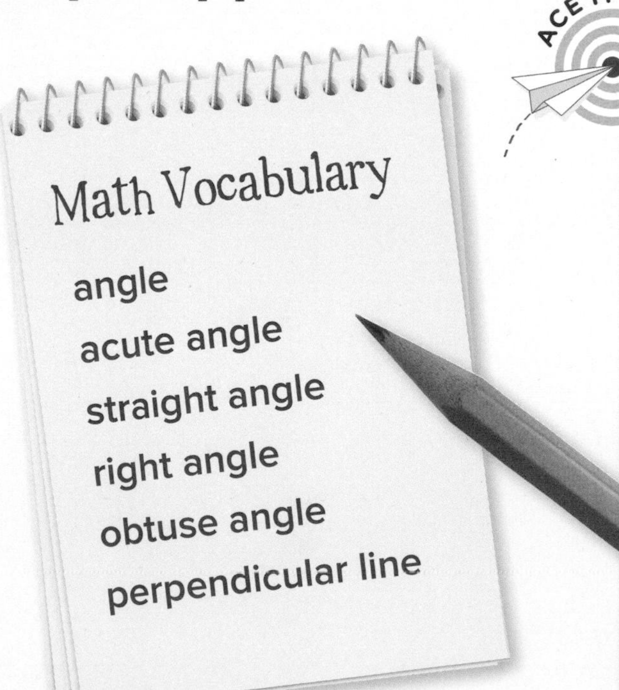

ACE IT TIME!

	yes	no
Did you underline the question in the word problem?		
Did you circle the numbers or number words?		
Did you box the supporting details or information needed to solve the problem?		
Did you draw a picture or a graphic organizer and write a math sentence to show your thinking?		
Did you label your numbers and your picture?		
Did you explain your thinking and use math vocabulary words in your explanation?		

Look around your house and find examples of different kinds of angles. Start a contest with a parent or family member. See who can find the most angles in 15 minutes.

CCSS.Math.Content.4.G.A.1; CCSS.Math.Practice.MP2; MP3; MP4; MP5; MP6

Triangles

UNPACK THE STANDARD
You will learn to identify different kinds of triangles.

LEARN IT: A ***triangle*** is a ***polygon*** or shape that has 3 connected sides that form 3 angles. Triangles can be named by their ***vertices*** or corners.

A

B C

Δ ABC Δ CBA
Δ BCA Δ ACB
Δ CAB Δ BAC

Right Triangle

If a triangle has a right angle, it is called a **right triangle**.

Acute Triangle

If a triangle has 3 acute angles, it is called an **acute triangle**.

If a triangle has 1 obtuse angle, it is called an **obtuse triangle**.

Obtuse Triangle

PRACTICE: Now you try Complete the problems.

1. Draw an acute triangle and name it in 3 different ways.

2. Draw a right triangle and name it in 3 different ways.

3. Draw an obtuse triangle and name it in 3 different ways.

Identify the triangles.

4.

5.

6.

7.

Use this figure to answer the questions.

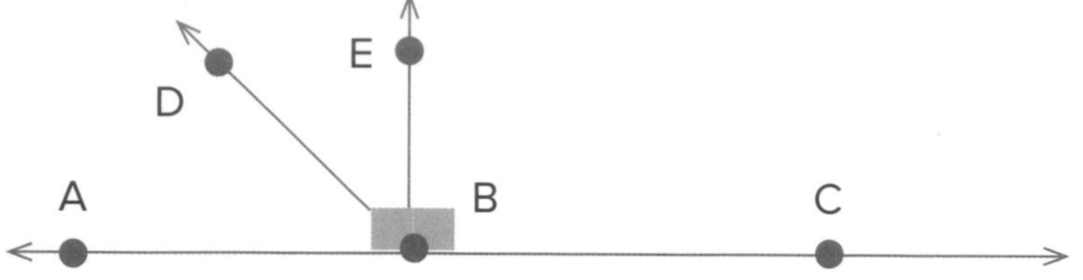

8. Name 2 right angles. ______________ ______________

9. Name an obtuse angle. ______________

10. Name 2 acute angles. ______________ ______________

11. What kind of angle is ∠ABC? ______________

If you took an acute triangle and divided it equally in two, what kind of triangles would you make? Show your work and explain your thinking on a piece of paper.

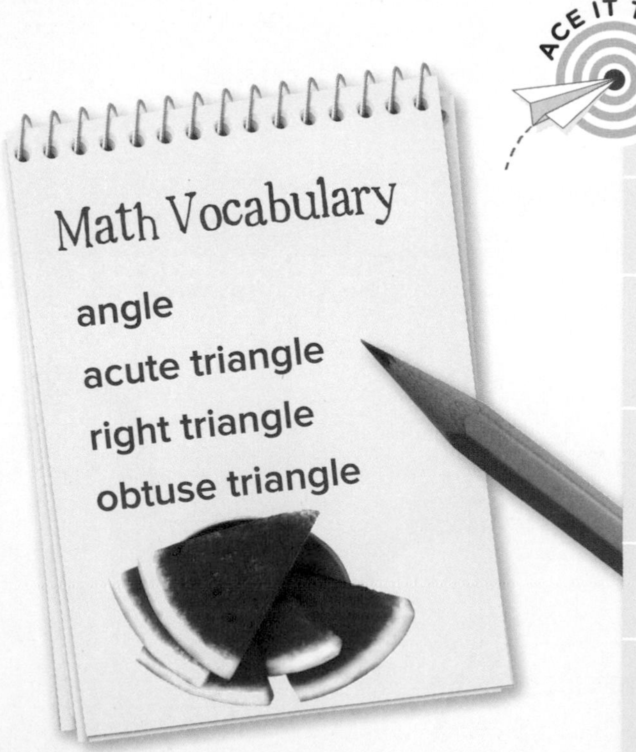

ACE IT TIME!

	yes	no
Did you underline the question in the word problem?	○	○
Did you circle the numbers or number words?	○	○
Did you box the supporting details or information needed to solve the problem?	○	○
Did you draw a picture or a graphic organizer and write a math sentence to show your thinking?	○	○
Did you label your numbers and your picture?	○	○
Did you explain your thinking and use math vocabulary words in your explanation?	○	○

Fold a piece of scrap paper several times, making as many triangles as you can with the folds. Open up the paper and try to label each triangle you made with the proper name. If you did not make any particular kind of angle, try it again with another piece of paper.

Geometric Shape Patterns

UNPACK THE STANDARD
You will learn to identify different kinds of quadrilateral shapes.

LEARN IT: A ***quadrilateral*** is a ***polygon*** that has 4 connected sides that form 4 angles. Quadrilaterals are named by the ***vertices*** of their angles. Since there are 4 vertices, quadrilaterals will have 4 letters in their name.

Term	Looks Like	Definition
trapezoid		1 set of parallel sides
parallelogram		2 sets of parallel sides 2 pairs of sides with equal length
rhombus		2 sets of parallel lines all 4 sides of equal length
rectangle		2 sets of parallel lines 2 sets of sides with equal length 4 right angles
square		2 sets of parallel lines 4 sides of equal length 4 right angles

To show when line segments have the same length, some markings are made on the sides that are alike.

Example:

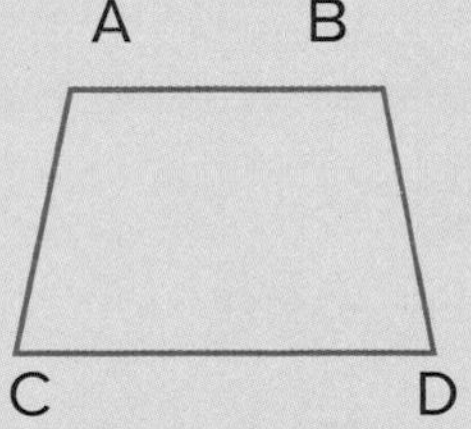

When you name a quadrilateral, you name it by **vertices**.

This example would be called trapezoid ABCD. You could not call it trapezoid ADCB because neither points A and D nor points C and B have endpoints on the same line.

PRACTICE: Now you try

Use the quadrilaterals to answer the questions below.

A. B. C. D. E.

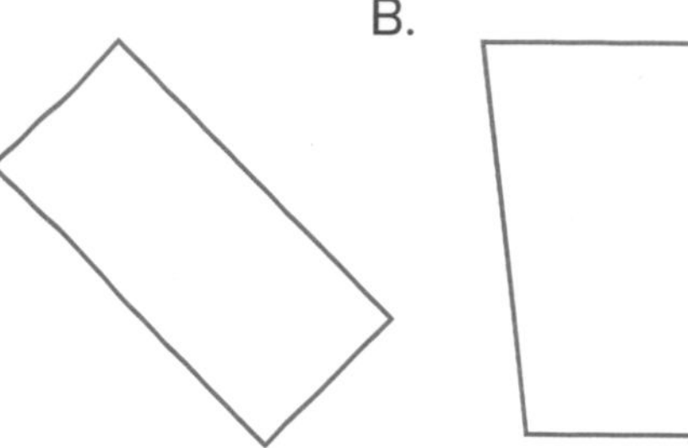

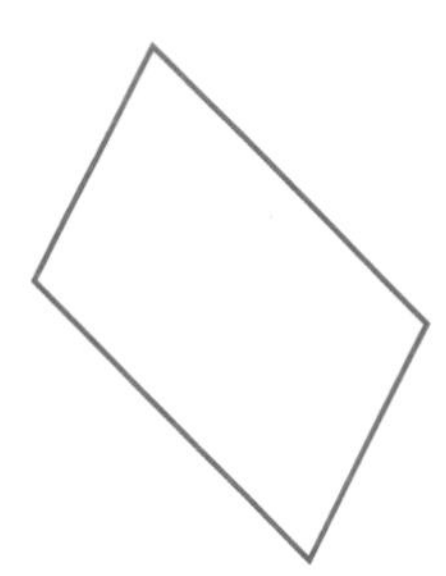

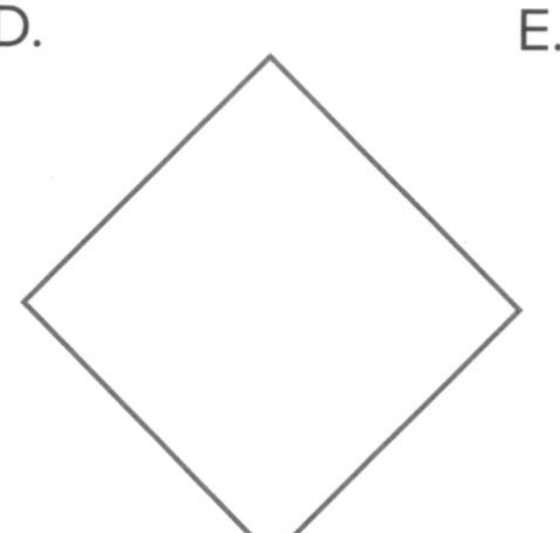

1. How is the figure in C different from D?

2. How is the figure in A different from E?

Explain how a square and a rhombus are alike and different.
Show your work and explain your thinking on a piece of paper.

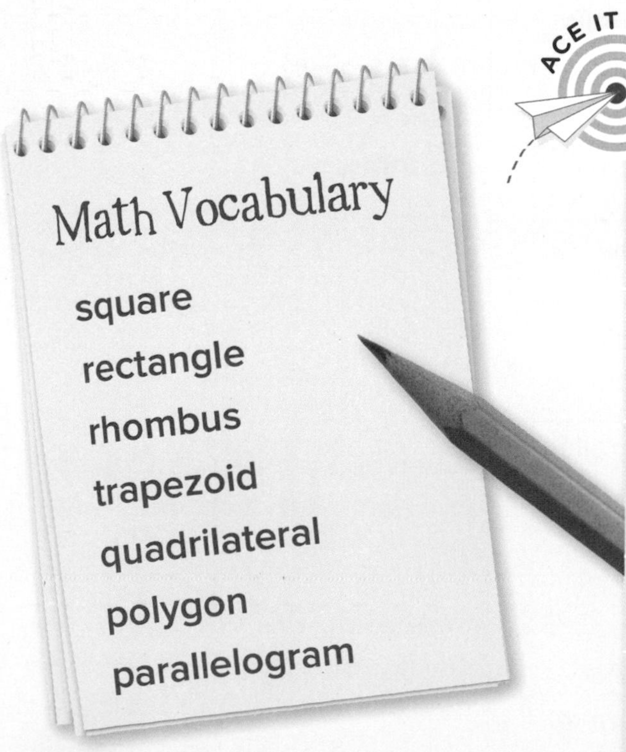

ACE IT TIME!

	yes	no
Did you underline the question in the word problem?		
Did you circle the numbers or number words?		
Did you box the supporting details or information needed to solve the problem?		
Did you draw a picture or a graphic organizer and write a math sentence to show your thinking?		
Did you label your numbers and your picture?		
Did you explain your thinking and use math vocabulary words in your explanation?		

Find examples of each type of quadrilateral in the real world. Can you find more than one example?

Symmetry

UNPACK THE STANDARD

You will learn to identify shapes that have lines of symmetry.

LEARN IT: Have you ever folded a piece of drawing paper into 2 even parts? If you have, you made a fold that can be called a ***line of symmetry***. A shape has a line of symmetry if it can be folded on a line so that both parts match exactly.

Many shapes have a line of symmetry, but others do not. A line of symmetry can be ***horizontal*** (go from left to right), ***vertical*** (go up and down), or ***diagonal*** (go corner to corner).

Line of Symmetry	Not a Line of Symmetry
Look at the letter A. We could draw a vertical line from the top to the bottom right in the middle to see if the left side and the right side are identical. Right Side Left Side  Looks like both sides match!	Look at the letter A. We could draw a horizontal line from the left to the right in the middle to see if the top side and the bottom side are identical. Top  Bottom The top and the bottom do not match!

The letter A had a vertical line of symmetry, but not a horizontal line of symmetry.

think!
Must triangles have sides of the same length to have a line of symmetry?

PRACTICE: Now you try

Solve.

1. Draw a line of symmetry in the following triangles and quadrilaterals. Some may have more than 1 line of symmetry.

 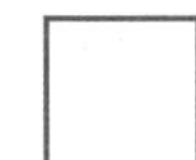   

2. Draw an obtuse triangle that does not have a line of symmetry.

Do the lines appear to show a line of symmetry? Write *yes* or *no*.

3. 

4. 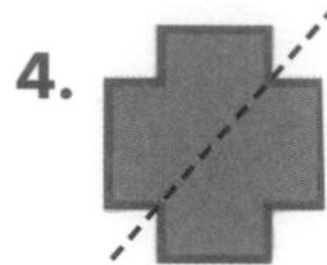

5. 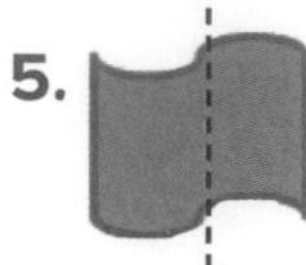

6. 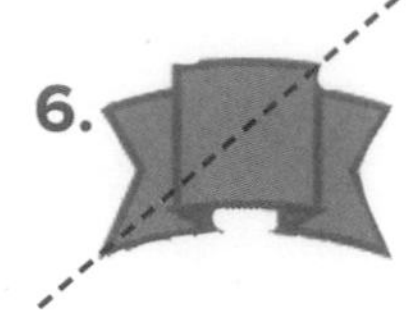

Draw dotted lines to show a line of symmetry.

7. 

8. 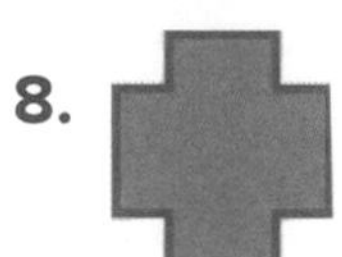

9. 

10. 

Martin says that five numbers from 0 through 9 have lines of symmetry. He also says that none of these numbers have 2 lines of symmetry. Prove that he is right or wrong. Show your work and explain your thinking on a piece of paper.

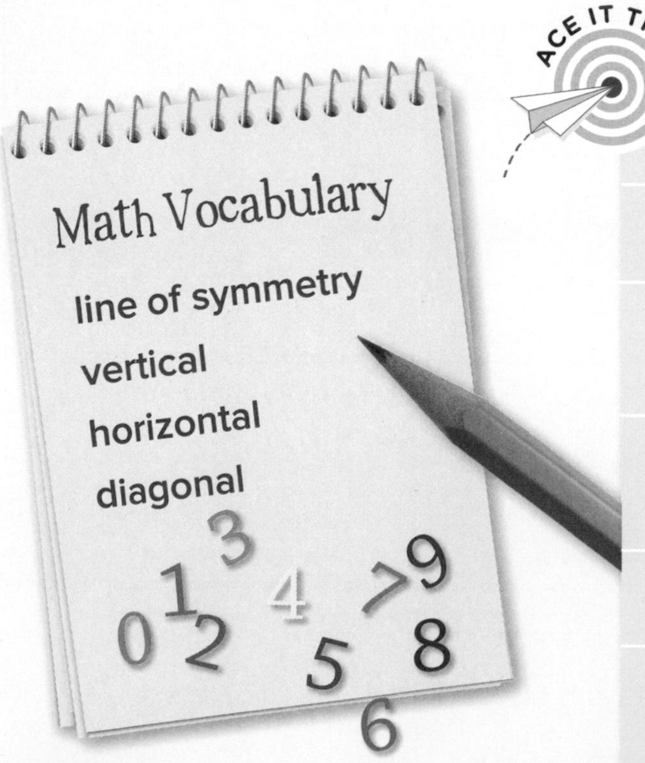

ACE IT TIME!

	yes	no
Did you underline the question in the word problem?	○	○
Did you circle the numbers or number words?	○	○
Did you box the supporting details or information needed to solve the problem?	○	○
Did you draw a picture or a graphic organizer and write a math sentence to show your thinking?	○	○
Did you label your numbers and your picture?	○	○
Did you explain your thinking and use math vocabulary words in your explanation?	○	○

MATH ON THE MOVE

Go through the letters of the alphabet to determine how many letters have no lines of symmetry, 1 line of symmetry, 2 lines of symmetry, or all 3 lines of symmetry.

Angles as Fractional Parts of a Circle

UNPACK THE STANDARD
You will learn that an angle is measured in reference to a circle.

LEARN IT: Think of a second hand on a clock. It rotates around the clock face as time passes. Each turn is 1 second. Now, think of a circle with 2 rays coming out from the center of the circle to form a small angle. Think of this small angle rotating around the circle just like the second hand moves around the clock. A clock is divided into 60 units (seconds or minutes). Mathematicians divide the circle into 360 parts called ***degrees***. Every time the angle moves 1 unit, mathematicians call this ***1 degree* or *1°*.** This small angle can rotate ***360 degrees*** before it starts over again.

There are 360 angles in a circle. Each angle is 1° of a circle. All circles have 360°. Their size does not matter.

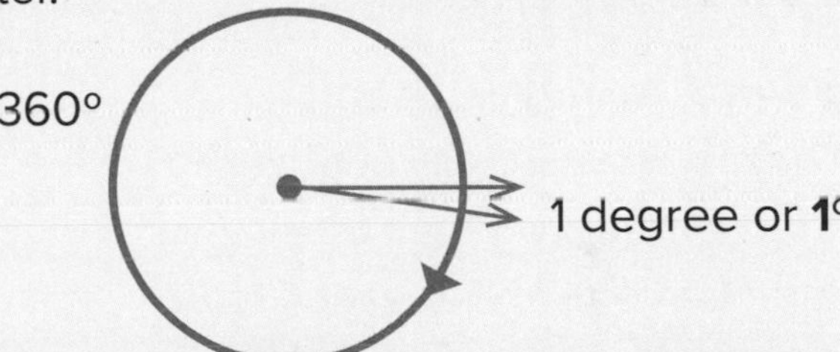

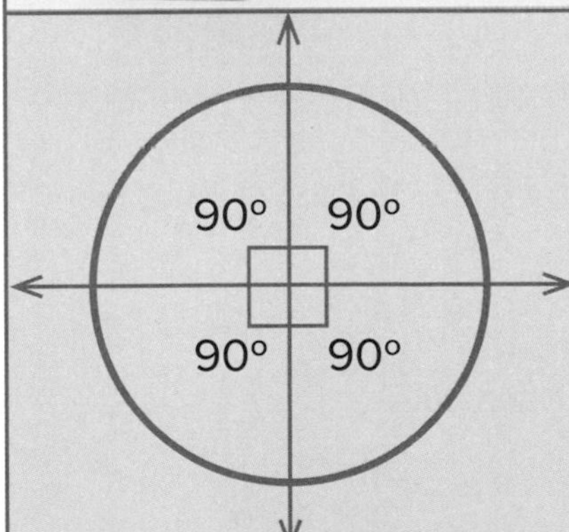

When a circle is divided into 4 equal parts, 4 angles are formed. These are right angles because they each form a square corner. There are 4 right angles in a circle. Each right angle is $\frac{1}{4}$ of 360.

$$\frac{1}{4} = \frac{\square}{360}$$

So each right angle is $\frac{90}{360}$. A right angle has 90 degrees. We write it as 90°.

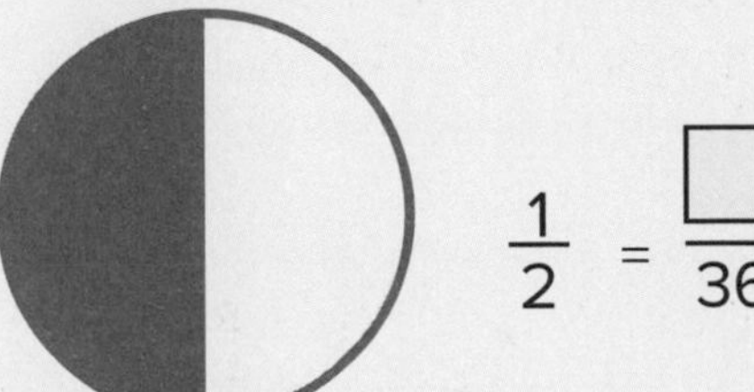

$$\frac{1}{2} = \frac{\square}{360}$$

$$\frac{1}{3} = \frac{\square}{360}$$

PRACTICE: Now you try

Tell what fractional part of the circle the shaded angle represents.

1. 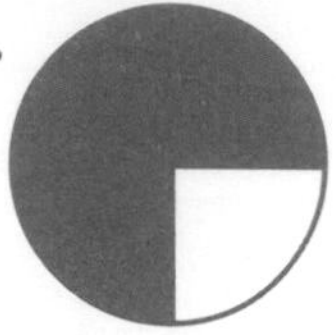
2. 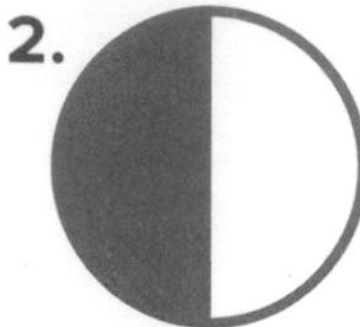
3. 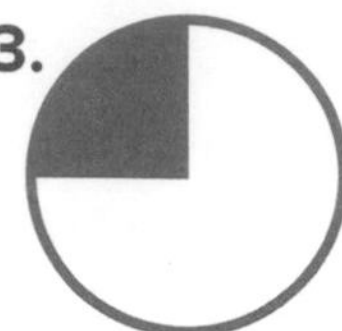
4. 
5. 

Circle the correct answer.

6. In circle #1, what type of angle is shaded?	Acute	Obtuse	Straight	Right
7. In circle #2, what type of angle is shaded?	Acute	Obtuse	Straight	Right
8. In circle #3, what type of angle is shaded?	Acute	Obtuse	Straight	Right
9. In circle #4, what type of angle is shaded?	Acute	Obtuse	Straight	Right
10. In circle #5, what type of angle is shaded?	Acute	Obtuse	Straight	Right

Let's say you have two circles and one is bigger than the other. Both circles have right angles shaded. Does one right angle have more degrees than the other? Show your work and explain your thinking on a piece of paper.

ACE IT TIME!

	yes	no
Did you underline the question in the word problem?		
Did you circle the numbers or number words?		
Did you box the supporting details or information needed to solve the problem?		
Did you draw a picture or a graphic organizer and write a math sentence to show your thinking?		
Did you label your numbers and your picture?		
Did you explain your thinking and use math vocabulary words in your explanation?		

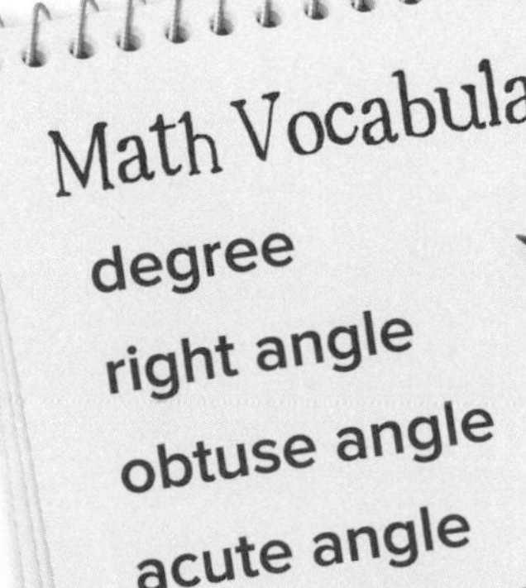

With an adult's permission, go on the Internet and search for professions that require an understanding of angles and angle size. Can you think of any ideas you may find?

Angles Are Measured in Degrees

UNPACK THE STANDARD
You will learn that because angles are measured in degrees, angles can be defined by their measurement unit.

LEARN IT: Angles can be further defined by their measure of degrees. Now that you know angles are defined by their relationship to a circle, many relationships between angles can be made.

Term	Definition	Addition to Definition	Looks Like
right angle	forms a square corner; uses 2 rays that are **perpendicular** to each other	angles that measure 90°	
straight angle	forms a line	angle that measures 180°	
acute angle	forms an angle that is smaller than a right angle	any angle that is less than 90°	
obtuse angle	forms an angle that is larger than a right angle	any angle that is greater than 90°	

Some New Ideas

2 right angles form 1 straight angle. $90° + 90° = 180°$

2 or more acute angles must be used to make a right angle.

If you put 2 obtuse angles together, you will have an angle greater than a straight angle.

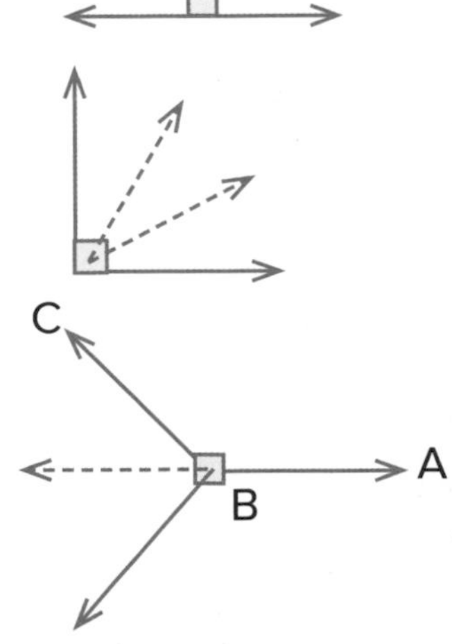

PRACTICE: Now you try

Estimate the size of the angles. Draw and name them.

1. 45°
2. 270°
3. 190°
4. 90°
5. 180°

think!
To draw an obtuse angle, ask yourself what size the other angle would be if you drew the angle inside a circle.

How many degrees are in an angle that turns $\frac{4}{6}$ of a circle? Show your work and explain your thinking on a piece of paper.

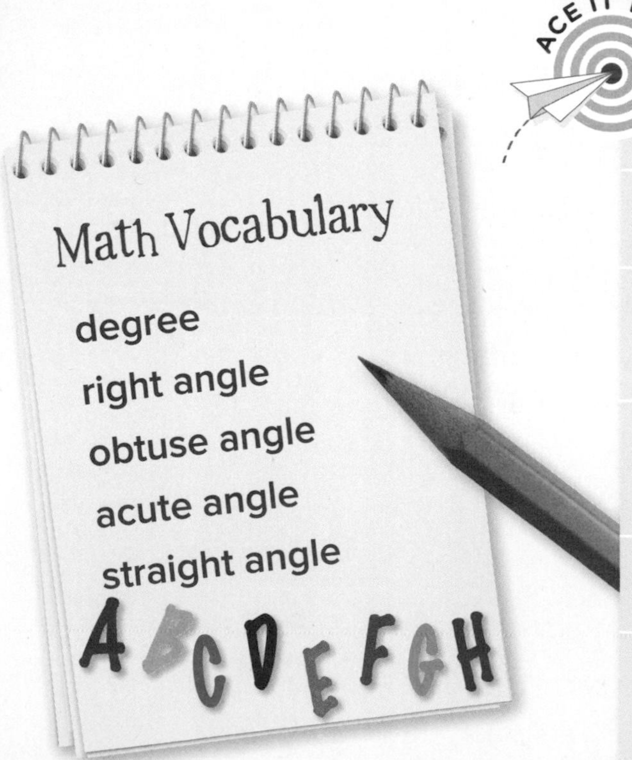

ACE IT TIME!

	yes	no
Did you underline the question in the word problem?		
Did you circle the numbers or number words?		
Did you box the supporting details or information needed to solve the problem?		
Did you draw a picture or a graphic organizer and write a math sentence to show your thinking?		
Did you label your numbers and your picture?		
Did you explain your thinking and use math vocabulary words in your explanation?		

Remember when you made a list of the alphabet to find different kinds of lines? Now write the alphabet again and see if you can find the kinds of angles each letter has, if any. Use capital letters!

How to Use a Protractor

UNPACK THE STANDARD
You will learn that angles are measured by a tool called a protractor. You can use a protractor to draw an angle with a specific degree measure.

LEARN IT: A ***protractor*** is a semi-circle instrument used for measuring and creating angles.

How to Measure with a Protractor	
Step 1	Place the center point on the vertex of angle ABC. (Point B)
Step 2	Align the 0 mark with $\overrightarrow{BC}$.
Step 3	Find the place where point A intersects with a degree mark on the protractor. (Extend the ray to pass the protractor if you need to.)
Step 4	Read the tick mark where the line crosses in degrees. Each mark counts as 1.

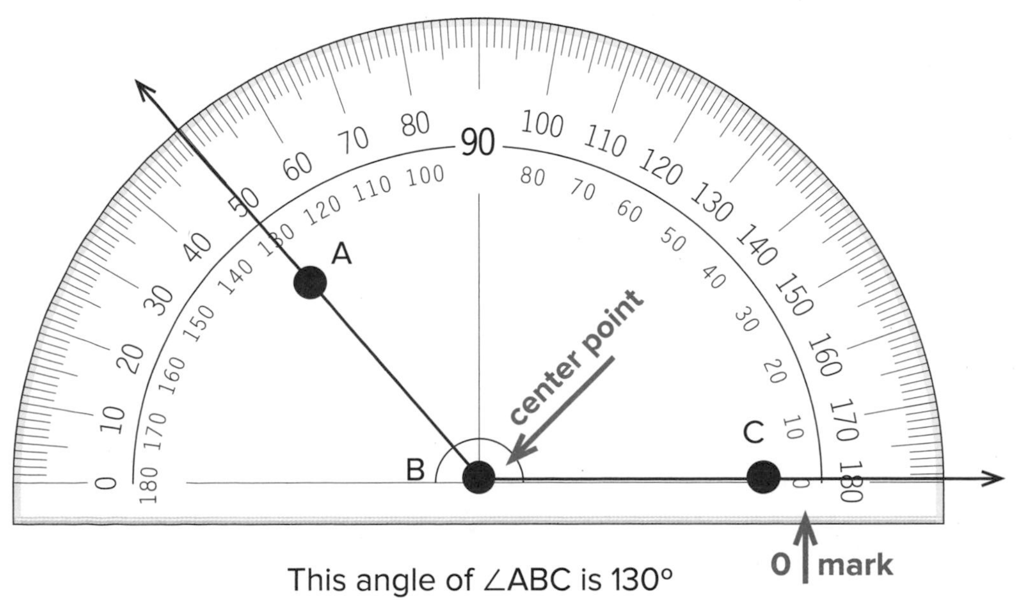

This angle of ∠ABC is 130°

How to Draw an Angle with a Protractor	
Step 1	Use the straight edge to draw $\overrightarrow{RS}$.
Step 2	Place the center point on the endpoint $\overrightarrow{RS}$. Make sure you align the ray to the 0 mark on the protractor.
Step 3	Find the degree point required. Let's use 45°. Use your pencil to mark the spot.
Step 4	Use the straight edge to draw the other ray.

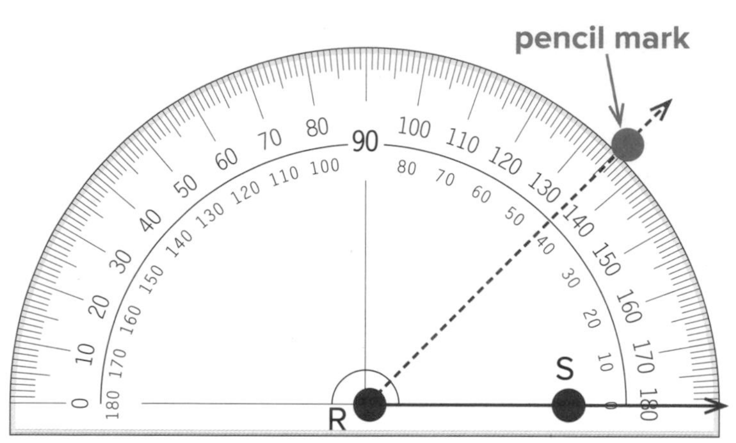

Hint: If you are measuring an angle that opens to the right, use the inside degree markings. If you are measuring an angle the opens to the left, use the outside degree markings.

PRACTICE: Now you try Use a protractor to draw the angles.

1. 48° **2.** 125° **3.** 67° **4.** 159° **5.** 90°

Use a protractor to measure the angles.

6. D E

7. F G I H

8.

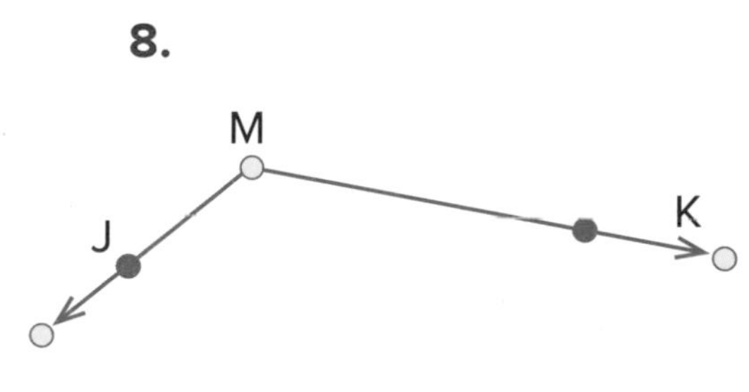

∠DE = ________

∠GIH = ________

∠FIH = ________

∠JMK = ________

Marci measured this angle incorrectly as 95° instead of 85°. What did she likely do wrong? Show your work and explain your thinking on a piece of paper.

ACE IT TIME!

	yes	no
Did you underline the question in the word problem?		
Did you circle the numbers or number words?		
Did you box the supporting details or information needed to solve the problem?		
Did you draw a picture or a graphic organizer and write a math sentence to show your thinking?		
Did you label your numbers and your picture?		
Did you explain your thinking and use math vocabulary words in your explanation?		

Math Vocabulary

degree
protractor
center point

Go to three different rooms in your house. Take your protractor with you. Find things that have angles and measure them with your protractor. Record your findings.

Angles Add Up

UNPACK THE STANDARD
You will learn to determine how to join and separate angles by determining the measure of an angle that is separated into parts.

LEARN IT: The measure of an angle equals the sum of the measure of its parts. First you measure the angles, then you add the sums together.

Imagine that you have 1 whole pizza. You can cut the pizza into 6 fair-share slices; each slice will have an angle of 60° (360° ÷ 6 = 60°).

Suppose you give 1 slice of pizza to a friend. He wants to cut this slice in half. He would be taking a piece of pizza with a 60° angle and making it into 2 pieces that have 30° each. If he knows that his slice is 60° of the whole pizza, he could determine the angles of the 2 new pieces he made.

What does this mean? If you cut ∠ABC into 2 different angles, the sum of those 2 angles will be the same as ∠ABC.

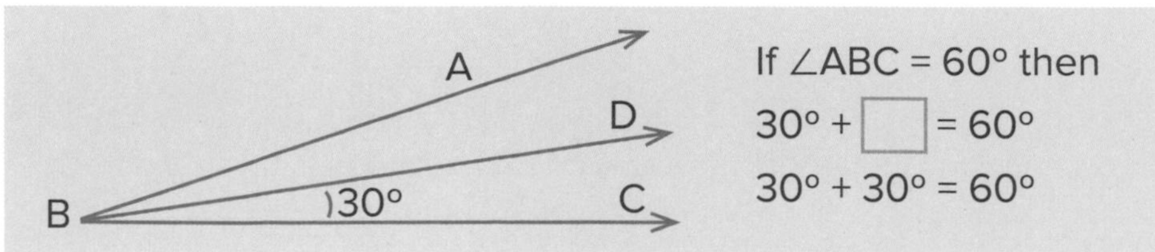

PRACTICE: Now you try

Find all the angle measurements in the circle below.

Measure only *one* angle with a protractor!

1. ∠ACD =
2. ∠ACB =
3. ∠BCD =
4. ∠BCE =
5. ∠ECD =
6. ∠BCF =
7. ∠FCE =

8. What equation would you use to find ∠FCE?

think!
What angles do you already know the measure of?

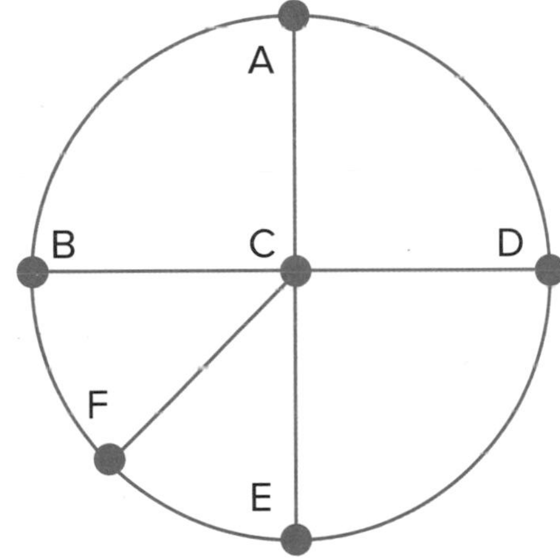

think!
What angle(s) might you need to measure using the protractor?

Find the measure of the angle. Write an equation to show your work.

9.

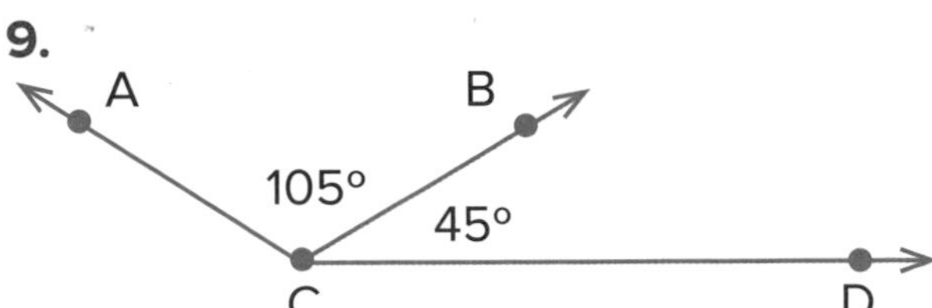

∠ACD = ______________

10.

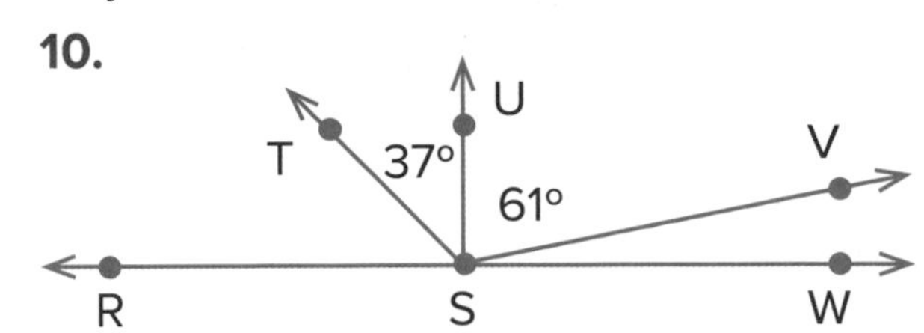

∠RST = ____________ ∠VSW = ____________

At a pizza party, Johnny and his 7 friends shared a pizza. Johnny decided to cut the pizza in fair shares to do this. Draw a picture to show how he cut the pizza and what the angle measurement for each piece would be. Write equations to show your thinking. Show your work and explain your thinking on a piece of paper.

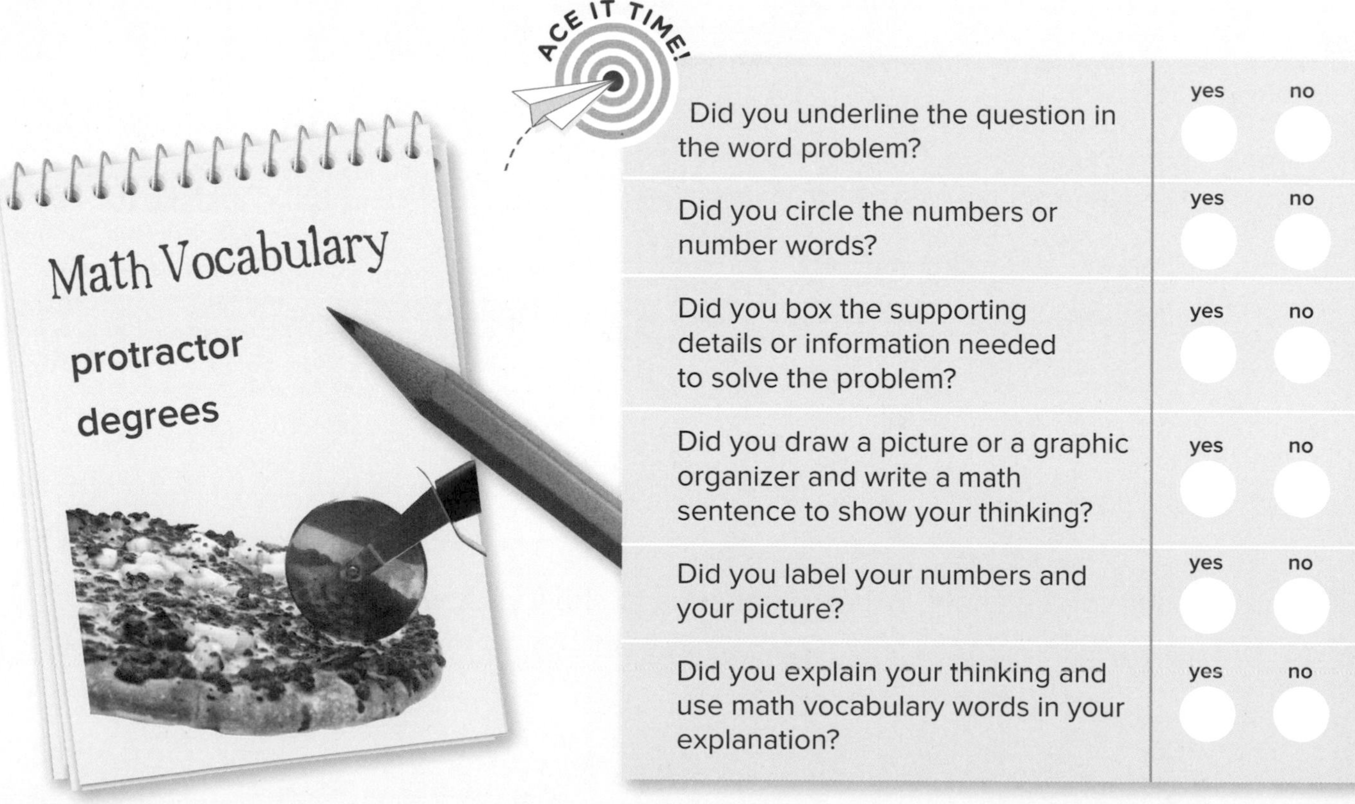

	yes	no
Did you underline the question in the word problem?		
Did you circle the numbers or number words?		
Did you box the supporting details or information needed to solve the problem?		
Did you draw a picture or a graphic organizer and write a math sentence to show your thinking?		
Did you label your numbers and your picture?		
Did you explain your thinking and use math vocabulary words in your explanation?		

Make a geometric piece of art. Use 20 different angles. Show right, straight, acute, and obtuse. Use your protractor to make sure you don't repeat a single size.

REVIEW

Stop and think about what you have learned.

Congratulations! You've finished the lessons for this unit. This means you learned about lines, angles, and geometric shapes. You have learned about which shapes have symmetry. You can identify shapes by the number of sides and the size of their angles. You know that angles are fractional parts of a circle and that they are measured in degrees. Finally, you can determine the size of angles by knowing the size of the angles within the same circle.

Now it's time to prove your skills with geometry! Solve the problems below. Use all of the methods you have learned.

Activity Section 1: Lines, Angles, and Triangles

Identify and name types of lines, angles, and triangles.

1. What is the error?	**2.**	**3.** Draw 2 lines that are perpendicular to each other and explain the definition.
V X M Sharon called this figure ∠MVX ____________	A B C Name this shape: ________ What kind of angles: A ________ B ________ C ________	

Activity Section 2: Geometric Shape Patterns

1. Mark the parallel lines in the figure.	**2.** Can a rhombus be a square?	**3.** Name quadrilaterals that have 2 sets of sides that are equal in length.

Activity Section 3: Symmetry Complete the table.

Polygon	▬	■	⏢	▲	⬢
Name					hexagon
# of sides					
Draw lines of symmetry					

Activity Section 4: Angles as Fractional Parts of a Circle

1. How many degrees does every circle have?	**2.** Define an obtuse angle. Draw a sample.	**3.** Define an acute angle. Draw a sample.	**4.** Define a right angle. Draw a sample.

Activity Section 5: Measuring Angles

1. What is the degree measurement of each angle in this diagram?

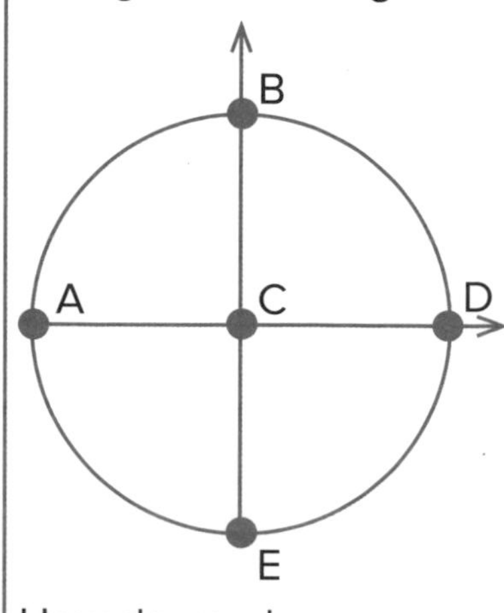

How do you know without using a protractor?

2. Draw a straight angle WZ that is divided by $\overrightarrow{XY}$. The 2 angles that $\overrightarrow{XY}$ forms with angle WZ should have 150° and 30° angles.

3. Name the degrees of all the angles. Show your work.

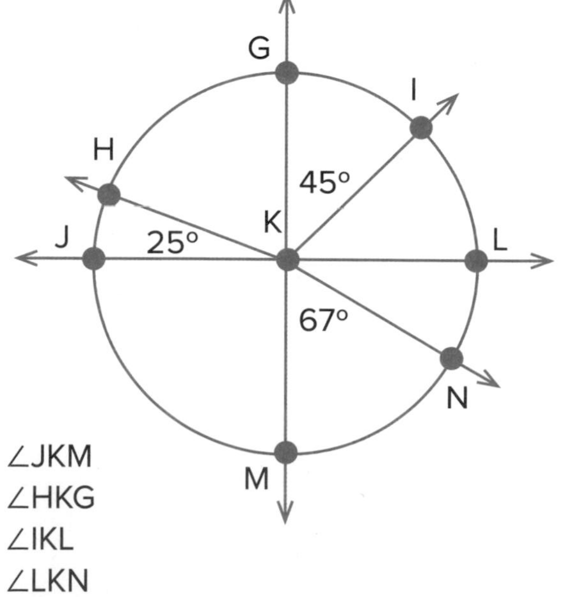

∠JKM
∠HKG
∠IKL
∠LKN

 CCSS.Math.Content.4.G.A.1; 4.G.A.2; 4.G.A.3;.4.MD.C.5; 4.MD.C.5a; 4.MD.C.5b; 4.MD.C.6; 4.G.MD.C.7; CCSS.Math.Practice.MP1; MP2; MP3; MP4; MP5; MP6; MP7; MP8

Understand the meaning of what you have learned and apply your knowledge.

We use geometry in our daily lives probably more than you realize! You can use what you've learned about measuring and estimating angles to get a better idea of "the big picture."

Activity Section

Katrina, Lorraine, and Phil had pizza for lunch. Katrina ate $\frac{1}{3}$ of the pizza, Lorraine ate $\frac{1}{4}$ of the pizza, and Phil ate the rest. Using what you know about how angles are measured, determine the angle size that was eaten by each person. Draw a diagram to show your thinking.

CCSS.Math.Content.4.G.A.1; 4.G.A.2; 4.G.A.3;.4.MD.C.5; 4.MD.C.5a; 4.MD.C.5b; 4.MD.C.6; 4.G.MD.C.7;
CCSS.Math.Practice.MP1; MP2; MP3; MP4; MP5; MP6; MP7; MP8

DISCOVER

Discover how you can apply the information you have learned.

Protractors are valuable tools. The more you practice using them, the easier it becomes to understand.

Activity Section

If a protractor can only measure up to 180°, how can you measure an angle over 180° using a protractor?

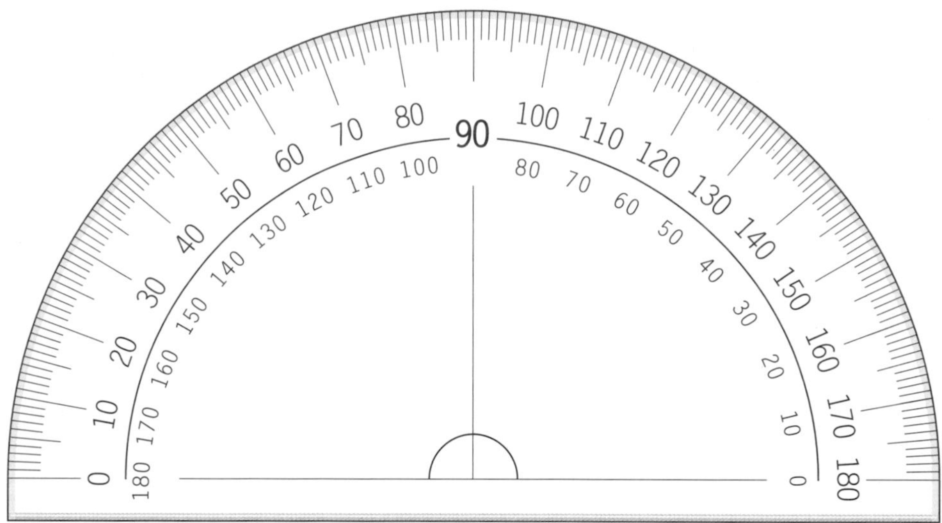

CCSS.Math.Content.4.G.A.1; 4.G.A.2; 4.G.A.3;.4.MD.C.5; 4.MD.C.5a; 4.MD.C.5b; 4.MD.C.6; 4.G.MD.C.7; CCSS.Math.Practice.MP1; MP2; MP3; MP4; MP5; MP6; MP7; MP8

CORE Measurement Concepts

Customary Measurement

UNPACK THE STANDARD

You will learn about customary units of measurement and how to convert measurements expressed in larger units as measurements in equivalent smaller units.

LEARN IT: ***Customary units*** **are the measurement units used in the United States' customary system of measurement. Look at the chart below to get an idea of some common, everyday items and their estimated measurements.**

Customary Units of **LENGTH**	Customary Units of **MASS**	Customary Units of **LIQUID VOLUME**
Length measures distance from one end of an object to the other end. about 1 inch about 1 foot	Mass measures the amount of matter in an object. about 1 ounce about 1 pound about 1 ton	Liquid volume is the amount of liquid that is in a container. about 1 cup about 1 pint about 1 quart about 1 half-gallon about 1 gallon

CUSTOMARY UNITS OF MEASUREMENTS

Practice learning customary measurements. Complete each conversion table below.

Length

1 foot = 12 inches
1 yard = 3 feet

Feet	Inches	think!
1	12	1 × 12 = 12 inches
2	24	2 × 12 = 24 inches
3		3 × 12 = ________
4		4 × 12 = ________
5		5 × 12 = ________

Since 1 foot is equal to 12 inches, you can rename feet as inches by multiplying the number of feet by 12.

Mass (Weight)

1 pound = 16 ounces
1 ton = 2,000 pounds

Pounds	Ounces	think!
1	16	1 × 16 = 16 ounces
2	32	2 × 16 = 32 ounces
3		3 × 16 = ________
4		4 × 16 = ________
5		5 × 16 = ________

Since 1 pound is equal to 16 ounces, you can rename pounds as ounces by multiplying the number of pounds by 16.

Liquid Volume

1 cup = 8 fluid ounces

1 pint = 2 cups = 16 fluid ounces

1 quart = 2 pints = 4 cups = 32 fluid ounces

1 gallon = 4 quarts = 8 pints = 16 cups = 128 fluid ounces

Gallons	Fluid Ounces	think!
1	128	1 x 128 = 128 fluid ounces
2		2 × 128 = ____ fl.oz.
3		3 × 128 = ____ fl.oz.
4		4 × 128 = ____ fl.oz.

Since 1 gallon is equal to 128 fluid ounces, you can rename gallons as fluid ounces by multiplying the number of gallons by 128.

Time

1 minute = 60 seconds

$\frac{1}{4}$ hour = 15 minutes

$\frac{1}{2}$ hour = 30 minutes

$\frac{3}{4}$ hour = 45 minutes

1 hour = 60 minutes

1 day = 24 hours

1 week = 7 days

Minutes	Seconds	think!
1	60	1 × 60 = 60 seconds
2		2 × 60 = ___ seconds
3		3 × 60 = ___ seconds
4		4 × 60 = ___ seconds

Since 1 minute is equal to 60 seconds, you can rename minutes as seconds by multiplying the number of minutes by 60.

PRACTICE: Now you try

Use the conversion tables on the previous page to complete or compare. Use >, <, or =.

1. 5 yards = _____ feet	**2.** 4 feet = _____ inches	**3.** 3 yards ◯ 9 feet
4. 4 tons = _____ pounds	**5.** 7 pounds = ____ ounces	**6.** 3 tons ◯ 3 pounds
7. 3 gallons = _____ pints	**8.** 5 quarts = _____ cups	**9.** 3 gallons ◯ 48 cups
10. 2 days = _____ hours	**11.** 3 minutes = _____ seconds	**12.** 36 hours ◯ 3 days

Godfrey and his sister eat 1 pound of peanuts every day. Their mom says that they should eat no more than 8 ounces of peanuts a day. How many extra ounces of peanuts do they eat in 1 week? Show your work and explain your thinking on a piece of paper.

ACE IT TIME!

	yes	no
Did you underline the question in the word problem?	◯	◯
Did you circle the numbers or number words?	◯	◯
Did you box the supporting details or information needed to solve the problem?	◯	◯
Did you draw a picture or a graphic organizer and write a math sentence to show your thinking?	◯	◯
Did you label your numbers and your picture?	◯	◯
Did you explain your thinking and use math vocabulary words in your explanation?	◯	◯

The next time you are at the grocery store with an adult, look for items that use customary units of length, mass, or liquid volume. Food packages and containers with liquids are a great place to start! For example, a box of pasta weighs 1 pound. How many ounces is this? How many ounces would 2 boxes weigh?

Metric Measurement

UNPACK THE STANDARD
You will learn about metric units of measurement and how to convert measurements expressed in larger units as measurements in equivalent smaller units.

LEARN IT: ***Metric units*** are measurement units used in the metric system. This is an international system of measurement. The metric system is another way we can measure objects, besides the customary system.

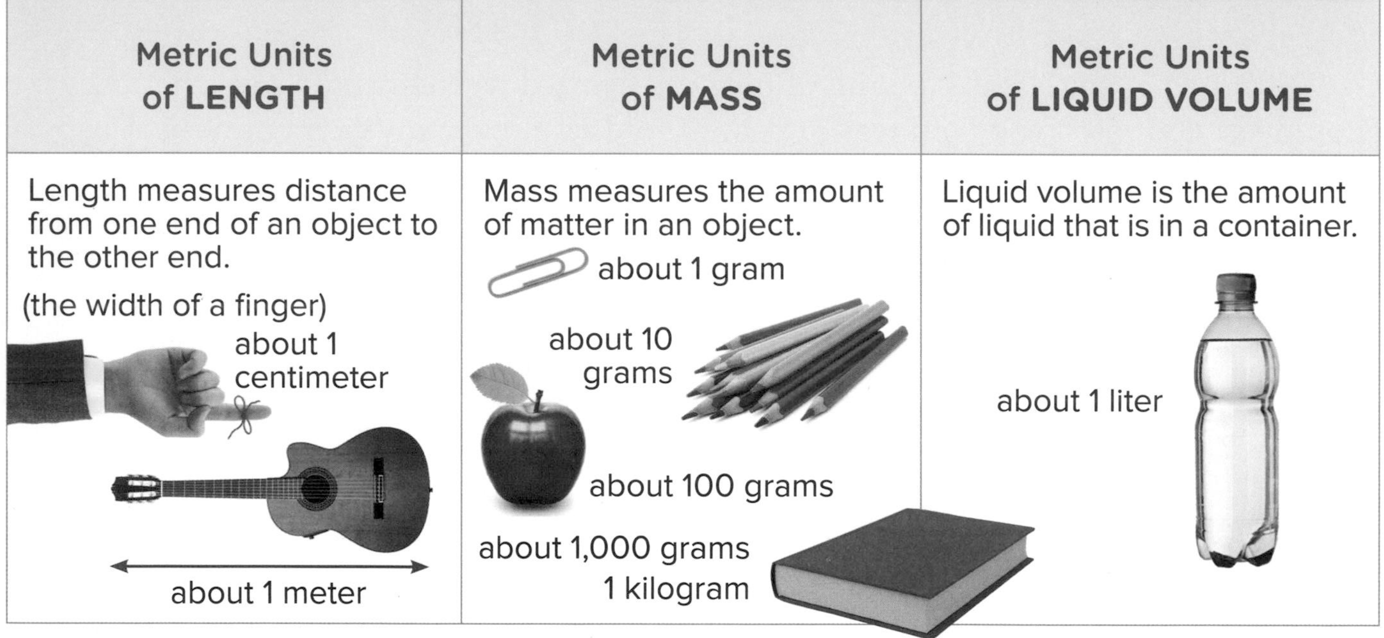

Metric Units of **LENGTH**	Metric Units of **MASS**	Metric Units of **LIQUID VOLUME**
Length measures distance from one end of an object to the other end.	Mass measures the amount of matter in an object.	Liquid volume is the amount of liquid that is in a container.
(the width of a finger) about 1 centimeter	about 1 gram	about 1 liter
about 1 meter	about 10 grams	
	about 100 grams	
	about 1,000 grams 1 kilogram	

METRIC UNITS OF MEASUREMENTS

Liquid Volume 1 liter = 1,000 milliliters

Complete the conversion table below.

Liters	Milli-liters	**think!**
1	1,000	1 × 1,000 = 1,000 millileters
2	2,000	2 × 1,000 = ______ millileters
3		3 × 1,000 = ______ millileters
4		4 × 1,000 = ______ millileters

Since 1 liter is equal to 1,000 milliliters, you can rename liters as milliliters by multiplying the number of liters by 1,000.

Mass 1 kilogram = 1,000 grams

Complete the conversion table below.

Grams	Kilo-grams	**think!**
1,000	1	1,000 ÷ 1,000 = 1 kilogram
2,000	2	2,000 ÷ 1,000 = 2 kilograms
3,000		3,000 ÷ 1,000 = _____ kilograms
4,000		4,000 ÷ 1,000 = _____ kilograms

Since 1,000 grams is equal to 1 kilogram, you can rename grams as kilograms by dividing the number of grams by 1,000.

Length 1 centimeter = 10 millimeters
1 meter = 10 decimeters =
100 centimeters = 1,000 milliliters
1 kilometer = 1,000 meters

Complete the conversion table below.

Meters	Centi-meters	**think!**
1	100	1 × 1,000 = 100 centimeters
2	200	2 × 1,000 = ____ centimeters
5		5 × 1,000 = ____ centimeters
8		8 × 1,000 = ____ centimeters

Since 1 meter is equal to 100 centimeters, you can rename meters as centimeters by multiplying the number of meters by 100.

PRACTICE: Now you try

Use the conversion tables at left and on the previous page to complete.

1. 5 centimeters = ____ millimeters
2. 7 kilograms = ____ grams
3. 2,000 milliliters = ____ liters

ACE IT TIME!

Aimee and her mom were going on a trip. Aimee's suitcase had a mass of 8 kilograms and her mom's suitcase had a mass of 19 kilograms. How many more grams did Aimee's mom's suitcase weigh than Aimee's suitcase? Show your work and explain your thinking on a piece of paper.

	yes	no
Did you underline the question in the word problem?	○	○
Did you circle the numbers or number words?	○	○
Did you box the supporting details or information needed to solve the problem?	○	○
Did you draw a picture or a graphic organizer and write a math sentence to show your thinking?	○	○
Did you label your numbers and your picture?	○	○
Did you explain your thinking and use math vocabulary words in your explanation?	○	○

The next time you are at the grocery store with an adult, look for items that use metric units of length, mass, or liquid volume. Food packages and containers with liquids are a great place to start! For example, a liquid detergent container might have 5 liters of detergent. How many milliliters is that?

Elapsed Time

UNPACK THE STANDARD
You will solve word problems involving addition and subtraction of time intervals in minutes.

LEARN IT: What time will it be when we get there? How long is the movie? If practice starts at 6:30, what time do we need to leave? These are the types of questions we ask that involve ***elapsed time***. When solving problems involving time, it is important to consider start time, end time, and elapsed time.

Finding the End Time

When solving time-interval problems, you may be asked to find the end time. In this case, you will be given a start time and the elapsed time. **End time** refers to how long an event took place.

Mya leaves to go to the mall at 10:05 a.m. It takes her 25 minutes to get there. What time does she get to the mall?

Start Time = 10:05 a.m. Elapsed Time = 25 minutes End Time = ___?___

Find the starting time on the clock. Skip-count around the clock by 5s and then by 1s until you count 25 minutes. Count forward 25 minutes to find that the end time is 10:30 a.m.

Use a number line to count or add 25 minutes. If Mya leaves at 10:05 a.m. to go to the mall and it takes her 25 minutes to get there, she gets to the mall at 10:30 a.m.

Finding Elapsed Time

To find elapsed time, you will be given a start time and an end time. **Elapsed time** is the difference from one time to another.

Eric starts his homework at 3:30 p.m. He finishes at 4:20 p.m. How long does Eric spend on his homework?

Start Time = 3:30 p.m. Elapsed Time = ___?___ End Time = 4:20 p.m.

Use a **clock** to figure out how long Eric spent on his homework.

Find the starting time on the clock. Skip-count around the clock by 5s and then by 1s until you get to the end time. Count forward from 3:30 p.m. to 4:20 p.m. The elapsed time is 50 minutes.

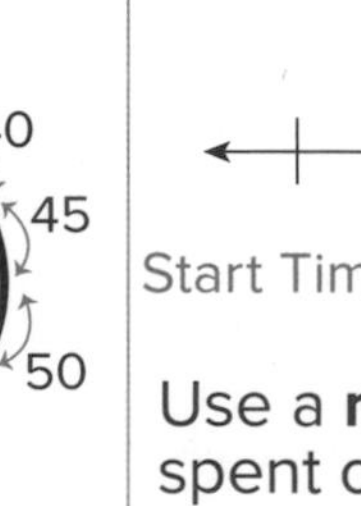

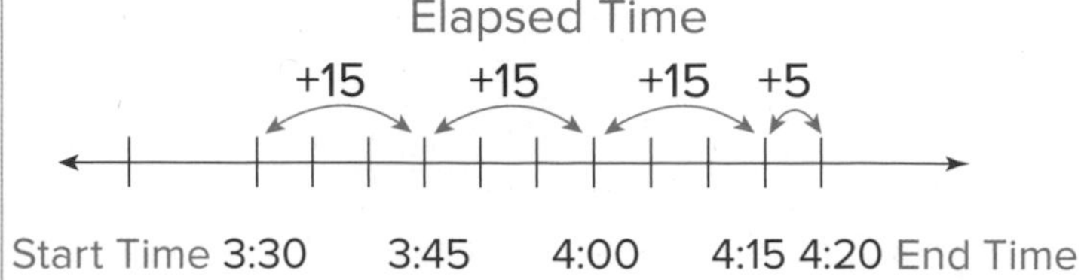

Use a **number line** to figure out how long Eric spent on his homework.

Finding the Start Time

Start time refers to the time an event began. To find the start time, you will be given an end time and an elapsed time.

Example: Julius has been at track practice for 1 hour and 15 minutes. It is now 6:25 p.m. What time did the practice start?

Start Time = ___?___   Elapsed Time = 1 hour 15 minutes   End Time = 6:25 p.m.

Find the end time on the clock. Count back 1 hour to 5:25. Count back by 5s until you count 15 minutes. This will give you the start time. The start time is 5:10 p.m.

Use a **number line** to figure out the time that Julius gets to practice.

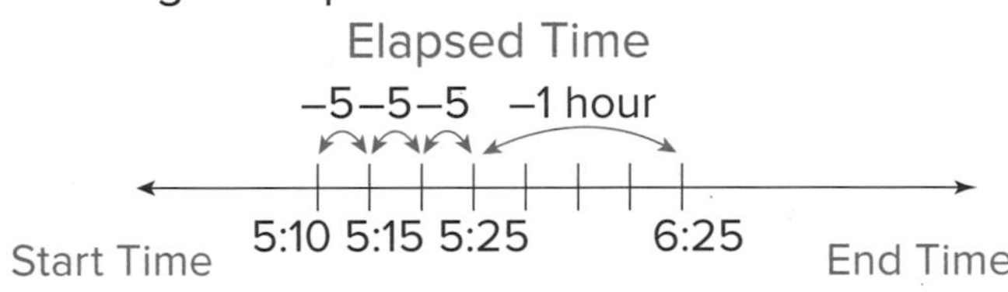

PRACTICE: Now you try

Draw a number line or clock to solve.

1. Marisol had a meeting that started at 4:15. The meeting finished at 5:46. How long was she in the meeting?

   Elapsed Time ____

2. Sophia started eating dinner at 6:10. She finished at 7:06. How long did it take her to eat?

   Elapsed Time ____

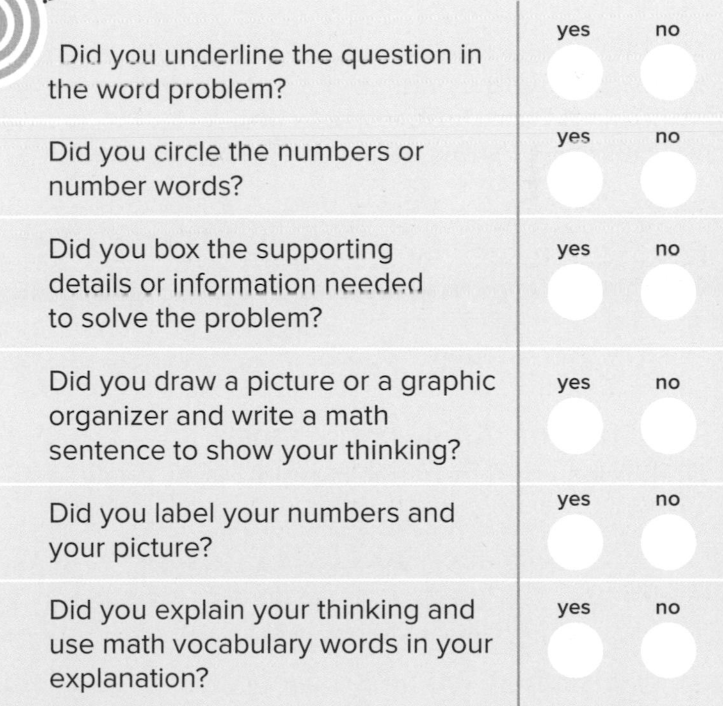

	yes	no
Did you underline the question in the word problem?		
Did you circle the numbers or number words?		
Did you box the supporting details or information needed to solve the problem?		
Did you draw a picture or a graphic organizer and write a math sentence to show your thinking?		
Did you label your numbers and your picture?		
Did you explain your thinking and use math vocabulary words in your explanation?		

When Michelle got to track practice, she warmed up for 18 minutes, stretched for 13 minutes, and then jogged around the track for 48 minutes. She left the track at 4:30 p.m. What time did she arrive? Show your work and explain your thinking on a piece of paper.

To practice solving time-interval problems, ask an adult to make up story problems and do the math to figure start times, end times, and elapsed times.

Line Plots

UNPACK THE STANDARD
You will understand and create line plots to display a data set of measurements in fractions. You will make observations about the data.

LEARN IT: A *line plot* graph is another way to visually represent data. A line plot records the number of times (frequency) data occurs. It shows the frequency of data along a number line.

Creating a Line Plot to Display Data

Janet has 8 pencils in her pencil case. The pencils are different lengths and were measured using feet as the unit. Let's make a line plot to represent the lengths of Janet's pencils.
($\frac{1}{2}$, $\frac{1}{2}$, $\frac{1}{4}$, $\frac{1}{2}$, $\frac{1}{4}$, $\frac{3}{4}$, $\frac{1}{4}$, $\frac{3}{4}$)

Step 1: Put the data in order from least to greatest. Record on a tally table.
$\frac{1}{4}$, $\frac{1}{4}$, $\frac{1}{4}$, $\frac{1}{2}$, $\frac{1}{2}$, $\frac{1}{2}$, $\frac{3}{4}$, $\frac{3}{4}$

Length of Janet's Pencils	
Length (in feet)	Tally
$\frac{1}{4}$	III
$(\frac{1}{2}) = \frac{2}{4}$	III
$\frac{3}{4}$	II

All of the measurements of Janet's pencils are between 0 and 1 foot. So let's draw and label a number line to show these numbers. Since all of the measurements are in fourths, we will draw the number line to show all of the fourths between 0 and 1.

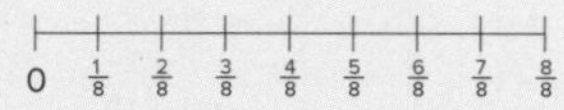

Step 2: Display the data. Draw an X above the location on the number line for each piece of data. If the data appears more than once, draw another X above the previous one. Notice how the title of the line plot matches the title of the tally table.

Length of Janet's Pencils

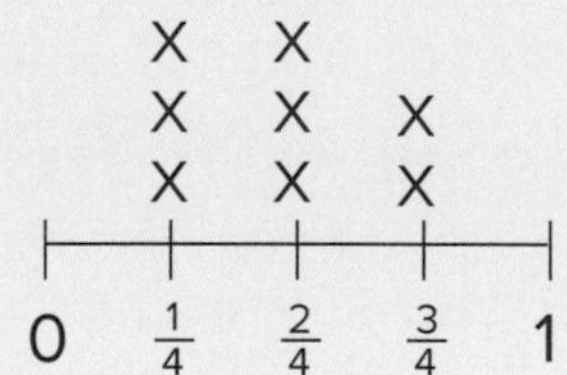

Reading and Analyzing a Line Plot

What can I learn from my line plot? Let's analyze it!

- There are 8 X's, so there are 8 pieces of data all together. Each X represents 1 pencil.
- I can look at my plot and see that all of my pencils are between $\frac{1}{4}$ and $\frac{3}{4}$ foot long.
- There were 3 pencils that were $\frac{1}{4}$ foot long, 3 pencils that were $\frac{2}{4}$ foot long, and 2 pencils that were $\frac{3}{4}$ foot long.
- Since there are no X's on the measurement of 1, I know that there were no pencils that were exactly 1 foot long. That would be a really long pencil!

You must also be able to solve problems regarding the line plot graph. Use the line plot of Lengths of Janet's Pencils to answer these questions:

1. How many pencils are $\frac{2}{4}$ of a foot and above?
   3 (measurement of $\frac{2}{4}$) + 2 (measurement of $\frac{3}{4}$) = 5 pencils
2. How many more $\frac{1}{4}$ of a foot pencils are there than $\frac{3}{4}$ of a foot?
   3 (measurement of $\frac{1}{4}$) – 2 (measurement of $\frac{3}{4}$) = 1 pencil
3. What is the difference between the length of the shortest pencil and the longest pencil? $\frac{3}{4} - \frac{1}{4} = \frac{2}{4}$

PRACTICE: Now you try

Use the data to complete the table. Complete the line plot. Answer the questions for the line plot.

The students in Mrs. O'Keefe's class had to walk 2 miles in gym class.

The following data shows the length of time the students in her class took to walk the 2 miles.

$(\frac{6}{8}, \frac{4}{8}, \frac{3}{8}, \frac{5}{8}, \frac{3}{8}, \frac{5}{8}, \frac{4}{8}, \frac{4}{8}, \frac{4}{8}, \frac{5}{8})$

Step 1: Put the data in order from least to greatest.

____, ____, ____, ____, ____, ____, ____, ____, ____, ____

Now record the data on the table.

Length of Time Students Walked in Mrs. O'Keefe's Class	
$\frac{3}{8}$	
$\frac{4}{8}$	
$\frac{5}{8}$	
$\frac{6}{8}$	

Step 2: Display the data. Draw an X above the location on the number line for each piece of data.

After creating the line plot, use the information to answer the questions on a separate piece of paper.

1. How many total students are in Mrs. O'Keefe's class?
2. How many more students walked for $\frac{4}{8}$ of an hour than walked for $\frac{3}{8}$ of an hour?
3. How many students walked for $\frac{5}{8}$ of an hour or more?
4. How many students walked for $\frac{4}{8}$ of an hour or more?

0 $\frac{1}{8}$ $\frac{2}{8}$ $\frac{3}{8}$ $\frac{4}{8}$ $\frac{5}{8}$ $\frac{6}{8}$ $\frac{7}{8}$ $\frac{8}{8}$

ACE IT TIME!

Use the line plot "Length of Time Students Walked in Mrs. O'Keefe's Class" to answer the following question: Which is greater, the number of students that walked $\frac{4}{8}$ of an hour or less, or the number of students that walked $\frac{5}{8}$ of an hour or more? Show your work and explain your thinking on a piece of paper.

	yes	no
Did you underline the question in the word problem?	◯	◯
Did you circle the numbers or number words?	◯	◯
Did you box the supporting details or information needed to solve the problem?	◯	◯
Did you draw a picture or a graphic organizer and write a math sentence to show your thinking?	◯	◯
Did you label your numbers and your picture?	◯	◯
Did you explain your thinking and use math vocabulary words in your explanation?	◯	◯

MATH ON THE MOVE

Create a line plot. Count the number of letters in each family member's name and plot them. Make up questions for your family members to answer.

REVIEW

Stop and think about what you have learned.

Congratulations! You've finished the lessons for this unit. This means you have learned about customary and metric units of measurement and how to convert them from larger units to smaller units. You practiced solving word problems involving distances, intervals of time, and money and using the 4 operations. You even understand line plots and can make observations about the data.

Now it's time to prove your skills with measurement! Solve the problems below. Use all of the methods you have learned.

Activity Section 1: Customary and Metric Measurement

1. Complete the conversion table

Gallons	Cups	**think!**
4		4 gallons × 16 = ___ cups
7		7 gallons × 16 = ___ cups
11		11 gallons × 16 = ___ cups

2. Complete the conversion table

Grams	Kilo-grams	**think!**
5,000		5,000 ÷ 1,000 = ___ kilograms
7,000		7,000 ÷ 1,000 = ___ kilograms
9,000		9,000 ÷ 1,000 = ___ kilograms

Activity Section 2: Customary Measurement

Use the conversion tables in the lesson on page 161 to complete or compare. Use >, <, or =.

1. 6 yards = ___ feet	**2.** 7 feet = ___ inches	**3.** 5 minutes ◯ 300 seconds

Activity Section 3: Metric Measurement

Use the conversion tables in the lesson on pages 163–164 to complete or compare. Use >, <, or =.

1. 14 kilograms = ___ grams	**2.** 5 kilograms = ___ grams	**3.** 5 liters ◯ 5,500 milliliters

Activity Section 4: Elapsed Time

Solve the problems below. Draw a number line or clock on a separate piece of paper to solve.

1. Mr. Maynor was done cooking dinner for his family at 7:05 p.m. He started at 3:45 p.m. How long did it take Mr. Maynor to cook dinner?

Start Time ______ Elapsed Time ______ End Time ______

2. The Hill family got to the park at 1:15 p.m. They were there for 2 hours and 58 minutes. What time did the Hills leave the park?

Start Time ______ Elapsed Time ______ End Time ______

UNDERSTAND

Understand the meaning of what you have learned and apply your knowledge.

You use measurement conversions in daily life all the time, especially when cooking in the kitchen! Problems like the one below are very true to real-life situations. You can use what you've learned about customary measurements and conversions.

Activity Section

Lindsey wants to have a large bowl of fruit punch for the guests at her birthday party. She mixes her favorite drinks together to make the punch. She mixes in 3 gallons of Very Berry punch, 1 quart of orange juice, 2 pints of apple juice, and 1 quart of cranberry juice.

1. How many quarts of fruit punch will she have for her guests? Use the conversion table on page 160 to help. Show your work. Explain your thinking.

2. If everyone who came to the party had 1 cup of fruit punch, how many guests could be served? Use the conversion table on page 160. Show your work. Explain your thinking.

DISCOVER

Discover how you can apply the information you have learned.

How many times during the day do you think about what time it is, or how much longer you need to do something, or how much money do you have or need? Situations based on time, distance, and money surround our daily lives. You can use the strategies you have learned to help you solve word problems involving these skills.

Activity Section

Charlize and her father want to go visit her aunt in New York. They decide to take an airplane to get there. Their plane leaves on Monday at 1:18 p.m. They must be at the airport to check in 1 hour before the plane leaves. The drive to the airport takes exactly 36 minutes. When they get to the airport, they have to park the car in the parking garage and take a shuttle over to the terminal (this will take 20 minutes). What time should they leave home? Is the time a.m. or p.m.? Show your work and explain your answer.

Answer Key

Unit 2: CORE Number Concepts

Place Value Relationships

Page 17 Practice: Now you try

1. 20,000 twenty thousand
2. 700 seven hundred
3. 80,000 eighty thousand
4. 300,000 three hundred thousand
5. 90 ninety
6. 1 one
7. 5,000 five thousand

Page 18 Practice: Now you try

1. 10
2. 10
3. 10
4. 10
5. 10
6. 10

Page 19 Practice: Now you try

1. 10
2. 100
3. 100

Ace It Time: Michelle is correct. The 5 in 367,258 is in the tens place while the 5 in 356,798 is in the ten-thousands place, which is 3 places to the left of the tens. You must multiply by 10 × 10 × 10 = 1,000 to get the amount larger. So it is 1,000 times greater.

Rename the Number

Page 20 Practice: Now you try

Number	How many 1,000s	How many 100s	How many 10s
26,000 (sample)	26	260	2,600
1. 74,000	74	740	7,400
2. 890,000	890	8,900	89,000
3. 93,000	93	930	9,300
4. 307,000	307	3,070	30,700
5. 650,000	650	6,500	65,000

Page 21 Practice: Now you try

1. 8,200
2. 1,290
3. 640,000
4. 78
5. 15,780
6. 120,000
7. 765,000

Ace It Time: The video game store needs to order 200 sets of 10.

Expanded and Word Form

Page 22 Practice: Now you try

1. 237,010
2. 519,116
3. three thousand, eight hundred seven
4. forty thousand, six hundred sixteen
5. nine hundred twenty-four
6. one hundred twenty-three thousand, four hundred fifty-six

Page 23 Practice: Now you try

1. D
2. E
3. G
4. F
5. C
6. B
7. A

Ace It Time: Kathryn wrote 70,000 and it should have been 7,000. There were no ten-thousands in this number. She also wrote 8,000 when it should have been 800, and the 4 should have been 40. Her answer should have been: 500,000 + 7,000 + 800 + 40.

Compare and Order Numbers to 1,000,000

Page 25 Practice: Now you try

1. <
2. <
3. >
4. 45,761; 44,766; 43,765
5. 142,894; 139,654; 135,976
6. 796,539; 796,538; 796,531
7. 21,736; 23,798; 26,750
8. 253,900; 253,901; 253,904
9. 521,755; 524,763; 529,745

Ace It Time: No, Micah was not correct; the stadiums should have been in the following order: Sun Life, Mile High, Arrowhead, Superdome.

Rounding Multi-Digit Numbers

Page 27 Practice: Now you try

1. 22,000
2. 600,000
3. 40,000
4. 562,000
5. 10,000
6. 400,000

Ace It Time: The student who had the correct range of numbers is Mariah.

Joshua: 549,000 to 649,000; these numbers round to 500,000 and 600,000

Jillian: 551,000 to 651,000; these numbers round to 600,000 and 700,000

Marcus: 540,000 to 640,000; these numbers round to 500,000 and 600,000

Mariah: 550,000 to 649,000 is the only answer that is correct; these numbers all round to 600,000

Addition and Subtraction of Multi-Digit Numbers

Page 28 Practice: Now you try

1. 910,419
2. 325,970
3. 78,693
4. 90,323
5. 569,065
6. 851,261
7. 57,535
8. 157,789
9. 419,412
10. 249,352
11. 1,076
12. 12,690

Page 29

13. 550,321
14. 31,172
15. 13,984
16. 32,798
17. 2
18. 9
19. 8
20. 5

Ace It Time: Sharon must travel 9,030 more feet to get to the library.

9,328 feet to Maria's
+ 8,629 feet to park
17,957

26,987 total feet to library
− 17,957 feet already ridden
9,030 more feet

Unit 3: CORE Factor and Divisibility Concepts

Factors

Page 30 Practice: Now you try

1. 1, 2 , 5, 10
2. 1, 2, 7, 14
3. 1, 3, 9
4. 1, 5, 25
5. 1, 2, 4, 8, 16
6. 1, 3, 7, 21
7. 1, 2, 3, 6
8. 1, 7, 49
9. 1, 2, 3, 4, 6, 8, 12, 24
10. 1, 2, 3, 6, 9, 18

Page 31 Ace It Time:

No, the largest number does not have the most factors:

30: 1, 2, 3, 5, 6, 10, 15, 30 – 8 factors

33: 1, 3, 11, 33 – 4 factors

36: 1, 2, 3, 4, 6, 9, 12, 18, 36 – 9 factors

39: 1, 3, 13, 39 – 4 factors

Multiples

Page 32 Practice: Now you try

1. 5: 5, 10, 15, 20, 25, 30
   10: 10, 20, 30, 40, 50, 60
   Common: 10, 20, 30
2. 3: 3, 6, 9, 12, 15, 18
   9: 9, 18, 27, 36, 45, 54
   Common: 9, 18
3. 4: 4, 8, 12, 16, 20, 24
   6: 6, 12, 18, 24, 30, 36
   Common: 12, 24

Page 33 Practice: Now you try

1. No, yes, no
2. Yes, yes, no
3. Yes, no, yes
4. No, yes, yes

Ace It Time:

Hot dogs: 6, 12, 18, 24

Hot dog buns: 8, 16, 24

He will need to buy 4 packages of hot dogs for 3 packages of hot dog buns.

Divisibility Rules

Page 35 Practice: Now you try

1. Yes, yes, yes

Ace It Time: There should be 5 of each item in each group. Each of the items listed is divisible by 5.

Prime and Composite Numbers

Page 36 Practice: Now you try

1. Composite
2. Composite
3. Composite
4. Composite
5. Composite
6. Composite
7. Prime
8. Composite
9. Composite
10. Prime
11. Prime
12. Composite
13. Prime
14. Composite

Page 37 Practice: Now you try

1. False: 9 is an odd number and it is not prime.
2. False: 9 is an odd number and it composite.
3. True: 1 has only 1 factor, itself. To be prime it must have 2 factors.
4. True: except for 2, the only even number that is prime, all prime numbers are odd.

Ace It Time: I am the number 47.

Number Patterns

Page 38 Practice: Now you try

1. 46, 41, 36: Rule: subtract 5
2. 128, 256, 512: Rule: multiply by 2
3. 42, 48, 54: Rule: add 6
4. 50, 40, 30: Rule: subtract 10

Page 39 Practice: Now you try

1. 4: 5, 6, 7, 8, 9, 10, 11, 12
2. 15: 19, 23, 27, 31, 35, 39, 43, 47
3. 2: 3, 5, 9, 17, 33, 65, 129, 257

Ace It Time: In 7 days the art studio will have 64 sculptures in stock.

Day 1: 52
Day 2: 54
Day 3: 56
Day 4: 58
Day 5: 60
Day 6: 62
Day 7: 64

Stop and Think! Units 2–3 Review

Page 40 Activity Section 1:

1. 10
2. 100
3. 100
4. 125,000
4. 3,100
5. 7,190
6. 120,000
7. 9,200
9. 1,641; 1000 + 600 + 40 + 1
10. two hundred thirty-seven thousand, ten; 237,010
11. 400,000 + 60,000 + 7,000 + 20 + 8; four hundred sixty-seven thousand, twenty-eight

Page 41

12. >
13. <
14. =

Activity Section 2:

1. 1, 5, 7, 35
2. 1, 2, 4, 8
3. 1, 2, 3, 4, 6, 12
4. 1, 2, 4, 7, 14, 28

Number	Is this divisible by?	Is this divisible by?	Is this divisible by?
5. 36	3: yes	5: no	9: yes
6. 50	10: yes	2: yes	6: no

7. Prime
8. Composite
9. Composite
10. Composite

Activity Section 3:

1. 536,177
2. 739,370
3. 1,162
4. 461,175

Stop and Think! Units 2–3 Understand

Page 42

1–10. Possible answers include numbers ranging from the smallest number possible, 650,123, through the largest number possible, 749, 865.

Possible answers could include:

650,124	651,238	749,860
650,127	651,239	749,858
650,128	651,240	749,856
650,129	749,864	749,853
650,132	749,863	749,852
650,134	749,862	749,851
651,237	749,861	

Students should understand there are more than 10 possible combinations that will round to 700,000.

Students should be able to explain or demonstrate in their work an understanding of rounding either up to 700,000 with numbers greater than 650,000 or rounding down to 700,000 with numbers less than 749,999.

Stop and Think! Units 2–3 Discover

Page 43 Activity Section:

Number of stamp packages	Rule: 5x + 4
1	(5 × 1) + 4 = 9
2	(5 × 2) + 4 = 14
3	(5 × 3) + 4 = 19
4	(5 × 4) + 4 = 24
5	(5 × 5) + 4 = 29
6	(5 × 6) + 4 = 34
7	(5 × 7) + 4 = 39
8	(5 × 8) + 4 = 44
9	(5 × 9) + 4 = 49
10	(5 × 10) + 4 = 54

Patterns noticed may be: The numbers alternate between odd and even numbers. Also you may notice the pattern in the ones place of 9 – 4 – 9 – 4, etc. You may also notice that each number increases by 5 (+5).

Unit 4: CORE Multiplication Concepts

Understanding Multiplication

Page 45 Practice: Now you try

1. 45 dimes 9 × 5 = 45
2. 36 = 9 × 4
3. 6 × 8 = 48

Ace It Time:

Dylan lifted 34 pounds and Dean lifted 17 pounds.

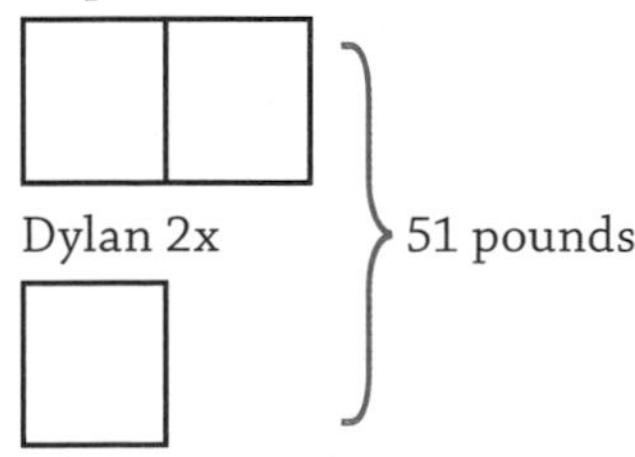

51 ÷ 3 = 17 pounds each box

So Dean lifted 17 pounds.

Dylan lifted 2 × 17 = 34 pounds.

Multiplying with Tens, Hundreds, and Thousands

Page 47 Practice: Now you try

1. 270, 2,700, 27,000
2. 24,000
3. 45,000

Ace It Time:

(200 x 2 = 400 for March and April)

+ (600 x 5 = 3,000 for May, June, July, August, September)

3,000 + 400 = **3,400** umbrellas rented during the 7 months

Methods of Multiplication

Page 49 Practice: Now you try

Methods will vary but should include either break apart, expanded form, area, and/or partial product strategies when computing each problem.

1. 936
2. 24,260
3. 212
4. 4,257

Ace It Time:

Christa will have 74 gigabytes left on her flash drives.

(32 × 3) + (128 × 2)

96 + 256 = 352

352 – 278 = 74 gigabytes

Multiply with Regrouping

Page 50 Practice: Now you try

1. Estimate: 21,000; Answer: 23,247
2. Estimate: 1,600; Answer: 1,424
3. Estimate: 30,000; Answer: 31,225
4. Estimate: 16,000; Answer: 15,386

Page 51

5. Estimate: 800; Answer: 760
6. Estimate: 2,100; Answer: 1,971
7. Estimate: 360; Answer: 342
8. Estimate: 5,400; Answer: 5,436

Ace It Time:

The Mitchells will pay $5,545.00

(1,499 × 2) + (849 × 3)

2,998 + 2,547

= $5,545

Multiply Two Two-Digit Numbers

Page 53 Practice: Now you try

1. Estimate: 6,300; Answer: 5,695
2. Estimate: 2,000; Answer: 1,632
3. Estimate: 1,500; Answer: 1,260
4. Estimate: 2,400; Answer: 2,400

Ace It Time:

Mrs. Peters: 21 × 25 = 525 cans

Ms. Hernandez: 24 × 21 = 504 cans

Mr. Juarez: 22 × 24 = 528 cans

Mr. Juarez's class won the contest.

Unit 5: CORE Concepts of Area and Perimeter

Area

Page 54 Practice: Now you try

1. 180 square kilometers
2. 60 square inches

Page 55

3. 84 square yards
4. 25 square feet

Ace It Time:

Lindsay's garden:
17 × 12 = 204 square feet

Catherine's garden:
15 × 15 = 225 square feet

Catherine's garden has the greatest area:

225
– 204

21 square feet more than Lindsay's garden.

Area Models and Partial Products

Page 56 Practice: Now you try

1. 32 × 16 = 512

30 x 10 = 300	10 x 2 = 20
30 x 6 = 180	6 x 2 = 12

Page 57

2. 35 × 27 = 945

30 x 20 = 600	20 x 5 = 100
30 x 7 = 210	5 x 7 = 35

3. 37 x 48 = 1,776

30 x 40 = 1,200	40 x 7 = 280
30 x 8 = 240	8 x 7 = 56

Ace It Time: No her model is not correct. She wrote 18 and it should have been 180. 20 × 9 = 180

Area by Combining Rectangles

Page 58 Practice: Now you try

1. Rectangle 1: 10 × 2 = 20 sq yds
   Rectangle 2: 1 × 4 = 4 sq yds

Total: 20 + 4 = 24 square yards

2. Square 1: 4 × 4 = 16 sq meters
   Rectangle 2: 8 × 4 = 32 sq meters

Total: 16 + 32 = 48 square meters

Page 59

3. Rectangle 1: 35 × 5 = 175 sq cm
   Rectangle 2: 8 × 15 = 120 sq cm

Total: 175 + 120 = 295 square centimeters

4. Square 1: 4 × 4 = 16 sq km
   Square 2: 8 × 8 = 64 sq km
   Square 3: 4 × 4 = 16 sq km

Total: 16 + 64 + 16 = 96 square kilometers

Ace It Time:

Corral A: Square 1: 3 × 3 = 9 sq yds
Rectangle 2: 6 × 5 = 30 sq yds

Total: 9 + 30 = 39 square yards

Corral B: Square 1: 6 × 6 = 36 sq yds
Square 2: 3 × 3 yds = 9 sq yds

Total: 36 + 9 = 45 square yards

It is Corral B that would be perfect for Keira's horse.

Area by Excluding Rectangles

Page 60 Practice: Now you try

1. Area of wall: 15 × 9 = 135 square feet
   Area of door: 3 × 7 = 21 square feet

Total area to be papered:
135 – 21 = 114 square feet

Page 61

2. Area of patio: 9 × 7 = 63 square meters
   Area of BBQ: 2 × 3 = 6 square meters

Total area to be tiled:
63 – 6 = 57 square meters

Ace It Time:

Area of dining room floor: 15 × 12 = 180 square feet; Area of rug: 5 × 7 = 35 square feet

Total area of dining room not covered by the rug: 180 – 35 = 145 square feet.

Perimeter

Page 62 Practice: Now you try

1. Rectangle: (2 × 23) + (2 × 65) = 46 + 130 = 176 meters
2. Square: 4 × 12 = 48 centimeters

Page 63

3. Rectangle: (2 × 2) + (2 × 85) = 4 + 170 = 174 inches
4. Square: 6 × 6 = 36 yards

Ace It Time:

Perimeter of the blanket: (2 × 60) + (2 × 30) = 120 + 60 = 180 inches

If 10 inches of fringe cost $1.00, she will need 18 units to cover the blanket. 18 units × 1.00 = $18.00

Apply Area and Perimeter Formulas

Page 65 Practice: Now you try

1. (2 × 12) = 24; 44 – 24 = 20;
   20 ÷ 2 = 10; missing side = 10 cm
2. 8 × b = 72; b = 9;
   missing side is 9 yards

Ace It Time: Lindsay needs to first calculate the perimeter around each cage.

Cage 1: (2 × 4) + (2 × 5) = 8 + 10 = 18 feet

Cage 2: (2 × 4) + (2 × 5) = 8 + 10 = 18 feet

Total: 36 feet of wire mesh

Stop and Think! Units 4–5 Review

Page 66 Activity Section 1:

1. 72 = 9 × 8
2. 88 = 11 × 8
3. 50 = 10 × 5
4. 20,000
5. 2,100
6. Estimate: 48,000; Product: 49,696
7. Estimate: 1,600; Product: 1,424
8. 882

40 x 20 = 800	20 x 2 = 40
40 x 1 = 40	2 x 1 = 2

9. 432

20 x 10 = 200	4 x 10 = 40
20 x 8 = 160	4 x 8 = 32

10. 957

30 x 20 = 600	20 x 3 = 60
30 x 9 = 270	3 x 9 = 27

Page 67

11. Estimate: 8,100; Answer: 7,998
12. Estimate: 1,600; Answer: 1,617
13. Estimate: 1,200; Answer: 1,408

Activity Section 2:

1. Area = 4 × 24 = 96 square yards;
   Perimeter = (2 × 4) + (2 × 24) = 8 + 48 = 56 yards
2. Area = 22 × 35 = 770 square centimeters;
   Perimeter = (2 × 22) + (2 × 35) = 44 + 70 = 114 centimeters
3. Rectangle 1: 45 × 3 = 135; Rectangle 2: 19 × 5 = 95 square centimeters
   Total: 135 + 95 = 230 square centimeters
4. Area of wall: 18 × 9 = 162; Area of the door: 3 × 7 = 21
   Total area of wall: 162 – 21 = 141 square feet

Stop and Think! Units 4–5 Understand

Page 68 Activity Section:

It is the student named Jared whose answer is wrong.

The mistake he made was he multiplied 50 × 8 incorrectly. The answer should have been 400, but he wrote 40.

The correct answer is 3,604.

Stop and Think! Units 4–5 Discover

Page 69 Activity Section:

Area = L x W Square units	Length L units	Width W units	Perimeter (2 x L) + (2 x W) units
36 (sample)	1	36	(2 x 1) + (2 x 36) 2 + 72 = 74
36	2	18	(2 x 2) + (2 x 18) 4 + 36 = 40
36	3	12	(2 x 3) + (2 x 12) 6 + 24 = 30
36	4	9	(2 x 4) + (2 x 9) 8 + 18 = 26
36	6	6	4 x 6 = 24

Rectangles

1. 1 × 36
2. 6 × 6

Unit 6: CORE Division Concepts

Understanding Division—Estimate a Quotient

Page 70 Practice: Now you try

Problem	Multiples	Quotient Estimate
33 ÷ 7	7, 14, 21, 28, 35, 42 1 2 3 4 5 6	5
48 ÷ 9	9, 18, 27, 36, 45, 54, 63 1 2 3 4 5 6 7	5
138 ÷ 5	50, 100, 150 10 20 30	30
710 ÷ 9	90, 180, 270, 360, 450, 540, 630, 720, 810 10, 20, 30, 40, 50, 60, 70, 80, 90	80
2,417 ÷ 4	400, 800, 1,200, 1,600, 2,000, 2,400, 2,800 100, 200, 300, 400, 500, 600, 700	600

Page 71

Ace It Time: Sample explanation: I will think about multiples of 8 starting with 8 × 10 because I have a total of 246.

Lunches	80,	160,	240,	320
Tables	10	20	30	40

25 tables will allow the school to serve less than 246 student lunches. Although 30 tables still doesn't seat 246 students, the 30 tables that Eric estimated is a better estimate because it is closer to 246.

Division with Partial Quotients

Page 73 Practice: Now you try

1. 69 ÷ 3

```
   23
3)69    3 x [] = 60    20
 - 60
    9   3 x [] = 9    + 3
 -  9                  23
    0
```

2. 555 ÷ 5

```
   111
5)555    5 x [] = 500   100
 - 500
    55   5 x [] = 50   + 10
 -  50
     5   5 x [] = 5    +  1
 -   5                  111
     0
```

3. 2,152 ÷ 4

```
    538
4)2,152   4 x [] = 2,000   500
 - 2,000
    152   4 x [] = 120    + 30
 -  120
     32   4 x [] = 32     +  8
 -   32                    538
      0
```

Ace It Time: First, Mikal confused the partial quotient column. He put 6,000, instead of 1,000. Then, he knew that he had to find a multiple of 6 that would equal about 426. He chose the wrong multiple. He multiplied incorrectly, 6 × 60 equals 360. The correct multiple is 70 because 6 × 70 = 420.

The last mistake he made is that he didn't finish the problem. There is still a multiple of 6 that has not been recorded. 6 × 1 = 6

```
   1,571                  1,000
6)9,426   6 × 1,000       ~~6,000~~
 - 6,000
   3,426
 - 3,000  6 × 500           500
     426      70             70
 -   420  6 × ~~60~~        ~~60~~
       6
 -     6  6 × 1           +   1
       0                  1,571
```

Repeated Subtraction Strategy

Page 75 Practice: Now you try

1. 42 ÷ 3 = 14

```
   42
 - 30   (subtract three 10 times)
   12
 - 12   (subtract three 4 times)
    0
```

2. 60 ÷ 4 - 15

```
   60
 - 40   (subtract four 10 times)
   20
 - 20   (subtract four 5 times)
    0
```

Ace It Time:

```
7)294    I think in multiples of ten
 - 280   (subtracting seven 40 times)
    14   I think in multiples of seven
 -  14   (subtracting seven 2 times)
     0
```

294 ÷ 7 = 42 pebbles will go in each jar

Division with the Distributive Property

Page 77 Practice: Now you try

1. 84 ÷ 4 =
   (80 + 4) ÷4 =
   (80 ÷ 4) + (4 ÷ 4) =
   20 + 1 = 21
   84 ÷ 4 = 21

2. 2,416 ÷ 8 =
   (2,400 + 16) ÷ 8 =
   (2,400 ÷ 8) + (16 ÷ 8) =
   300 + 2 = 302
   2,416 ÷ 8 = 302

Ace It Time:

Group 1

```
1,000  +  100  100  + 10  10 + 1
             100        10  10
                1,341
```

Group 2

```
1,000  +  100  100  + 10  10 + 1
             100        10  10
                1,341
```

Distributive Property

2,682 ÷ 2 =
(2,000 + 600 + 80 + 2) ÷ 2 =
(2,000 ÷ 2) + (600 ÷ 2) + (80 ÷ 2) + (2 ÷ 2) =
1,000 + 300 + 40 + 1 = 1,341

Remainders

Page 78 Practice: Now you try

1. 29 ÷ 6 =	2.
Think what times 6 = 29? 6 × 4 = 24 ~~6 × 5 = 30~~ 4 R5 6)29 - 24 5	41 R1 3)124 - 120 (subtract three 40 times) 4 - 3 (subtract three 1 time) 1 Subtracted three 41 times with 1 left over.

Page 79

3.	4. 768 ÷ 9 =
656 R4 Partial Quotient 6)3,940 - 3,600 6 × 600 600 340 - 300 6 × 50 50 40 - 36 6 × 6 6 4 656 4 left	Estimate: 85 because 9 × 80 = 720 9 × 5 = 45 765 with 3 left

Ace It Time:

Estimate your answer first: About 90 books on each shelf.

Explain your estimation: 90 × 5 = 450. She has a little over 450. So each shelf will have a few more than 90 books. 100 × 5 = 500 is too many. The number has to be between 90 and 100.

Solve/Explain: First, I know that the number 12 doesn't have to do with books. It is a number that is extra. Second, I know that 467 – 450 = 17. So I have subtracted the divisor (5), 90 times. That is my partial product. Now I have to figure out how many times I can subtract 5 from 17. That would be 3.

So I can add my two partial products to get 93. 17 – 15 = 2. Since 2 is less than the divisor, the 2 books will be left over. She can place 93 books on each shelf, and she has 2 left over.

Understanding Remainders

Page 81 Practice: Now you try

1. 39 ÷ 4 = 9 R3. 9 booths can be covered.
2. Since there is a remainder of 3, three booths could have extra helpers.

Ace It Time:

24 ÷ 8 = 3. Each piece will be 3 feet long if there are 8 packages.

24 ÷ 9 = 2 and $\frac{6}{9}$ feet of ribbon can be used on each package if there are 9 packages.

Divide by 10, 100, or 1,000

Pages 82–83 Practice: Now you try

1. 2,700 ÷ 9	2. 240 ÷ 6
Name the basic fact: 27 ÷ 9 = 3	Name the basic fact: 24 ÷ 6 = 4
2,700 = 27 hundreds	240 = 24 tens
27 hundreds ÷ 9 = 3 hundreds	24 tens ÷ 6 = 4 tens
2,700 ÷ 9 = 300	240 ÷ 6 = 40
3. 3,500 ÷ 7	**4. 640 ÷ 8**
Name the basic fact: 35 ÷ 7 = 5	Name the basic fact: 64 ÷ 8 = 8
3,500 = 35 hundreds	640 = 64 tens
35 hundreds ÷ 7 = 5 hundreds	64 tens ÷ 8 = 8 tens
3,500 ÷ 7 = 500	640 ÷ 8 = 80

Page 83 Ace It Time:

Sherri used 6 buckets to collect her shells. If she put 50 in each bucket, then she would only put 300 shells in the buckets. 50 × 6 = 300. She has 420 shells.

Since she is dividing the total, 420 shells into 6 buckets, she should think of the related basic fact 420 ÷ 6 or 42 ÷ 6, which equals 7.

420 = 42 tens, so 42 tens ÷ 6 = 7 tens or 70. She should put 70 shells in each bucket.

Divide by One Digit

Page 85 Practice: Now you try

1. 369 ÷ 3

	1	2	3		
3	3	6	9		
-	3				
	0	6			
	-	6			
		0	9		
		-	9		
			0		

2. 4,584 ÷ 6

		7	6	4	
6	4	5	8	4	
-	4	2			
		3	8		
	-	3	6		
			2	4	
		-	2	4	
				0	

Ace It Time:

		3	6	R	1
4	) 1	4	5		
	1	2			
		2	5		
		2	4		
			1		

Answer: The PE teacher had to separate 145 students into groups of 4.

I thought about 145 having 14 tens so I divided 4 into 14 tens and knew that 30 × 4 would get me closest. I subtracted the 120 from 140 and got 2 tens. I brought the ones down so now I had to think about what times 4 would equal 25. 4 × 6 equals 24. There can be 36 teams but there will be one student left over.

Stop and Think! Unit 6 Review

Page 86 Activity Section 1:

1. 230 ÷ 8

+10 +10 +10 +10

10 20 30 40

8, 80, 160, 240, 320

The estimate would be 30 because 240 is closest to 230.

2. 4,505 ÷ 9

+100 +100 +100 +100 +100

100 200 300 400 500

9, 900, 1,800, 2,700, 3,600, 4,500

The estimate would be 500 because 4,500 is closest to 4,505.

3. 408 ÷ 8 =

	PQ
8 × 50 = 400	50
8 × 1 = 8	1
408	51

The quotient is 51.

4. 291 ÷ 3 =

	PQ
3 × 90 = 270	90
3 × 7 = 21	7
291	97

The quotient is 97.

5. 2,049 ÷ 5 = 409 R4

2,049
−2,000 (subtract five 400 times)
49
− 45 (subtract five 9 times)
4

6. 3,062 ÷ 3 = 1,020 R2

3,062
−3,000 (subtract three 1000 times)
62
− 60 (subtract three 20 times)
2

7. 255 ÷ 5 =

(200 + 50 + 5) ÷ 5 =
(200 ÷ 5) + (50 ÷ 5) + (5 ÷ 5) =
40 + 10 + 1 =
51

255 ÷ 5 = 51

8. 424 ÷ 7 =

(420 + 4) ÷ 7 =
(420 ÷ 7) + (4 ÷ 7) =
60 + (4 ÷ 7) =
60 R4

424 ÷ 7 = 60 R4

OR 60 $\frac{4}{7}$

9. 3 cats × 4 ounces = 12 ounces a day

68 ÷ 12 = 5 R8

68
−60 (subtract twelve 5 times)
8

Mary can feed her cats for 5 days.

10. There are 8 ounces left.

11. 2 $\frac{2}{3}$ ounces

$$3\overline{)8} = 2\ R\tfrac{2}{3}$$

−6
2

12.

$$\begin{array}{r} 905 \text{ R1} \\ 5\overline{)4{,}526} \\ -45 \\ \hline 26 \\ -25 \\ \hline 1 \end{array}$$

13.

$$\begin{array}{r} 1{,}376 \text{ R3} \\ 6\overline{)8{,}259} \\ -6 \\ \hline 22 \\ -18 \\ \hline 45 \\ -42 \\ \hline 39 \\ -36 \\ \hline 3 \end{array}$$

Stop and Think! Unit 6 Understand

Page 87

Activity Section 2

First, Luke needs to know if he has enough money to spend $10 a day for 14 days:

14 × $10 = $140

Yes, he has enough money for his plan because he saved $280.

How much does he have left over?

$280 – $140 = $140.

He will have $140 left if he spends $10 a day for 14 days.

How much more could he spend each of the 14 days? Actually, Luke can spend $20 a day because $280 is double $140.

Luke will have an additional $10 a day to spend.

To check, divide

$280 ÷ 14 = $20

– 140 (subtract fourteen 10 times)

140

– 140 (subtract fourteen 10 times)

0

Stop and Think! Unit 6 Discover

Page 88

Activity Section 3

This student got everything correct except for the number of days they needed to request for vacation. It will take 10 days to get to California and 10 days to return to Florida. This student forgot to add the 10 days visiting family and friends. So the total number of days they need for vacation is 30 days, not 20.

Unit 7: CORE Fractions Concepts

Equivalent Fractions

Page 91 Practice: Now you try

1. $\frac{3}{3}, \frac{3}{9}$
2. $\frac{2}{2}, \frac{4}{8}$
3. $\frac{4}{4}, \frac{4}{8}$
4. $\frac{3}{5} \times \frac{2}{2} = \frac{6}{10}$
5. $\frac{3}{4} \times \frac{3}{3} = \frac{9}{12}$
6. $\frac{1}{2}, \frac{3}{6}, \frac{5}{10}$
7. $\frac{1}{3}, \frac{4}{12}, \frac{2}{6}$

Ace It Time: $\frac{1}{3}$ **cup**

Fractions in Simplest Form

Page 92 Practice: Now you try

1. $\frac{3}{5}$
2. $\frac{1}{2}$
3. $\frac{2}{3}$
4. $\frac{1}{2}$
5. $\frac{1}{2}$
6. $\frac{2}{5}$

Page 93

7. Yes
8. No
9. No
10. Yes
11. $\frac{3}{4}$
12. $\frac{1}{3}$
13. $\frac{2}{3}$
14. $\frac{9}{10}$
15. $\frac{1}{3}$
16. $\frac{7}{8}$

Ace It Time: Trevon needs $3\frac{1}{4}$ cups of nuts. $\frac{6}{8} = \frac{3}{4}$

Common Denominators

Page 95 Practice: Now you try

1. Common denominator = 8, $\frac{2}{8}, \frac{3}{8}$
2. Common denominator = 12, $\frac{8}{12}, \frac{4}{12}$
3. Common denominator = 16, $\frac{4}{16}, \frac{6}{16}$

Page 96

4. Multiples of 3: 3, 6, 9, 12, 15, 18
   Multiples of 4: 4, 8, 12, 16, 20, 24
   Common denominator = 12; $\frac{1}{3} \times \frac{4}{4} = \frac{4}{12}$; $\frac{1}{4} \times \frac{3}{3} = \frac{3}{12}$
5. Multiples of 12: 12, 24, 36
   Multiples of 8: 8, 16, 24, 32
   Common denominator = 24; $\frac{3}{12} \times \frac{2}{2} = \frac{6}{24}$; $\frac{7}{8} \times \frac{3}{3} = \frac{21}{24}$

Ace It Time: No. Nigel added the denominators. He should have found multiples for 5 and 3 and picked the one they have in common, 15.

Compare Fractions

Page 98 Practice: Now you try

1. $\frac{8}{10} > \frac{4}{8}$
2. $\frac{1}{3} < \frac{4}{5}$
3. $\frac{1}{4} < \frac{3}{6}$
4. $\frac{2}{10} < \frac{1}{4}$
5. $\frac{4}{5} = \frac{8}{10}$
6. $\frac{5}{12} > \frac{2}{6}$

Ace It Time: Troy did more vacuuming. $\frac{4}{10}$ in simplest form is $\frac{2}{5}$. $\frac{2}{3}$ is greater than $\frac{2}{5}$, so Troy did more vacuuming.

Order Fractions

Page 100 Practice: Now you try

1. $\frac{1}{2}, \frac{2}{3}, \frac{5}{6}$
2. $\frac{2}{8}, \frac{2}{4}, \frac{5}{8}$
3. $\frac{5}{8}, \frac{1}{2}, \frac{1}{4}$
4. $\frac{4}{5}, \frac{6}{10}, \frac{2}{10}$
5. $\frac{4}{8} = \frac{2}{4}$
6. $\frac{3}{4} > \frac{2}{6}$

Ace It Time: $\frac{5}{12}, \frac{3}{6}, \frac{2}{3}$. Majella walked the most on Monday.

Break Apart Fractions

Page 101 Practice: Now you try

1. $\frac{5}{6} = \frac{1}{6} + \frac{1}{6} + \frac{1}{6} + \frac{1}{6} + \frac{1}{6}$
2. $\frac{3}{4} = \frac{1}{4} + \frac{1}{4} + \frac{1}{4}$
3. $\frac{7}{8} = \frac{1}{8} + \frac{1}{8} + \frac{1}{8} + \frac{1}{8} + \frac{1}{8} + \frac{1}{8} + \frac{1}{8}$
4. The numerators must add up to 5. There are various ways to write the sum of $\frac{5}{6}$. Ex: $\frac{2}{6} + \frac{3}{6} = \frac{5}{6}$
5. The numerators must add up to 3. There are various ways to write the sum of $\frac{3}{4}$. Ex: $\frac{1}{4} + \frac{2}{4} = \frac{3}{4}$
6. The numerators must add up to 7. There are various ways to write the sum of $\frac{7}{8}$. Ex: $\frac{6}{8} + \frac{1}{8} = \frac{7}{8}$

Page 102

7. $\frac{6}{10} = \frac{1}{10} + \frac{1}{10} + \frac{1}{10} + \frac{1}{10} + \frac{1}{10} + \frac{1}{10}$
8. $\frac{3}{5} = \frac{1}{5} + \frac{1}{5} + \frac{1}{5}$
9. $\frac{9}{6} = \frac{1}{6} + \frac{1}{6} + \frac{1}{6} + \frac{1}{6} + \frac{1}{6} + \frac{1}{6} + \frac{1}{6} + \frac{1}{6} + \frac{1}{6}$
10. The numerators must add up to 6. There are various ways to write the sum of $\frac{6}{10}$. Ex: $\frac{4}{10} + \frac{2}{10} = \frac{6}{10}$
11. The numerators must add up to 3. There are various ways to write the sum of $\frac{3}{5}$. Ex: $\frac{2}{5} + \frac{1}{5} = \frac{3}{5}$
12. The numerators must add up to 9. There are various ways to write the sum of $\frac{9}{6}$. Ex: $\frac{3}{6} + \frac{3}{6} + \frac{3}{6} = \frac{9}{6}$

Ace It Time: No, Nakeesha is not right because the sum of the numerators must add up to 3.

Rename Fractions and Mixed Numbers

Page 104 Practice: Now you try

1. $1\frac{1}{5}$
2. $2\frac{2}{4}$
3. $4\frac{1}{2}$
4. $\frac{23}{5}$
5. $\frac{16}{6}$
6. $\frac{11}{8}$

Ace It Time: $\frac{16}{5}$. $3\frac{1}{5}$ is 3 wholes and $\frac{1}{5}$. There are 15 fifth-sized pieces in 3 wholes and one fifth-sized piece in $\frac{1}{5}$, so there are a total of 16 fifth-sized pieces in $3\frac{1}{5}$. $3\frac{1}{5} = \frac{16}{5}$

Stop and Think! Unit 7 Review

Page 105 Activity Section 1:

1. $\frac{5}{5}, \frac{5}{10}$
2. $\frac{2}{2}, \frac{4}{12}$
3. $\frac{4}{4}, \frac{12}{16}$
4. $\frac{3}{3}, \frac{2}{3}$
5. $\frac{4}{4}, \frac{1}{5}$
6. $\frac{2}{2}, \frac{4}{6}$
7. $\frac{1}{2}, \frac{3}{6}, \frac{6}{12}$
8. $\frac{1}{3}, \frac{4}{12}, \frac{5}{15}$

Activity Section 2:

1. $\frac{2}{3}$
2. $\frac{1}{2}$
3. $\frac{2}{5}$
4. $\frac{1}{4}$
5. Yes
6. No
7. Yes
8. No

Page 106 Activity Section 3:

1. Multiples of 3: 3, 6, 9, 12, 15, 18
   Multiples of 5: 5, 10, 15, 20, 25, 30
   Common denominator = 15; $\frac{1}{3} \times \frac{5}{5} = \frac{5}{15}$; $\frac{1}{5} \times \frac{3}{3} = \frac{3}{15}$
2. Multiples of 12: 12, 24, 36, 48, 60, 72
   Multiples of 8: 8, 16, 24, 32, 40, 48
   Common denominator = 24; $\frac{3}{12} \times \frac{2}{2} = \frac{6}{24}$; $\frac{6}{8} \times \frac{3}{3} = \frac{18}{24}$

Activity Section 4:

1. $\frac{2}{10} < \frac{2}{4}$
2. $\frac{5}{6}, \frac{2}{3}, \frac{1}{2}$

Activity Section 5:

1. $\frac{1}{8} + \frac{1}{8} + \frac{1}{8} + \frac{1}{8} + \frac{1}{8}$
2. The numerators must add up to 3. There are various ways to write the sum of $\frac{3}{5}$. Ex: $\frac{1}{5} + \frac{2}{5}$

Activity Section 6:

1. $1\frac{2}{5}$
2. $\frac{19}{5}$

Stop and Think! Unit 7 Understand

Page 107

No they did not eat the same amount of pizza. Carla ate the most pizza. $\frac{2}{5} < \frac{4}{6}$

Stop and Think! Unit 7 Discover

Page 108

Brian came in first place ($3\frac{1}{4}$ minutes). Terry came in last place ($3\frac{5}{6}$ minutes).

Unit 8: CORE Operations with Fractions

Add and Subtract Fractions with Like Denominators

Page 110 Practice: Now you try

1. $\frac{9}{12}$
2. $\frac{4}{6}$
3. $\frac{9}{10}$

Ace It Time: No it will not be enough because he only has $\frac{8}{8}$ yard of rope and he will need $\frac{9}{8}$ yards.

Add and Subtract Mixed Numbers

Page 112 Practice: Now you try

1. $3\frac{3}{4}$
2. $6\frac{4}{5}$
3. $3\frac{2}{10}$
4. $6\frac{2}{5}$

Ace It Time: Kirk traveled a total of $7\frac{2}{6}$ miles.

Subtract Mixed Numbers with Renaming

Page 114 Practice: Now you try

1. $2\frac{3}{6}$
2. $2\frac{6}{8}$
3. $1\frac{10}{12}$
4. $1\frac{8}{10}$

Ace It Time: Carlene's snake is $1\frac{5}{8}$ feet bigger.

Multiply Unit Fractions by Whole Numbers

Page 116 Practice: Now you try

1. $\frac{2}{3}$
2. $\frac{3}{5}$
3. $\frac{1}{5}, \frac{2}{5}, \frac{3}{5}, \frac{4}{5}, \frac{5}{5}, \frac{6}{5}, \frac{7}{5}, \frac{8}{5}, \frac{9}{5}, \frac{10}{5}, \frac{11}{5}, \frac{12}{5}$
4. $2 \times \frac{1}{6}$
5. $7 \times \frac{1}{8}$
6. $4 \times \frac{1}{10}$

Ace It Time: Chris walked for 4 hours. After the answer Chris walked for 4 hours, add this text: $\frac{1}{2} \times 8 = \frac{8}{2}$, which reduces to 4.

Multiply Fractions or Mixed Numbers by Whole Numbers

Page 118 Practice: Now you try

1. $\frac{6}{8}$
2. $3\frac{3}{4}$
3. 2
4. $3\frac{1}{5}$
5. 2
6. $1\frac{1}{8}$

Ace It Time: Mitch read for $13\frac{3}{4}$ hours.

Unit 9: CORE Decimals Concepts

Tenths and Hundredths

Page 120 Practice: Now you try

1. Shade 4 tenths, $\frac{4}{10}$, 0.4
2. Shade 25 boxes out of 100, $\frac{25}{100}$, 0.25
3. 0.2
4. 0.34
5. 3.1

Page 121

6. $\frac{3}{10}$, 0.3
7. $\frac{73}{100}$, 0.73

Ace It Time: Roberto has 0.3 of his sandwich left to eat.

Equivalent Fractions and Decimals

Page 122 Practice: Now you try

1. 0.30, $\frac{30}{100}$
2. 0.10, $\frac{10}{100}$
3. $\frac{6}{10}$
4. $\frac{3}{10}$

Page 123

5. 2.30
6. 1.80
7. 4.60
8. 3.4
9. 5.1
10. 2.5

Ace It Time: Shauntaey is correct.

Fractions—Decimals—Money

Page 125 Practice: Now you try

1. Shade 27 boxes out of 100, 0.27

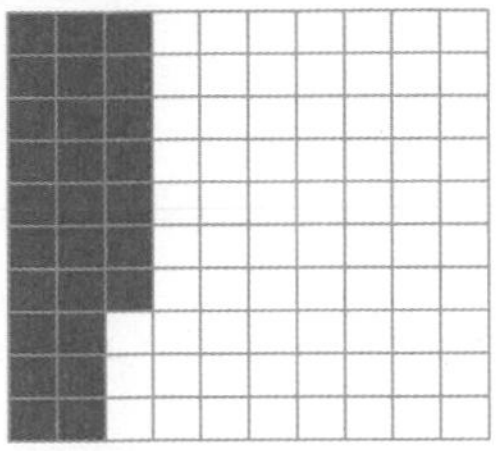

2. Shade 31 boxes out of 100, 0.31

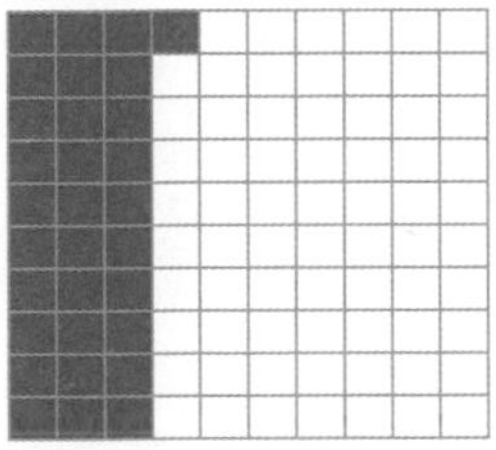

3. Shade 1 full hundred and 70 boxes out of the second 100, 1.70

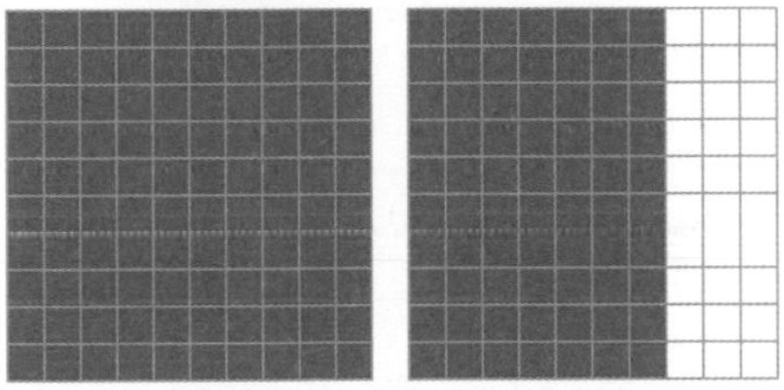

4. Sample: 4 dimes and 1 penny.
5. Sample: 2 quarters, 1 dime, 1 nickel, and 2 pennies

Page 126

6. Sample: 3 dollar bills, 2 dimes, and 3 pennies
7. Sample: 2 dollar bills, 3 quarters, 1 nickel, and 3 pennies

Ace It Time: Iyanna has 0.40 or 40 cents left over after buying her chips.

$$\begin{array}{r} 1.00 \\ -\ .60 \\ \hline .40 \end{array}$$

Compare Decimals

Page 128 Practice: Now you try

1. 0.7 > 0.62
2. 0.24 < 2.45
3. 0.32 > 0.23
4. 0.07 < 0.70

Ace It Time: No. Nyla is not correct. Shane's worm is longer because 8.6 is greater than 8.06.

Add Fractions and Decimals with Tenths and Hundredths

Page 130 Practice: Now you try

1. $\frac{61}{100}$
2. $\frac{55}{100}$
3. $\frac{86}{100}$
4. $\frac{57}{100}$, .57
5. $\frac{45}{100}$, .45
6. $\frac{84}{100}$, .84

Ace It Time: The correct answer is $\frac{62}{100}$. Landon's error was when he added the numerators together and he added the denominators together. He did not rename the fractions so that the denominators were the same before adding.

Stop and Think! Units 8–9 Review

Page 131 Activity Section 1:

1. $\frac{11}{15}$
2. $\frac{5}{6}$
3. $\frac{5}{8}$
4. $\frac{4}{10}$

Activity Section 2:

1. $7\frac{1}{8}$
2. $5\frac{2}{6}$

Activity Section 3:

1. $3\frac{7}{10}$
2. $\frac{4}{6}$

Page 132 Activity Section 4:

1. $4 \times \frac{1}{6}$
2. $5 \times \frac{1}{8}$

Activity Section 5:

1. $1\frac{4}{5}$
2. $1\frac{1}{4}$

Activity Section 6:

1. 0.4
2. 4.66
3. 6.78

Activity Section 7:

1. 0.60 $\frac{60}{100}$
2. 0.40 $\frac{40}{100}$
3. 0.90 $\frac{90}{100}$
4. $\frac{2}{10}$
5. $\frac{7}{10}$
6. $\frac{5}{10}$

Activity Section 8:

1. Answers may vary; 3 quarters, 1 penny
2. Answers may vary; 1 quarter, 4 pennies

Activity Section 9:

1. 0.8 > 0.52
2. 0.37 < 3.75

Activity Section 10:

1. $\frac{64}{100}$
2. $\frac{56}{100}$

Stop and Think! Units 8–9 Understand

Page 133 Activity Section:

$\frac{5}{100}$, .05 There will be 5 seats left on the bus.

Stop and Think! Units 8–9 Discover

Page 134 Activity Section:

1. Roy can make 13 servings because there are 12 fourths in 3 wholes, and $\frac{3}{12}$ is equivalent to 1 fourth.
2. First he must subtract $1\frac{6}{12}$ from $3\frac{3}{12}$; that equals $1\frac{9}{12}$. He can make 7 servings of salsa out of $1\frac{9}{12}$.

Unit 10: CORE Geometry Concepts

Lines and Relationships

Page 136 Practice: Now you try

1. 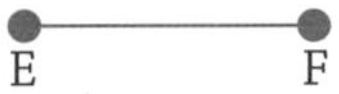

2. 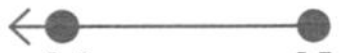

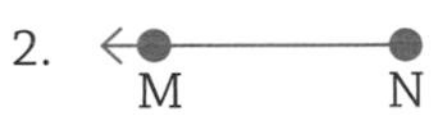

3. 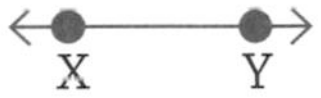

4. 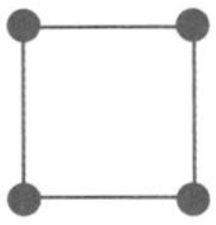

5. Some possible answers: Stripes on a flat flag, staircase banister, legs on a chair, floor planks, legs on a table, columns, paper edges.
6. A line does not end. A segment is only a small part of the line. It has two endpoints.
7. A line extends forever from both ends. A ray has an endpoint and extends forever in one direction only.
8. These rays extend in different directions, one to the right and one to the left.

Ace It Time:

Sample:

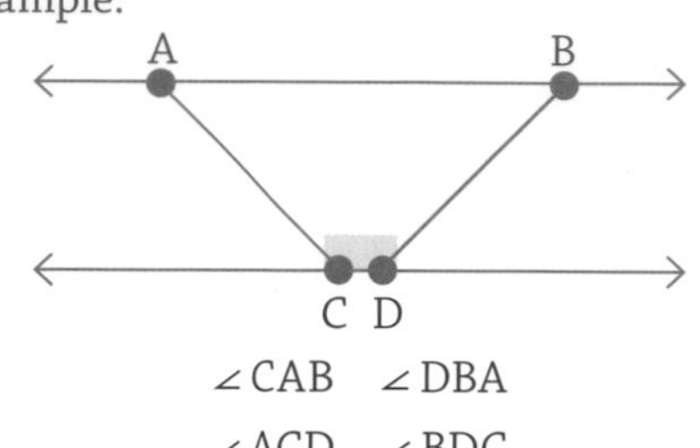

∠CAB ∠DBA

∠ACD ∠BDC

Angles

Page 138 Practice: Now you try

1.
2.
3.
4.
5.

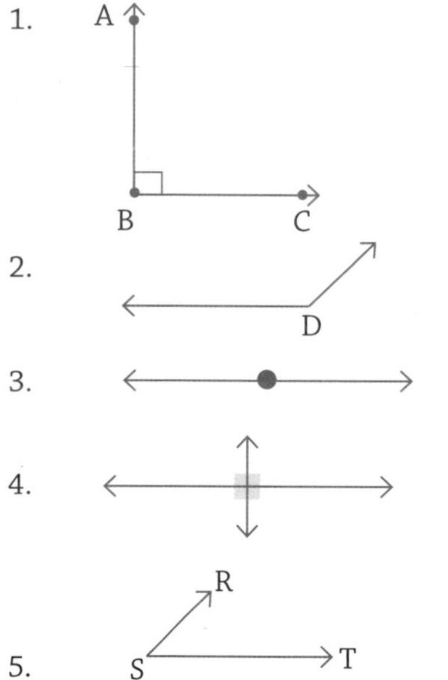

Figure 1

6. KH KJ KL LM HM LH HK JK LK ML MH HL
7. ∠MHJ ∠MLK ∠JHM ∠KLM
8. ∠HLK ∠LKH ∠LHK
   ∠HKL ∠KLH ∠KHL

Ace It Time: No, two acute angles can't make a straight angle. It takes two right angles to make a straight angle.

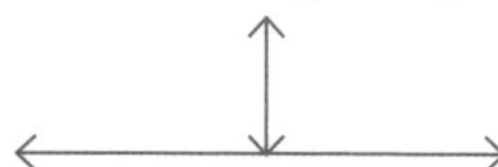

An acute angle has to be less than a right angle. So if you put two acute angles together, both are less than two right angles together.

Triangles

Page 139 Practice: Now you try

1. Possible answers:

Δ ABC Δ BCA

Δ CAB Δ ACB

Δ BAC Δ CBA

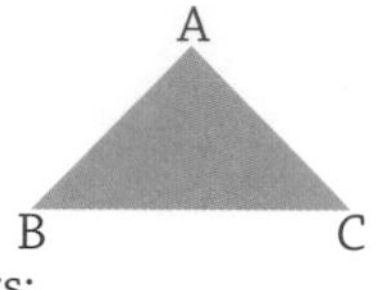

2. Possible answers:

Δ XYZ Δ YZX

Δ ZXY Δ YXZ

Δ XZY Δ ZYX

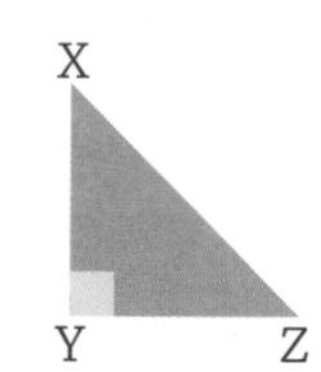

3. Possible answers:

Δ DEF Δ EFD

Δ FDE Δ FED

Δ DFE Δ EDF

D E F

4. Right
5. Obtuse
6. Acute
7. Acute

Page 140

Possible answers:

8. ∠ABE ∠EBC ∠EBA ∠CBE
9. ∠DBC ∠CBD
10. ∠ABD ∠DBE ∠DBA ∠EBD
11. Straight angle

Ace It Time:

I would have to make a perpendicular line from the top vertex to the bottom base. There would be two right triangles formed. One would be to the right of the line and the other to the left.

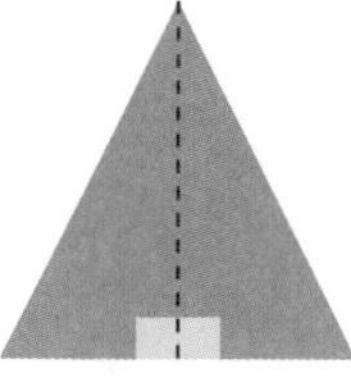

Geometric Shape Patterns

Page 142 Practice: Now you try

1. Figure C is a parallelogram and Figure D is a rhombus. A parellelogram has 2 sets of sides that are the same length. A rhombus has all sides the same length.
2. Figure A is a rectangle and Figure E is a square. A rectangle has two sets of same size sides. The square has all four of the sides the same size.

Ace It Time: A rhombus does not have any right angles. A square does. Both have 4 sides the same length.

Symmetry

Page 143 Practice: Now you try

1.

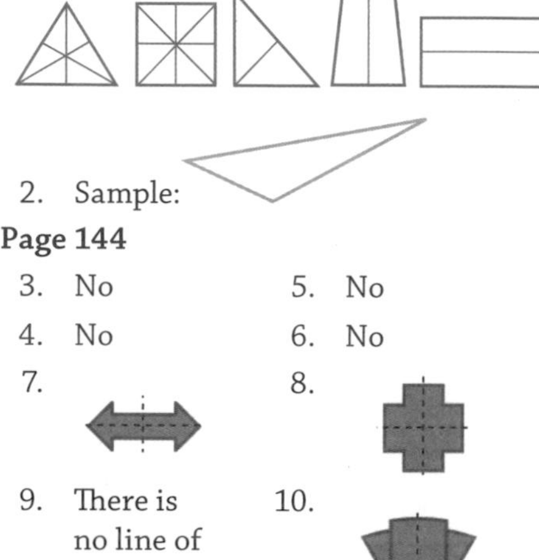

2. Sample:

Page 144

3. No
4. No
5. No
6. No
7.
8.
9. There is no line of symmetry.
10.

Ace It Time:

0 has two lines of symmetry.

1, 2, 4, 5, 6, 7, 9 have no lines of symmetry.

3 has one line of symmetry and 8 has two lines of symmetry.

Martin is wrong on both statements.

Angles as Fractional Parts of a Circle

Page 146 Practice: Now you try

1. $\frac{3}{4}$ is shaded
2. $\frac{1}{2}$ is shaded
3. $\frac{1}{4}$ is shaded
4. $\frac{1}{6}$ is shaded
5. $\frac{1}{8}$ is shaded
6. Obtuse
7. Straight
8. Right
9. Acute
10. Acute

Ace It Time: No. All circles are measured in 360°. So if circle A is bigger than circle B, the size (area) of the right angle in circle A will be bigger than the size (area) of the right angle in circle B. However, they both will have 90°, because they both represent $\frac{1}{4}$ of 360°, which is 90°.

Angles Are Measured in Degrees

Page 148 Practice: Now you try

1. 45° acute

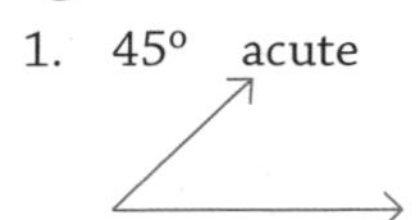

2. 270° obtuse

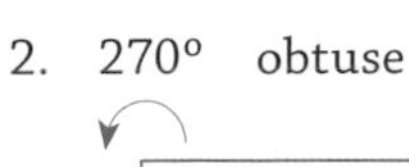

3. 190° obtuse

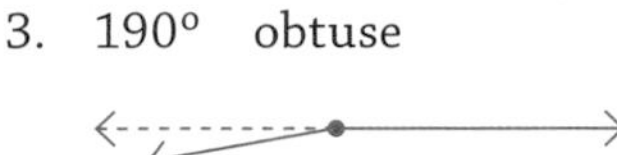

4. 90° right

5. 180° straight

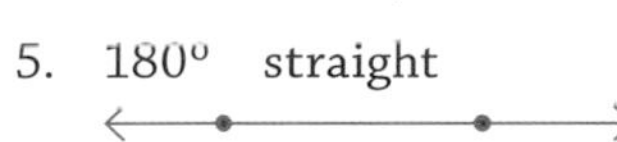

Ace It Time:

Each of the parts of the circle will be 60° because there are 360° in the complete circle. 4 of the 6 angles would be 240°.

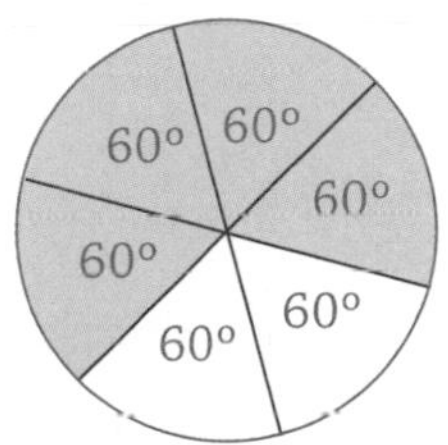

How to Use a Protractor

Page 150 Practice: Now you try

Students will use a protractor to draw the following angles:

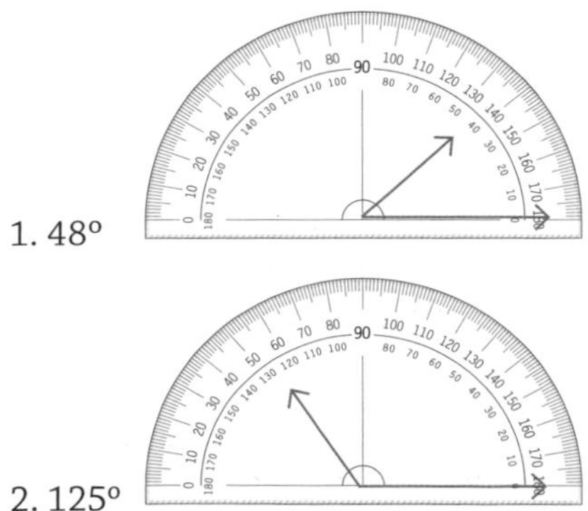

1. 48°

2. 125°

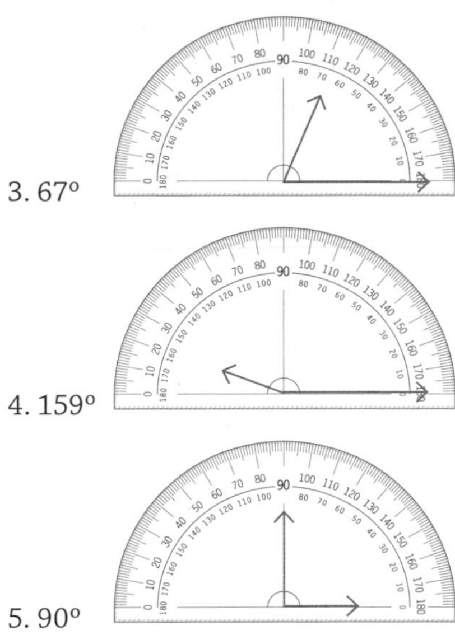

3. 67°

4. 159°

5. 90°

Students will use a protractor to measure the following angles:

6. ∠DE = 135°
7. ∠GIH = 99°
   ∠FIH = 81°
8. ∠JMK = 142°

Page 151 Ace It Time:

Marci measured the angle to be 95°, but she should have realized that this angle is smaller than a right angle. The one ray is not perpendicular to the other. This angle has to be smaller than 90°. When she used the protractor, she used the wrong scale. She used the inner scale, instead of the outer scale. When an angle opens to the left, you have to use the outer scale.

Angles Add Up

Page 153 Practice: Now you try

1. ∠ACD = 90°
2. ∠ACB = 90°
3. ∠BCD = 180°
4. ∠BCE = 90°
5. ∠ECD = 90°
6. ∠BCF = 45°
7. ∠FCE = 45°
8. 45° + 45° = 90°
   OR
   90° – 45° = 45°
9. ∠ACD = 105° + 45° = 150°
10. ∠RST = 90° – 37° = 53°
    ∠VSW = 90° – 61° = 29°

Page 154

Ace It Time:

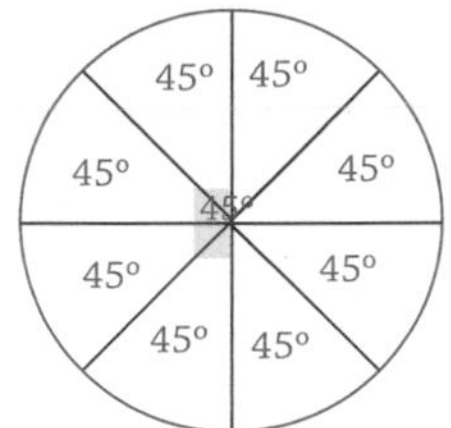

Johnny cut the pizza into 8 equal parts. Since the pizza is 360°, each of the 8 pieces would be 45°.

45° + 45° + 45° + 45° +
45° + 45° + 45° + 45° = 360°.

Stop and Think! Unit 10 Review

Page 155 Activity Section 1:

1. Sharon called this figure ∠MVX. An angle must have the name of the vertex in the middle. It should be ∠MXV or ∠VXM.
2. Right triangle
   A: right
   B: acute
   C: acute
3. 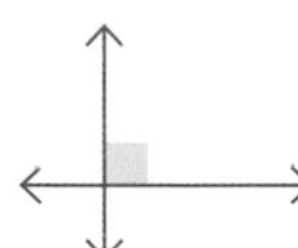

Perpendicular lines are two lines that come together to form a square corner (90° angle).

Activity Section 2:

1. 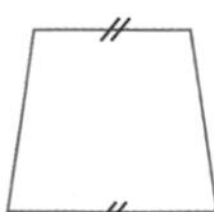
2. Yes, because both the rhombus and the square have 4 sides that are all the same length. What makes them different is that the square must have 4 right angles, while the rhombus could have angles that are not 4 right angles.
3. rectangle
   parallelogram
   square (both sets are equal to each other)
   rhombus (both sets are equal to each other)

Page 156 Activity Section 3:

Polygon					
Name	rectangle	square	trapezoid	triangle	hexagon
# of sides	4	4	4	3	6
Draw lines of symmetry					

Activity Section 4:

1. 360°
2. An obtuse angle is one that is larger than 90°.

3. An acute angle is less than 90°.

4. A right angle is 90°.

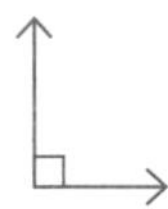

Activity Section 5:

1. Each angle is 90° because the $\overleftrightarrow{BE}$ and $\overleftrightarrow{AD}$ are perpendicular. This means they form 90° angles. You don't need a protractor to know that.
2. Sample:

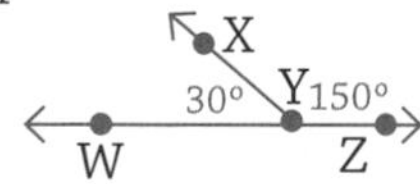

A straight angle has 180°
30° + 150° = 180°

3.

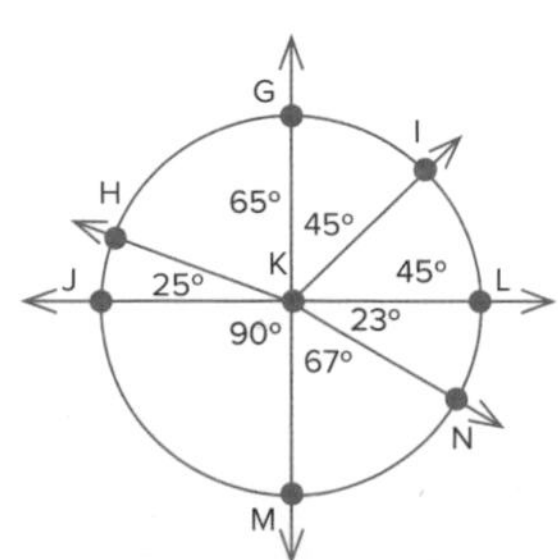

4. ∠JKM = 90° right angle
∠HKG = 90° – 25° = 65°
∠IKL = 90° – 45° = 45°
∠LKN = 90° – 67° = 23°

Stop and Think! Unit 10 Understand
Page 157 Activity Section:

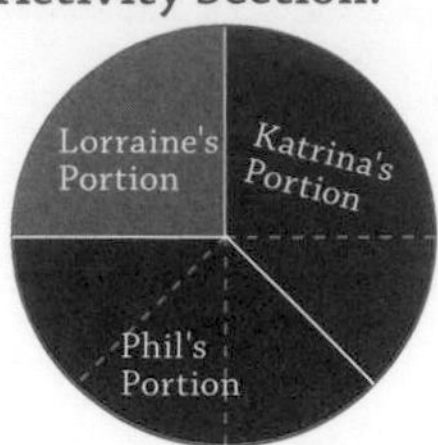

Lorraine's portion is $\frac{1}{4}$ of the pizza, which is 90°: 360° ÷ 4 = 90°

Katrina's portion is $\frac{1}{3}$ of the pizza, which is 120°: 360° ÷ 3 = 120°

Phil's portion will be the difference of the total of Lorraine's and Katrina's portion.

360° – (90° + 120°) =
360° – 210° = 150°

Phil had the largest portion of the pizza.

Stop and Think! Unit 10 Discover
Page 158 Activity Section:

Since an angle is part of a circle, and a circle is always 360°, then you could measure the smaller angle that makes up the rest of the circle. Then you would have to subtract the smaller angle from 360°.

∠MLP = 50°
180° – 50° = 130°

Unit 11: CORE Measurement Concepts

Customary Measurement

Page 160

Length:

Feet	Inches	Think:
1	12	1 × 12 = 12 inches
2	24	2 × 12 = 24 inches
3	36	3 × 12 = 36 inches
4	48	4 × 12 = 48 inches
5	60	5 × 12 = 60 inches

Mass (Weight):

Pounds	Ounces	Think:
1	16	1 × 16 = 16 ounces
2	32	2 × 16 = 32 ounces
3	48	3 × 16 = 48 ounces
4	64	4 × 16 = 64 ounces
5	80	5 × 16 = 80 ounces

Liquid Volume:

Gallons	Fluid Ounces	Think:
1	128	1 × 128 = 128 fluid ounces
2	256	2 × 128 = 256 fluid ounces
3	384	3 × 128 = 384 fluid ounces
4	512	4 × 128 = 512 fluid ounces

Time:

Minutes	Seconds	Think:
1	60	1 × 60 = 60 seconds
2	120	2 × 60 = 120 seconds
3	180	3 × 60 = 180 seconds
4	240	4 × 60 = 240 seconds

Page 161 Practice: Now you try

1. 15 feet
2. 48 inches
3. 3 yards = 9 feet
4. 8,000 pounds
5. 112 ounces
6. 3 tons > 3 pounds
7. 24 pints
8. 20 cups
9. 3 gallons = 48 cups
10. 48 hours
11. 180 seconds
12. 36 hours < 3 days

Ace It Time: They eat 56 extra ounces of peanuts in 1 week.

Metric Measurement

Page 162

Liquid Volume:

Liters	Milliliters	Think:
1	1,000	1 × 1,000 = 1,000 milliliters
2	2,000	2 × 1,000 = 2,000 milliliters
3	3,000	3 × 1,000 = 3,000 milliliters
4	4,000	4 × 1,000 = 4,000 milliliters

Mass:

Grams	Kilograms	Think:
1,000	1	1,000 ÷ 1,000 = 1 kilogram
2,000	2	2,000 ÷ 1,000 = 2 kilograms
3,000	3	3,000 ÷ 1,000 = 3 kilograms
4,000	4	4,000 ÷ 1,000 = 4 kilograms

Page 163

Length:

Meters	Centimeters	Think:
1	100	1 × 100 = 100 centimeters
2	200	2 × 100 = 200 centimeters
5	500	5 × 100 = 500 centimeters
8	800	8 × 100 = 800 centimeters

Practice: Now you try

1. 50 millimeters
2. 7,000 grams
3. 2 liters

Ace It Time: 11,000 grams

First, subtract 19 kilograms – 8 kilograms = 11 kilograms. Aimee's mom's suitcase is 11 kilograms heavier than Aimee's suitcase. Then, multiply to convert kilograms to grams. 11 kilograms × 1,000 = 11,000 grams.

Elapsed Time

Page 165 Practice: Now you try

1. 1 hour 31 minutes
2. 56 minutes

Ace It Time: 3:11 p.m.

Line Plots

Page 167 Practice: Now you try

Step 1. $\frac{3}{8}, \frac{3}{8}, \frac{4}{8}, \frac{4}{8}, \frac{4}{8}, \frac{4}{8}, \frac{5}{8}, \frac{5}{8}, \frac{5}{8}, \frac{6}{8}$

Length of Time Students Walked in Mrs. O'Keefe's Class	
$\frac{3}{8}$	II
$\frac{4}{8}$	IIII
$\frac{5}{8}$	III
$\frac{6}{8}$	I

Step 2. There should be 0 x's above the 0;

There should be 0 x's above the $\frac{1}{8}$;

There should be 0 x's above the $\frac{2}{8}$;

There should be 2 x's above the $\frac{3}{8}$;

There should be 4 x's above the $\frac{4}{8}$;

There should be 3 x's above the $\frac{5}{8}$;

There should be 1 x above the $\frac{6}{8}$;

There should be 0 x's above the $\frac{7}{8}$;

There should be 0 x's above the 1.

Questions:

1. 10 students
2. 2 more students
3. 4 students
4. 8 students

Ace It Time: The number of students that walked $\frac{4}{8}$ of an hour or less is greater.

Stop and Think! Unit 11 Review

Page 168 Activity Section 1:

1.

Gallons	Cups	Think!
4	64	4 gallons × 16 = 64 cups
7	112	7 gallons × 16 = 112 cups
11	176	11 gallons × 16 = 176 cups

2.

Grams	Kilograms	Think!
5,000	5	5,000 ÷ 1,000 = 5 kilograms
7,000	7	7,000 ÷ 1,000 = 7 kilograms
9,000	9	9,000 ÷ 1,000 = 9 kilograms

Activity Section 2:

1. 18 feet
2. 84 inches
3. 5 minutes = 300 seconds

Activity Section 3:

1. 14,000 grams
2. 5,000 grams
3. 5 liters < 5,500 milliliters

Activity Section 4:

1. Start time: 3:45 p.m.
   Elapsed time: 3 hours and 20 minutes
   End time: 7:05 p.m.
2. Start time: 1:15 p.m.
   Elapsed time: 2 hours 58 minutes
   End time: 4:13 p.m.

Stop and Think! Unit 11 Understand

Page 169

1. Lindsay will have 15 quarts of punch for her guests.
2. 60 guests can be served 1 cup of punch each.

Stop and Think! Unit 11 Discover

Page 170

11:22 a.m.

sponge painting

fast & fun techniques for creating beautiful art

sponge painting

fast & fun techniques for creating beautiful art

NORTH LIGHT BOOKS
CINCINNATI, OHIO
www.artistsnetwork.com

 Published by North Light Books, an imprint of F+W Publications, Inc., 4700 East Galbraith Road, Cincinnati, Ohio, 45236. (800) 289-0963. First Edition.

Other fine North Light Books are available from your local bookstore, art supply store or direct from the publisher.

11 10 09 08 07 5 4 3 2 1

Distributed in Canada by Fraser Direct
100 Armstrong Avenue
Georgetown, ON, Canada L7G 5S4
Tel: (905) 877-4411

Distributed in the U.K. and Europe by David & Charles
Brunel House, Newton Abbot, Devon, TQ12 4PU, England
Tel: (+44) 1626 323200, Fax: (+44) 1626 323319
Email: postmaster@davidandcharles.co.uk

Distributed in Australia by Capricorn Link
P.O. Box 704, S. Windsor NSW, 2756 Australia
Tel: (02) 4577-3555

Library of Congress Cataloging in Publication Data

Tse, Terrence
Sponge painting : fast & fun techniques for creating beautiful art / Terrence Tse. -- 1st ed.
p. cm.
Includes index.
ISBN-13: 978-1-58180-962-6 (pbk. : alk. paper)
ISBN-10: 1-58180-962-X (pbk. : alk. paper)
1. Acrylic painting--Technique. 2. Sponge painting--Technique. I. Title.

ND1535.T73 2007
751.4'9--dc22

2006102620

Edited by Kathy Kipp
Designed by Clare Finney
Production coordinated by Greg Nock
Photography by Christine Polomsky, Tim Grondin and Al Parrish

Metric Conversion Chart

to convert	to	multiply by
Inches	Centimeters	2.54
Centimeters	Inches	0.4
Feet	Centimeters	30.5
Centimeters	Feet	0.03
Yards	Meters	0.9
Meters	Yards	1.1

About the Author

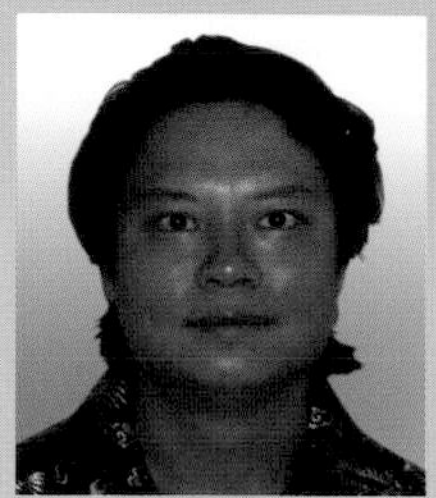

Terrence Lun Tse was born in Hong Kong, moved to the United States at an early age and grew up in the small town of Salinas, California. He began his art career as a freelance artist and supplemented his studies by reading many art instruction books, mostly by North Light. Employed as an artist by a company in Tampa that produced hand-painted artworks for retail stores and other mass markets, Terry gained invaluable experience in learning how to paint quickly while producing high-quality work. He continues to produce new designs and commissioned works for Deljou Art Group in Atlanta, Georgia, where he lives with his family. Terry is the co-author of *Painting Murals Fast & Easy*, and has been featured in *Painter's Quick Reference: Trees & Foliage* and *Painter's Quick Reference: Landscapes*, all by North Light.

Dedication

For my Tseh family.
For Sunlun, Mousey and Chuii.

Acknowledgments

Unreserved gratitude to Kathy Kipp, my editor at North Light Books.

table of contents

introduction

PAINTING ORIGINAL ARTWORK on canvas is one of today's most popular and creative ways to enjoy our leisure time and to improve our artistic skills. No other painting technique puts such a unique and personal stamp on our surroundings, or brings such joy and satisfaction to both the artist and the viewer.

In the past, painting landscapes or floral still-lifes on canvas meant spending many hours in preparation, copying a pattern or drawing, assembling just the right brushes and paints, buying special equipment, painting with slow, deliberate strokes, repainting mistakes and starting over again....

No more! In this book you will discover a new and innovative way to paint quickly and easily using acrylic paints and common household sponges. No brushes needed! No experience required!

Painting with sponges is downright fun—and it frees you from the fear and frustration of making mistakes. Don't like what you've just painted? Spray the area with water and remove it with a clean sponge. It's that easy.

The sponges used to paint the projects in this book are the inexpensive cellulose ones you can find in any grocery, hardware or home improvement store. A natural sea sponge is also used to achieve some interesting effects, such as layers of colorful foliage on trees and bushes.

To clean the paint out of your sponges, just squeeze them out in a bucket of clean water. The paints used in this book are all acrylics, which are water-based, have no odor, and can be thinned or removed with plain water.

In this book, you will learn many simple techniques for achieving a wide variety of painted effects you can use in any painting, from scenic country landscapes to oceanfront beaches to floral still lifes and more. You will see how easy it is to speed-paint clouds and skies, sandy shorelines, sun-dappled palm trees, bold and colorful flowers, plus grassy hills, tree-shaded rivers, and so much more.

None of the artwork demonstrated in this book will take longer than three hours to paint! Many paintings can be finished in under two hours. Each demo begins with a clock timer that indicates how much time you can expect to spend on painting that design. Sponges allow you to cover a large amount of space in a matter of minutes. They also let you shade and highlight quickly to achieve depth and realism.

Try your hand at mixing and matching the ideas you see in these pages to create your own unique artwork, and discover how much fun it is to paint with sponges!

"Enticing Palms"
18" x 24" (45.7 x 61 cm)

getting started with the sponge

MATERIALS NEEDED

The materials used to create all the paintings in this book are shown here. These items can be purchased at your local home center and craft supply store. Sponges and paper towels are available at grocery stores.

The following pages show all the sponge-painting techniques used in this book. Try them out on a scrap piece of canvas first to get the feel and rhythm of working with a sponge. It's fun and relaxing!

Household cleaning sponge. This is the kind of sponge you see everywhere in different colors and sizes. It is a cellulose composite with breadlike pores and texture. It's more economical to buy the large ones (7-1/2 x 4 x 2 inches) (19 x 10 x 5cm) and cut them into smaller, easier-to-handle sizes with scissors.

Natural sea sponge. This type of sponge is grown and cultivated. Generally, the sea sponge has deep tunneling pores and a coral-like surface. The natural surface texture is ideal for random effects such as foliage and sand. If your sea sponge is large, tear off smaller pieces to use for painting.

Water bucket. A small one or two gallon bucket of water will be needed to rinse out the sponge as you paint. Place an old towel underneath to catch drips.

Spray bottle of water. Use to mist or moisten the canvas, keep your paint wet on your sponge, and thin the paint on your palette if needed.

Rubber gloves. Sponge painting requires physical contact with paint, so you may want to use thin disposable rubber gloves to keep your hands clean.

Scissors. Scissors may be used to cut large sponges into smaller sizes.

Pencil. Use a sharp pencil to lightly sketch the main outlines of your design on your canvas.

Foam plates. Inexpensive foam plates can serve as a palette for your paints. When you're finished painting your project, just throw the plate away. No need to wash unused paint down the drain.

Canvases. All of the paintings in this book were done on 18x24-inch (46x61cm) pre-stretched, pre-gessoed canvases bought at an art supply store. For a more inexpensive option, buy rolls of unstretched canvas at a craft supply store and cut them 2 inches (51mm) larger on each side, then staple them to wooden stretcher bars, also available at any art or craft store.

Acrylic paints. Acrylic waterbased paints can be found at art and craft supply stores and come in a wide variety of colors. For the paintings in this book, I used two brands. Liquitex Acrylic Artist Color (high viscosity/heavy body) comes in tubes. Utrecht Artists' Colors, Series 1 Acrylic (high viscosity) comes in one-pint (16 fluid ounce) jars. Both are perfect for sponge painting because they are thicker-bodied than the bottled craft acrylics—a little dollop on your palette goes a long way. For more information on these brands, contact Liquitex at www.liquitex.com or phone 1-888-4-Acrylic. Contact Utrecht at www.utrecht.com or phone toll-free 1-877-Utrecht.

CUTTING AND LOADING THE SPONGE WITH PAINT

1 **Cut the Sponge with Scissors.** Cutting a large sponge into thirds makes them the right size for most painting needs. They're also more comfortable to hold at this size and easy to load with paint.

2 **The Flat Side.** In the painting demonstrations in this book, you will see instructions about loading or painting with the flat side of the sponge. This is the largest area on the sponge.

3 **The Top Edge.** This sharp edge separates the flat side and the top side of the sponge. You will be using the top edge often to make thin brushlike lines and crisp edges in your paintings.

4 **Corner Loading.** Load one corner of the sponge to paint small areas and to make brushlike strokes.

5 **Loading the Top Edge.** Hold the sponge at an angle and dip just the top edge of the flat side into your puddle of paint. This will allow you great control when drawing sharp or precise edges.

6 **Loading the Top Half.** Loading just the top half will keep the sponge from getting too saturated with paint.

7 **Loading the Flat Side.** To paint large areas of your canvas quickly, such as backgrounds or horizontal washes of color, load the entire flat side by pressing the sponge into a puddle of paint and working the paint in using circular motions on your palette.

8 **Double-loading the Sponge.** You can double-load a sponge just as you can a brush. Dip one corner into your main color, then dip the other corner into your shading or highlighting color.

PINCHING THE SPONGE TO CREATE EFFECTS

1 **No Pinch.** Depending on how tightly you pinch the top of the sponge as you paint, you can achieve different effects just as you would using large or small brushes. Here I'm not pinching the sponge at all.

2 **The Effect.** Painting with no pinch to the sponge allows you to cover large areas and create long sweeps of color. I use the sponge this way to block in the horizon line in a landscape, or to paint the flat top of a table in a floral still life.

3 **Medium Pinch.** Squeeze the sides slightly to reduce the width of the sponge's painting area.

4 **The Effect.** Use the top edge to "draw" the outside shape of a vase. This will allow you great control when drawing sharp or precise edges.

5 **Tight Pinch.** Squeeze the sides tightly between your thumb and first two fingers to achieve a tight pinch that reduces the painting area on the sponge even more.

6 **The Effect.** Use a tight pinch to "draw" details such as leaves and flower petals, tree trunks and branches, or any other area where you need the greatest control.

MORE NEAT TRICKS WITH THE SPONGE

1 **Loading a Natural Sea Sponge.** The sea sponge is a product of nature and therefore a great tool for painting any area where randomness is important. To load a sea sponge, tear off a small piece and dip it lightly into paint.

2 **Stippling with a Sea Sponge.** Load the sponge first with the darkest value of your color and stipple on the first layer. Turn the sponge to a clean spot and load with a medium value of your color. Stipple on the next layer without totally covering the first layer. Turn the sponge again, load with the lightest value and stipple the final layer in a few areas. All three values should be visible.

1 **Flipping the Sponge to the Clean Side.** The same sponge can be used to both paint an area or object and blend it out or wipe off a mistake. Here's the loaded side of a damp sponge.

2 **The Flip.** Using your thumb and index finger as pivot points, flip the bottom of the sponge upward.

3 **The Clean Side.** Now you have the clean side of the sponge ready in an instant to wipe off paint, clean up an edge, or blend out and soften color or shading. No need to wash out your sponge in clean water again and again. Just flip it to the clean side!

Spritz with Water to Moisten Paint. Sometimes the paint on your sponge may need to be thinned to create a large wash, or it may feel as if it's dragging on your canvas. Just keep a spray bottle of clean water handy and mist the paint as needed. If the paint on your canvas is drying too quickly, mist it lightly to keep it moist and workable.

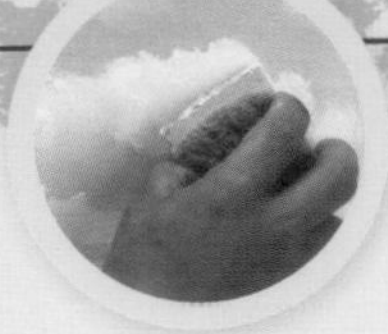

14 quick sponge-painting demos

BLUE SKIES

1 **Load the Sponge.** Load the flat side of the sponge with your blue sky color.

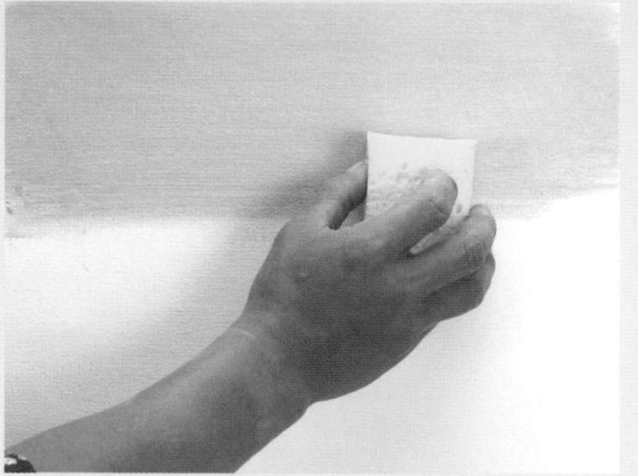

2 **Apply Wash.** Mist the canvas with clean water and wash the sky color on in horizontal motions, starting at the top of your canvas and working downward.

3 **Blend and Fade Out.** Flip the sponge over to the clean side and blend and fade the blue color out as you near the horizon line.

WHITE PUFFY CLOUDS

1 **Load the Sponge.** Load a clean sponge on the top edge of the flat side with Titanium White.

2 **Draw in Cloud Shapes.** Draw in irregular shapes for the clouds using the edge of the sponge. Leave areas of blue sky showing through here and there to indicate translucency.

3 **Soften and Fade Out.** Flip the sponge over to the clean side and blend and fade the white downward. The bottoms of the clouds should always be very diffuse. If you want to show that the clouds are flat on the bottom, stroke your sponge laterally.

SUNSET SKIES

1 **Apply Color Washes.** Mist your canvas with clean water. Wash in a dark blue for the upper sky, a yellow for the mid sky, an orange for the lower sky, and an orange-red near the horizon. Blend out all the colors where they meet.

2 **Place Cloud Shapes.** Place in puffy cloud shapes with white, blending and fading out their edges and lower sides. Add a few streaky cirrus clouds in among the puffy clouds using lateral strokes of the sponge. Let dry.

3 **Add Sunset Colors on the Clouds.** To light the cloud bottoms with the sunset colors of the sky, lightly scrub a red such as Alizarin Crimson over some of the white areas.

4 **Shade the Clouds.** With a very thin cool gray such as Payne's Gray, shade and shape the clouds to show that the sky is darkening and evening is coming on.

5 **Strengthen White Cloud Tops.** Finish by strengthening the white of the cloud tops using the pinched top edge of your sponge and Titanium White. Streak in some very thin and wispy cirrus clouds in among the puffy clouds using lateral strokes, almost like dry-brushing.

CALM OCEAN WATER

1 **Load the Sponge.** Load the flat side of the sponge with your lighter blue color (here I'm using Bright Aqua Green) to suggest shallow water.

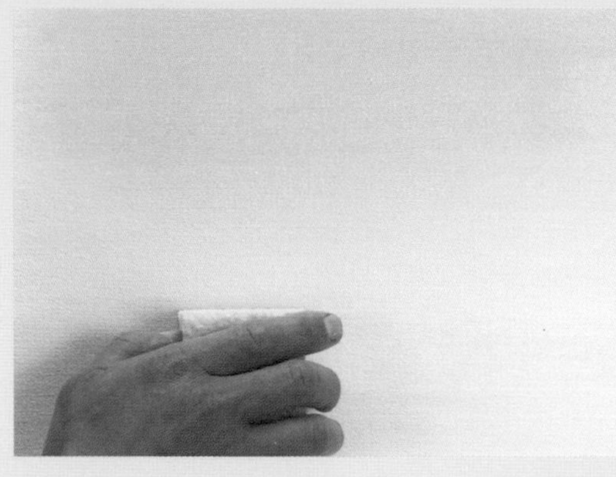

2 **Apply Wash.** Wash on the light aqua blue color with horizontal sweeps of the flat of the sponge. Let this color soften and fade out a little towards the bottom of the canvas.

3 **Load the Sponge.** Load the top half of the flat side of a clean sponge with a darker blue (such as Ultramarine Blue) to suggest deeper water.

4 **Apply Wash.** Establish your horizon line by drawing it in across your canvas with the sharp edge of the sponge. Wash on the darker blue with horizontal strokes here and there to imply areas of deeper ocean water in the mid- and far-distance.

BREAKING WAVES

1 **Load the Sponge.** Load the top half of the flat side of a clean sponge with Titanium White.

2 **Draw Wave Shapes.** Draw in rough-edged, random shapes to indicate the foamy water of waves breaking in the shallow water.

3 **Blend Upward.** Flip the sponge over to the clean side and use upward motions to blend and fade the waves out from the top part of the foam. Leave the leading edges of the breaking waves sharp and distinct. Streak in a few horizontal whitecaps in the distant blue water.

SANDY BEACH

1 **Load the Sponge.** Load the top half of the flat side of your sponge with a cream color such as Unbleached Titanium.

2 **Wash in Beach Area.** Wash in this color where the beach will be in your painting, using lateral strokes. Soften and blend it into the shallow water.

3 **Shape the Sand.** Apply a darker brown such as Raw Sienna here and there to indicate the dips and low places in the sandy beach.

4 **Add Breaking Waves.** With white, dab on places where the waves are rolling up onto the beach, using the same technique as you did for the breaking waves on the previous page.

1 **Load the Sponge.** Load the flat side of your sponge with a medium warm green.

2 **Apply Wash.** Mist your canvas with clean water and wash the first green in your field area.

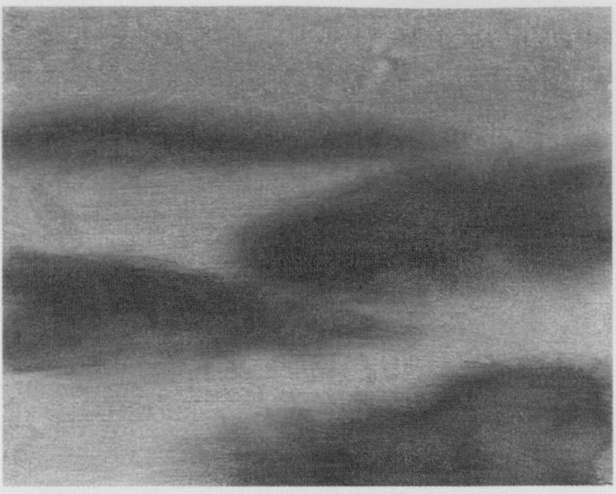

3 **Add Valleys.** Indicate valleys and low places in the field with a dark green, such as Sap Green Permanent plus Raw Umber.

4 **Indicate Hills.** Add white to your first medium green to make a lighter green, and scrub in the areas where the field rises or where there are low hills.

5 **Add Dried Grasses.** Stroke in patches of dried grasses with an earth tone or brownish-yellow color such as thinned yellow ochre.

6 **Finish with Highlights.** Add more white to the lighter green and scrub in the final highlights where the sun hits the tops of the hills and high places.

DISTANT LAND MASSES

1 **Load the Sponge.** Load the top corner part of the flat side of the sponge with a dark brown.

2 **Draw Shapes.** Draw the top edge of the land masses with the edge of your sponge, then fill in with a scrubbing motion.

3 **Add Grass.** Dab in a medium warm green to indicate grassy areas on the hillsides. Let the dark brown show through in spots.

4 **Highlight the Grass.** Highlight the green grass areas with a lighter yellow-green where the sunlight hits them.

5 **Shape the Landforms.** Use raw sienna to shade and shape the slopes and hillsides, and to ground the land masses at the bottom.

6 **Final Highlights.** Finish with a few cream or white highlights on the highest portions of the land masses and on areas where the sunlight is strongest.

1 **Wash In Water Area.** Mist the canvas with clean water, load the flat side of your sponge with paint and apply thin washes of a blue water color using long horizontal sweeps of the sponge. Scrub the canvas to fill in and blend.

2 **Draw Distant Land Mass.** Place in your land mass with a dark brown, and while the paint is wet, draw your sponge downward with light pressure to indicate the reflection in the water below.

3 **Add Warm Brown.** Warm up the dark brown of the land mass and shape the hillsides with a warm reddish-brown such as burnt sienna. Draw your sponge lightly downward to add this color to the reflection in the water.

4 **Indicate Treeline.** Add a dark green treeline along the shore and, again, draw your sponge lightly downward to add the dark green color to the reflection.

5 **Highlight Trees.** Highlight the trees both in the main land mass and in the reflection with some light greens and a few spots of yellow.

6 **Load the Sponge.** Load the very top edge of a clean sponge with white.

7 **Show Movement in the Water.** Draw in short horizontal streaks of white with the sharp edge of the sponge to begin the areas where there are small waves and movement in the water.

8 **Blend Out.** Turn your sponge over to the clean side and blend out the white areas with horizontal motions of the sponge. Make sure these white areas are thin enough that the reflections of the trees and land masses show through. Opaque white paint will ruin the illusion of the reflections.

TREE TRUNKS AND BRANCHES

1 **Load the Sponge.** Load the top edge corner of the flat side of your sponge with a dark brown.

2 **Draw Trunk and Branches.** Draw the shape of the trunk and branches with a medium pinch of the sponge edge.

3 **Shade.** Shade and enrich the color here and there on the trunk and branches with raw sienna.

4 **Highlight.** Highlight the parts of the branches that are lit by the sun with Unbleached Titanium or another warm cream color.

TREE FOLIAGE

1 **Darkest Leaves.** Load the top corner of your sponge with a dark green and dab on the innermost, darkest layer of leaves. Don't fill in too much—leave areas where the background and the branches show through.

2 **Medium Green Leaves.** Enrich the color of the foliage by adding a bright yellow to your dark green and dabbing in another layer of leaves. Again, don't fill in too much.

3 **Lightest Leaves.** With a very light green, highlight the leaves on the outermost areas where the sun hits them. Here I've added white to the yellow-green mix used in the previous layer.

PALM TREES

1 **Palm Tree Trunk.** Load the top edge of the flat side of a sponge with dark brown. Make a tight pinch and draw in the palm tree trunk. Widen the area at the top where the palm fronds attach to the trunk.

2 **Growth Segments.** Touch on the diagonal growth segments of the palm trunk with a cream color using the top edge of the sponge.

3 **Load the Sponge.** Load the top edge of the sponge with a dark green.

4 **Stroke Palm Fronds.** Draw four or five curving lines outward from the top to form the spines of the palm fronds, then lightly pull color downward from that line to create the darkest leaves. Keep these airy and open.

5 **Fill In.** Fill in with more palm fronds as needed, foreshortening the fronds facing the back and the front to indicate roundness and depth.

6 **Enrich the Color.** Enrich the color with a medium yellow-green, lightly overpainting the dark green fronds here and there.

7 **Indicate Dried Leaves.** Streak in a few areas of raw sienna to indicate dried-up leaves.

8 **Final Highlights.** Add a little white to the medium yellow-green you used in step 6 and highlight the fronds where the sunlight hits them.

1 Load the Sponge. Load the top edge of the flat side of a clean sponge with Titanium White.

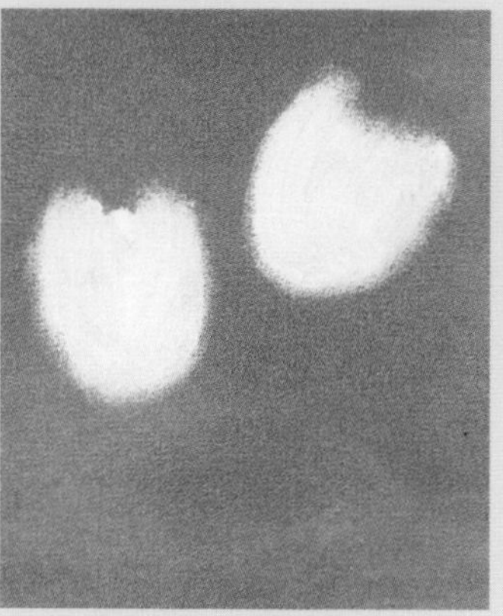

2 Draw the Basic Shape. Using the top edge of the sponge in a tight pinch, draw in the basic shape of your flower. In this demo, we are painting white tulips.

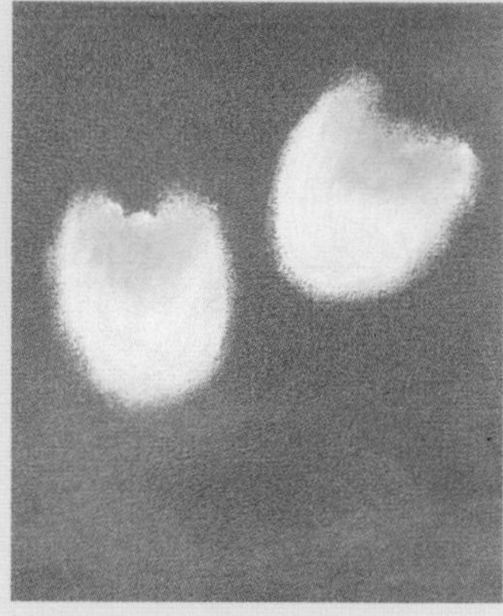

3 Define the Throat. Place a bright yellow at the tulip's throat where it is open at the top.

4 Shade the Base. Shade the base of the tulip with a very pale light gray, letting it fade out toward the top edge.

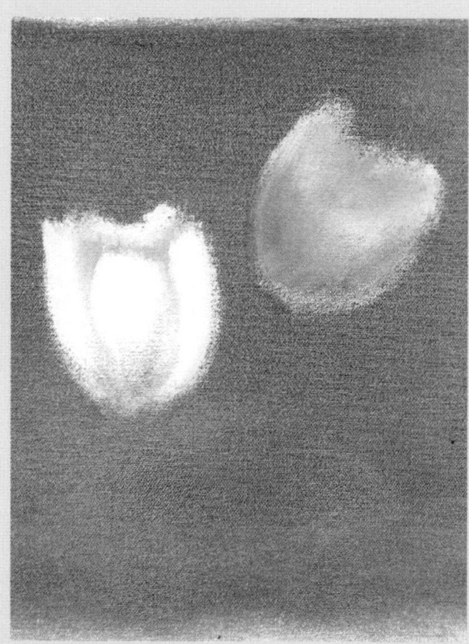

5 Indicate the Petals. Use pure Titanium White to draw in the tulip petals in front, letting a few light gray lines show to indicate the petal sections.

6 Add Stems. Draw the stems and the base where they connect to the tulip petals with a dark green.

7 Highlight Stems. Add yellow to your dark green and highlight the stems, pulling this color up into the base of the tulip.

CHERRY BLOSSOMS

1 Load the Sponge. To paint the tiny branches, leaves and petals of a flowering tree such as a cherry, load just the corner of your sponge as shown. This will give you greater control when making very small shapes.

2 Draw Branches, Leaves and Petals. Draw in the branches with a dark brown. Place in a few tiny leaves with a medium green using the tightly pinched edge of the sponge. Draw in the four-petal blossoms with a medium red such as Alizarin Crimson.

3 Overpaint with Lighter Color. Add white to your medium red to make a bright pink and overpaint the red petals using a tight pinch of your sponge, leaving some of the red showing along the edges to give form and shading to the petals.

4 Add Centers. Dot the centers of the open blossoms with a bright yellow.

20 timed step-by-step paintings

NOW LET'S USE THE SPONGE PAINTING TECHNIQUES you have learned so far to create a wide variety of beautiful paintings on canvas! Presented in this next section are 20 complete, step-by-step painting demonstrations, including colorful floral still lifes and scenic landscapes in all seasons.

All of these paintings can be finished in three hours or less. That's because they are speed-painted with sponges! No brushes or palette knives are used on any of the paintings.

Each of the following demonstrations begins with a clock timer icon that tells you how much time the painting will take to complete. The first seven demonstrations on pages 28-57 all take 90 minutes or less to paint. The final thirteen paintings on pages 58-125 take 90 minutes to three hours to complete. Of course, the more you practice with the sponge, the faster and more confident you will be and the quicker you can complete each painting.

Painting with sponges allows you, even encourages you, to work in a looser, freer way without getting bogged down in tiny details or worrying about mistakes. (Remember, any mistake can simply be wiped off with a clean damp sponge!) It's fun and relaxing, and the results are very rewarding.

"Mountain River Bloom"
24" x 18" (61 x 45.7 cm)

1 HR 10 MIN

daffodil dance

Brown-green mix

Blue-green mix

Burnt Sienna

Brilliant Purple

Shading purple mix

Dark leaf green mix

Bright yellow mix

Burnt Sienna (thinned)

Cadmium Yellow Medium

Medium leaf green mix

Light leaf green mix

Light purple mix

Titanium White

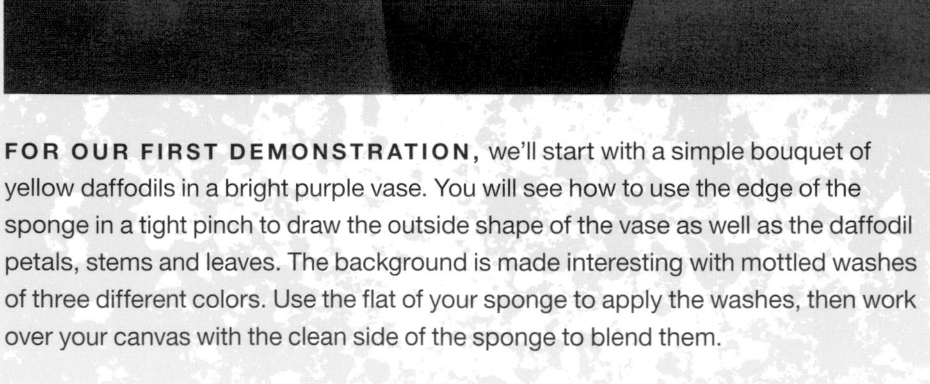

FOR OUR FIRST DEMONSTRATION, we'll start with a simple bouquet of yellow daffodils in a bright purple vase. You will see how to use the edge of the sponge in a tight pinch to draw the outside shape of the vase as well as the daffodil petals, stems and leaves. The background is made interesting with mottled washes of three different colors. Use the flat of your sponge to apply the washes, then work over your canvas with the clean side of the sponge to blend them.

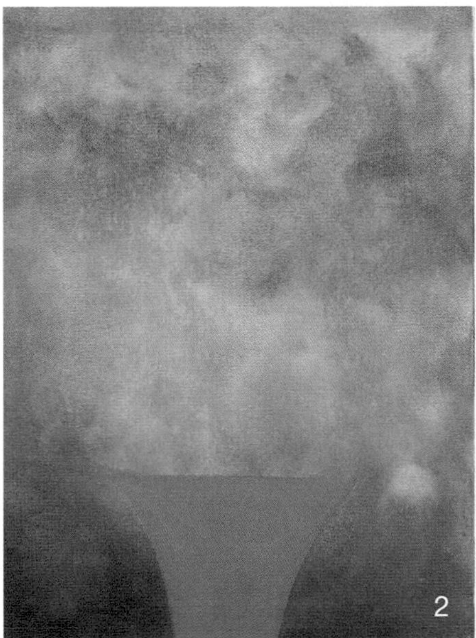

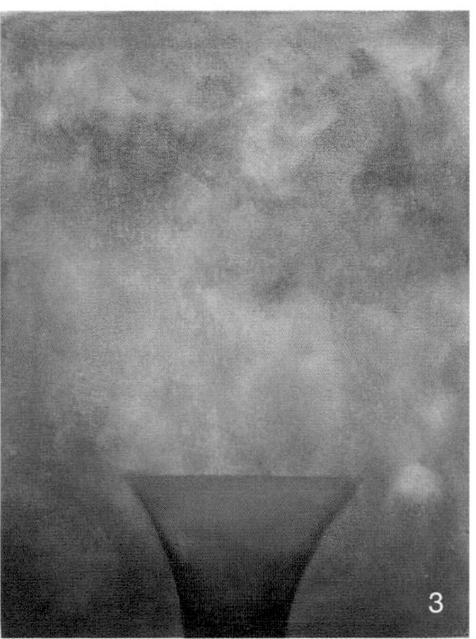

1 Mist the canvas with water and wash in a mottled green with the brown-green mix (Sap Green Permanent + Raw Umber). Mottle in a blue-green mix (brown-green mix + Cobalt Blue) in the upper right. Mottle in Burnt Sienna in the lower part of the canvas, then blend it up toward the middle to meet the greens.

2 Block in the vase shape with Brilliant Purple. Use the edge of your sponge to draw the outer edge of the vase, then fill in the middle with a scrubbing motion.

3 Shade the outer edges and the lower part of the vase with shading purple mix (Dioxazine Purple + Burnt Umber) to give the illusion of roundness and shape to the vase. Let the vase dry.

4 With dark leaf green mix (Sap Green Permanent + Raw Umber), draw in the daffodil leaves, starting at the top of each leaf and drawing downward toward the vase. Don't worry if your leaves extend over the vase's edge; as long as the vase is dry you can wipe off the excess green with a clean sponge.

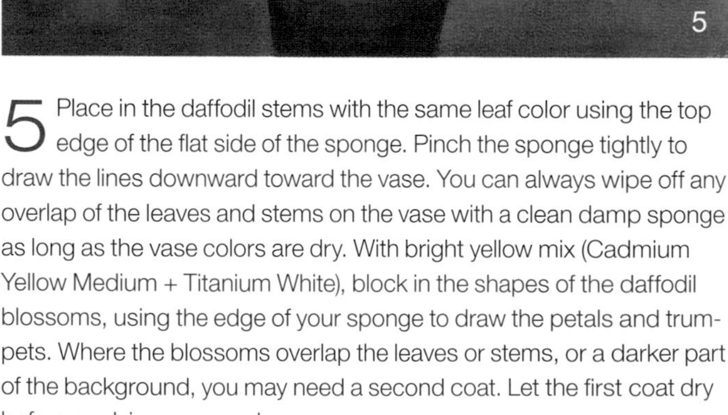

5 Place in the daffodil stems with the same leaf color using the top edge of the flat side of the sponge. Pinch the sponge tightly to draw the lines downward toward the vase. You can always wipe off any overlap of the leaves and stems on the vase with a clean damp sponge as long as the vase colors are dry. With bright yellow mix (Cadmium Yellow Medium + Titanium White), block in the shapes of the daffodil blossoms, using the edge of your sponge to draw the petals and trumpets. Where the blossoms overlap the leaves or stems, or a darker part of the background, you may need a second coat. Let the first coat dry before applying a second.

6 With thinned Burnt Sienna, shade the openings of the trumpets and on the petals where they attach to the base of the trumpet.

7 Load Titanium White onto the edge of a clean sponge and highlight the tops of the yellow trumpets and the outer portions of the petals. Don't cover up all the yellow, and allow the shading applied in step 6 to show.

8 Come back in with straight Cadmium Yellow Medium and re-establish the bright yellow color of the blossoms in the areas where they are in shade, opposite the white highlights. Let dry.

9 With your dark leaf green mix, redraw any stems that were covered by the blossoms. Finish the leaves by adding a stroke of medium leaf green mix (dark leaf green + Cadmium Yellow Medium) down the middle of each leaf, maintaining the dark edges. Use the same color to highlight part of each stem. Then highlight the toplit part of most of the leaves with the light leaf green mix (medium leaf green + Titanium White) using very little pressure on your sponge.

critique

Step back and take a critical look at your painting. Here the top edge of the purple vase needed to be cleaned up and resharpened after all the leaves and stems overlapped it. A soft highlight of light purple mix (Brilliant Purple + Titanium White) was added to the front of the vase at the top to give the illusion of roundness. Let this highlight fade out where the bottom part of the vase is shaded.

1 HR 15 MIN

bamboo bundle

Sap Green Permanent

Light Blue Violet

Burnt Umber

Unbleached Titanium

Inca Gold Metallic

Dark shading mix

Burnt Sienna

Titanium White

Dark green mix

Vivid Lime Green

Yellow Oxide

Raw Sienna

Highlight green mix

IN THIS SECOND DEMONSTRATION, we'll paint an interesting clay pot with rounded shapes and heavy shading, plus some texturing done with a lid dipped in gold paint. Easy! Bamboo canes are fun to paint with a sponge—just pinch the top edge of the sponge to draw the canes and indicate the growth segments, then use a corner to paint the little leaves.

1

2

3

1 Mist your canvas with clean water, then wash in the background with very thin Light Blue Violet using the flat side of the sponge. Alternate between vertical strokes and horizontal strokes to create texture.

2 Wash in Sap Green Permanent in a few areas, again alternating strokes to create texture. Spritz your sponge with water to keep your paint thin and transparent.

3 The final background color is thinned Burnt Umber to warm up the tone and to tie in the background color with the clay pot. Place the darker areas behind where the edges of the pot will be for good contrast.

4 Block in the shape of the clay pot with Unbleached Titanium, using the edge of the sponge to draw in the shape, then filling in with the flat of the sponge. Keep working the edges to get them symmetrical and well-shaped.

4

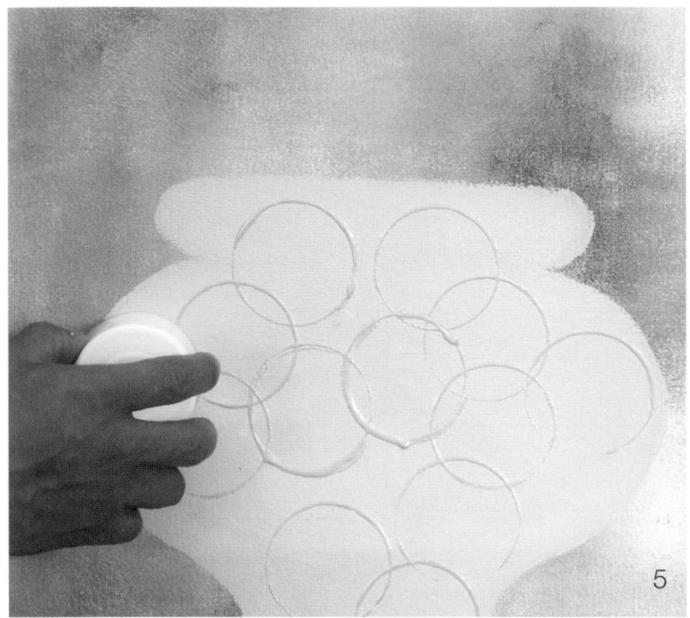
5

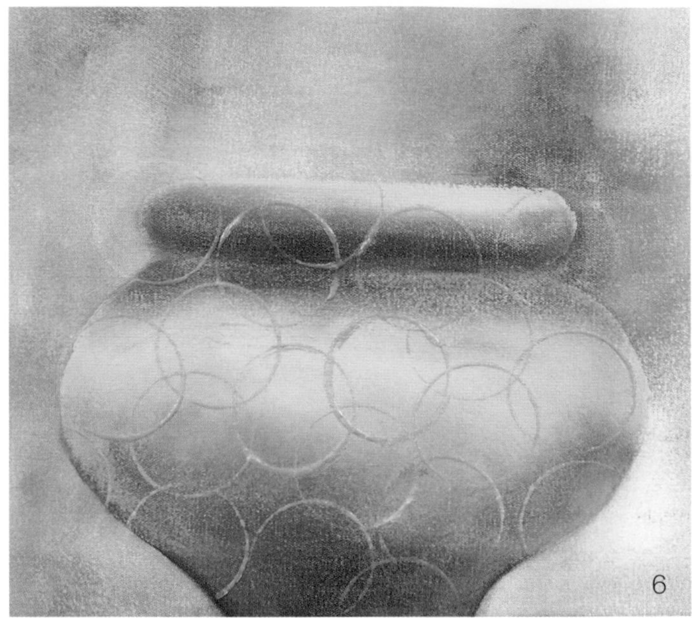
6

5 Using the lid to a can or some other ring-shaped item, dip into Inca Gold Metallic paint with the rim of the lid and apply overlapping rings to the clay pot. Some of the rings will have gaps in them and that's fine. Allow the gold paint to dry completely before going on.

6 Shade the lower part of the pot and underneath the rim with the dark shading mix (Burnt Umber + Payne's Gray), then come back in with Burnt Sienna to warm up the shading color.

7 With thinned Titanium White, highlight the top of the rim and the widest part of the pot to give it a bulbous, rounded shape.

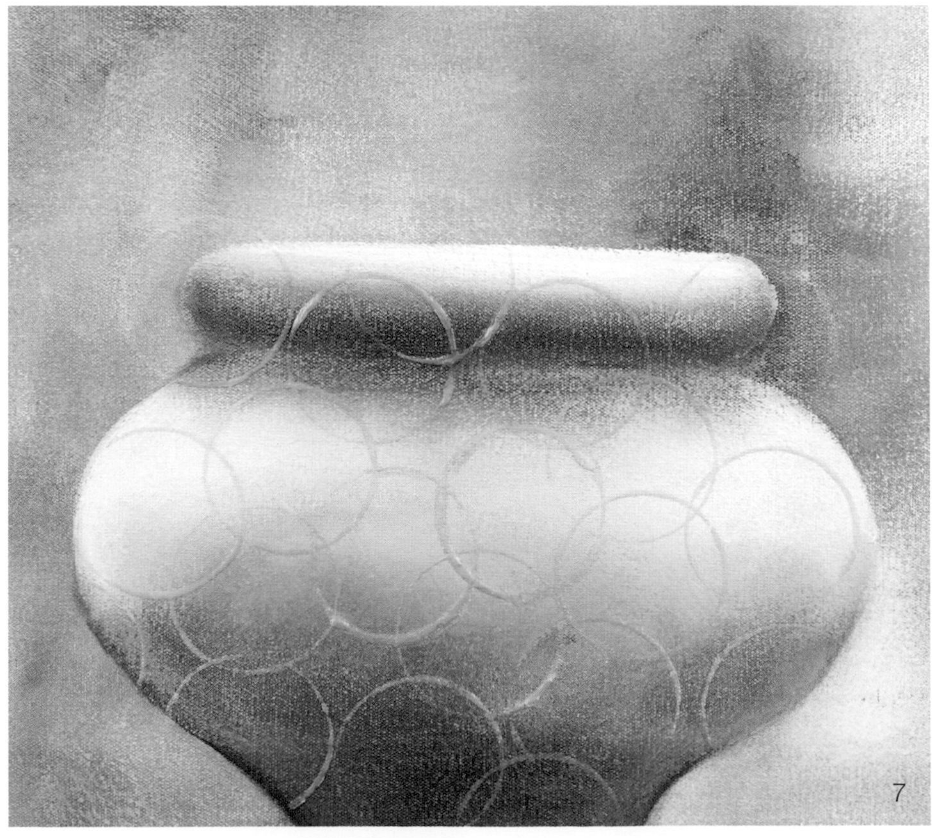
7

8 With the dark green mix (Sap Green Permanent + Burnt Umber + Payne's Gray), place in the canes of the bamboo, starting at the top of each cane and stroking downward toward the opening of the pot. Use the edge of your sponge in a medium pinch to draw each cane and the new little canes coming off them. Use the corner of the sponge and the same dark green mix to pull the darkest leaves, starting where the leaf attaches to the cane and pulling outward to a point.

9 With Vivid Lime Green, highlight the centers of the canes to give the illusion of roundness, using stop and start motions to segment the canes. With the same color, pull more little bamboo leaves.

critique

Step back and take a look at your painting so far. The bamboo needs more interesting textures. With Yellow Oxide and Raw Sienna, accent some of the canes to give variety to the cane colors, and add some more leaves with Raw Sienna. Highlight the leaves with a few strokes of highlight green mix (Vivid Lime Green + Titanium White). If needed, come back in and clean up the edges of the clay pot, either by re-stroking the edges or by re-establishing the background colors around the pot, especially if the gold rings you painted in Step 5 inadvertently extended over the edge and onto the background.

1 HR 20 MIN

calla elegance

Light Blue Violet

Ultramarine Blue

Burnt Umber

Ultramarine Blue mix

Olive green mix

Dioxazine Purple

Titanium White

Payne's Gray

Raw Sienna

Yellow Oxide

Light olive mix

CALLA LILIES MAKE BEAUTIFUL painting subjects because their shapes are so graceful and elegant, and easy to draw with the edge of your sponge! In this demonstration you'll also see how simple it is to paint reflections in glass using streaks of thinned Titanium White that follow the shape of the vase.

1

2

3

4

1 Mist the canvas lightly with clean water. Wash in the first background color with the flat side of the sponge and Light Blue Violet. Let dry.

2 Shade the upper portion and left side with Ultramarine Blue mix (Ultramarine Blue + a little Payne's Gray) on the flat side of the sponge. Wash in Burnt Umber on the bottom part where the vase will be, keeping the darkest part toward the bottom of the canvas and fading it upward into the blue background.

3 Block in the blue glass vase shape with Ultramarine Blue. With olive green mix (Payne's Gray + Cadmium Yellow Medium), draw in the shapes of the stems starting at the top and pulling down all the way over the vase shape using the top edge of the sponge in a medium pinch. Let dry.

4 To achieve a transparent look to the blue glass vase, shade first with curved vertical streaks of Dioxazine Purple.

5 With Titanium White, draw the water line in the vase using the sharp edge of the sponge. Highlight the top rim of the vase and add curved vertical streaks of thinned Titanium White to indicate the glass reflections. These should be whiter at the top and fade out to nothing at the bottom.

6 Draw in the shapes of the calla lilies with Titanium White using the edge of your sponge in a tight pinch. Let dry.

7 With thinned Payne's Gray, wash shading in the middle area of each calla lily, maintaining the white edges all around.

8 Pick up Titanium White on the edge of your sponge, make a tight pinch, and draw the spiral shape of the top edge of the lily trumpet.

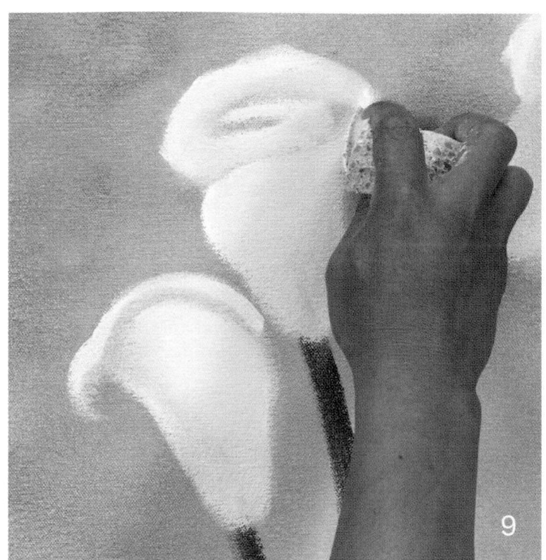

9 Blend the edges that you just drew in using the flat of the sponge and pulling downward into the trumpet of the lily. Don't cover the gray entirely. This maintains the shape and shading. Let dry.

10 Warm up small areas of the white on the shaded parts of the trumpets with thinned Raw Sienna. Draw in the large yellow stamens with Yellow Oxide on the corner of your sponge.

critique

Step back and check your painting for any final details needed. Shade the bottom of the each lily trumpet where it attaches to its stem with a light olive mix (add a little more Cadmium Yellow Medium to the olive green mix used in Step 3). Deepen the shading and pull from the stem up one side of the base of the calla lily with the olive green mix. This softens the area where the stem attaches to the base of the flower. Compare this to Step 10 to see how much better it looks now. If necessary, clean up any edges by re-establishing the background colors where they meet the flowers.

1 HR 20 MIN

orchid rhythm

Raw Sienna

Burnt Sienna

Burnt Umber

Bronze Yellow

Titanium White

Mars Black

Cadmium Yellow Medium

Mars Black + white mix

Highlight green mix

Dark olive mix

Unbleached Titanium

Dioxazine Purple

Cadmium Orange

Cadmium Yellow Medium + Payne's Gray

Bronze Yellow + Titanium White

THE SIMPLICITY OF THIS DESIGN—a white orchid in a black vase against a warm brown background—lends itself to almost any home decor and makes a lovely focal point over a mantelpiece or as part of a series of floral paintings on a wall. Orchid petals are large and open and can be drawn with the top edge of the sponge in a medium pinch. The richly colored background helps set off the white of the petals.

1 Begin by misting the canvas with water. Sponge in the background with Raw Sienna using the flat side of the sponge. Work over your canvas with vertical and horizontal strokes, but leave some areas lighter and some darker.

2 Shade and texture the background using large strokes of Burnt Sienna. Allow the Raw Sienna background to show through, mostly in the upper right.

3 With Burnt Umber, shade on the diagonal from the upper left corner to the lower right corner of the background area. Place the horizontal line of the tabletop at the bottom of the canvas with Bronze Yellow. Highlight the table with Bronze Yellow + Titanium White; shade with Burnt Umber.

4 Block in the vase shape with Mars Black using the top edge of the sponge in a tight pinch to draw the outline. Then fill in with the flat of the sponge. Work to make the shape even and symmetrical.

5 With Mars Black still in the sponge, pick up a little Titanium White and apply reflective highlights on both sides that indicate the rounded shape of the vase. These should be lightest at the top and fade to nothing at the bottom of the vase.

6

6 Draw in the stems of the orchid with Burnt Umber and highlight them with highlight green mix (Cadmium Yellow Medium + Payne's Gray + Titanium White). Base in the leaves with dark olive mix (Cadmium Yellow Medium + more Payne's Gray).

7 Shape the leaves with a mix of Cadmium Yellow Medium + Payne's Gray and highlight with highlight green mix. With a small piece of natural sea sponge, pick up Bronze Yellow + a tad of Titanium White and dab on dried moss around and between the leaves.

7

8

8 Begin blocking in the orchid petals with Unbleached Titanium using the top edge of the sponge in a medium pinch. Vary the sizes of the flowers and add a bud toward the top.

9 Add color to the centers of the orchid petals with Cadmium Yellow Medium. Use a tight pinch of the sponge and stroke outward on each petal. Leave plenty of white showing.

9

10 Shade the centers of the orchids with Dioxazine Purple. With a natural sea sponge, pick up a tiny bit of Cadmium Orange and dot in some stamens in the centers.

11 To lighten and brighten the orchids, highlight the outer edges of each petal with straight Titanium White using the top edge of the sponge in a medium pinch.

critique

Step back and take a critical look at your painting. You do not want to overwork a simple design such as this one, but you may find a few small areas that can be improved upon. Lighten the top of the vase in the center with very thin Titanium White to show a reflective highlight and to reinforce the roundness of the vase. Reapply some dried moss if needed to overlap this highlight. Check that the outside edges of the vase are sharp and distinct. If not, clean them up with the background color, not the vase color. The orchid petals in the foreground should be brighter white than the flowers further back; if they're not, add a little more Titanium White to the edges of the foreground petals.

1 HR 25 MIN

shady respite

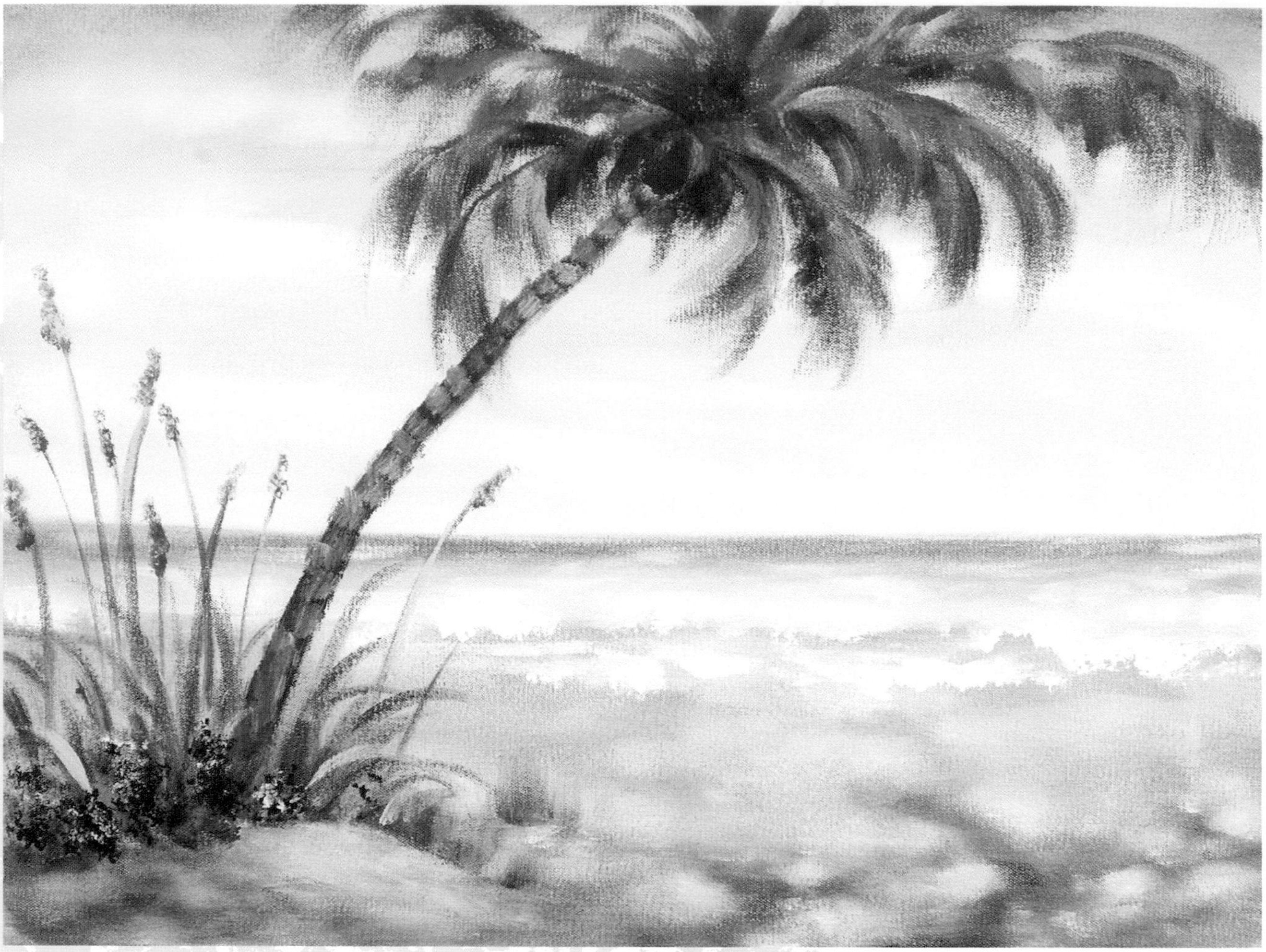

INSPIRED BY THE WHITE sand beaches of Florida, this painting is the stuff of dreams. Who hasn't fantasized about a deserted tropical island and having all the time in the world to relax and watch the waves roll in? Painting palm trees with sponges is the fastest, easiest way to do them. Refer to the step-by-step instructions on page 23, and check out pages 16-17 to see how to paint blue ocean water, breaking waves and a sandy beach.

1 Mist the canvas with clean water. Load the flat side of the sponge with Light Blue Permanent and wash in the sky area. Darken the top of the sky area and establish the horizon line of the distant blue water with thinned Ultramarine Blue.

1

2 Streak in cloud shapes in the sky using Titanium White on the top edge of your sponge. Keep your movements horizontal. With the very top edge of the sponge and Titanium White, use short streaking motions for the distant waves.

2

3

3 With Raw Sienna, establish the shape of the sandy beach. The darkest part of the sand is toward the bottom part of the picture, fading out toward the lightest part of the beach where the sand meets the water.

4 In the area where the sand meets the water, wash in some Bronze Yellow to indicate wet sand. With thinned Payne's Gray, establish the shaded or low parts of the sandy beach, and with Titanium White add the bright reflective parts of the beach where the sun hits the sand.

4

5

7

7 With the darkest foliage green mix (Payne's Gray + Raw Umber + Sap Green Permanent), stroke in the darkest palm fronds and the darkest grasses at the base of the tree. Pull the grass blades upward from the ground and bring them to a point.

8 Lighten the dark palm fronds with medium foliage green mix (add Cadmium Yellow Medium to the darkest foliage green mix used in step 7), then highlight with light foliage green mix (add Titanium White to the medium foliage green mix). Do the same with the grasses beneath the palm tree.

5 With Titanium White on the edge of your sponge, dab in the white water of the breaking waves rolling up onto the sandy beach. Allow the blues of the water to show through between and around the waves.

6 Draw the shape of the palm tree trunk with Burnt Umber on the edge of your sponge. Widen the top of the trunk where the palm fronds will attach. With Titanium White on the same sponge, dab in the growth segments on the trunk.

6

8

9 Add accents of color into the palm fronds with Raw Sienna and occasional spots of Cadmium Yellow Medium. Draw in the stems and the tops of the sea oats beneath the palm tree with Raw Sienna on the edge of your sponge. Highlight the tops of the palm fronds and the flowers of the sea oats with Unbleached Titanium.

10 Dab in the flowers in the lower foliage area with Magenta, Dioxazine Purple, and Cadmium Red Medium Hue all together on a small piece of your natural sea sponge. Highlight the flowers with small dots of Titanium White. Shade the sand beneath the foliage with Payne's Gray.

critique

Step back and take a critical look at your painting. In the center of the cluster of palm fronds, shade this area with dark palm shading mix (Phthalocyanine Blue + Payne's Gray) to give the tree more depth. Pull one or two more short fronds underneath the main cluster using this same shading mix. These darker fronds contrast with the lightest fronds at the top of the tree and strengthen the feeling of bright sunlight.

1 HR 10 MIN

valley of enlightenment

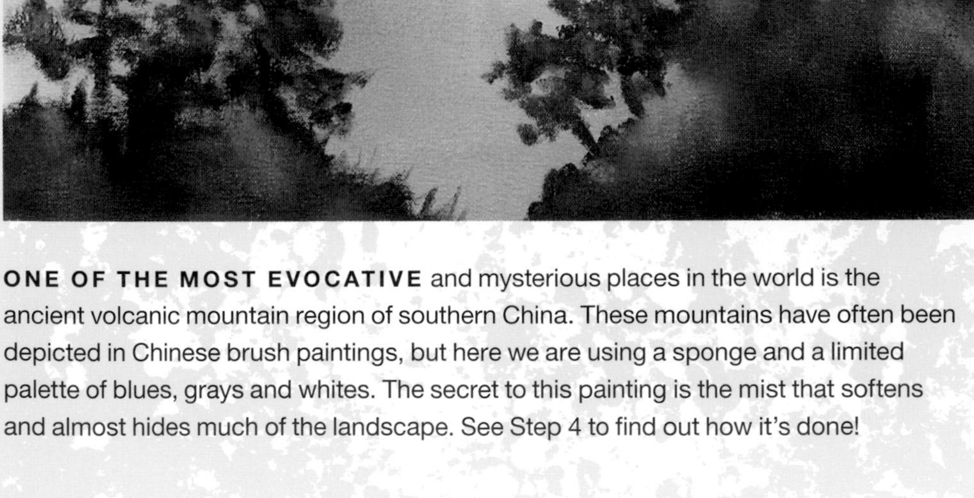

Dark blue-gray mix

Unbleached Titanium

Titanium White

Burnt Umber

Light Blue Violet

Warm gray mix

Burnt Sienna

Foliage green mix

ONE OF THE MOST EVOCATIVE and mysterious places in the world is the ancient volcanic mountain region of southern China. These mountains have often been depicted in Chinese brush paintings, but here we are using a sponge and a limited palette of blues, grays and whites. The secret to this painting is the mist that softens and almost hides much of the landscape. See Step 4 to find out how it's done!

1

2

3

1 Load the top edge of a clean sponge with the dark blue-gray mix (Phthalocyanine Blue + Payne's Gray + Burnt Umber) and draw the sides of the distant mountains, starting on the far left and overlapping as you go. Use the same color on the corner of the sponge to dab on the silhouetted trees on the mountaintops.

2 As you finish drawing each shape, flip to the clean side of the sponge and pull the color away from the edge, blending it and working it into the canvas to create the look of deep valleys.

3 Continue adding more mountain and tree shapes in the mid- and foreground using the same technique. To vary the colors, sometimes pick up more Phthalocyanine Blue on your sponge, and other times more Burnt Umber, and other times, more Payne's Gray. Let dry.

4

5

6

4 Soften the background with areas of Unbleached Titanium on the flat of your sponge, allowing it to overwash the tops of the mountains and the trees to set them back. Wash this same color up from the bottoms of the mountains to lose those bottom edges in the mists of the valleys. Blend and work this color into all areas.

5 With the flat of the sponge, wash Titanium White over the same areas you overwashed with Unbleached Titanium in Step 4. Use the edge of the sponge to sharpen some of the mountainside edges in the middleground. Leave the distant mountains alone. Also use the corner of the sponge and Titanium White to draw a few little waterfalls in the midground mountaintops.

6 Wash in some thinned Burnt Umber in some of the mountainsides to warm them up. Thin some Light Blue Violet and apply a very thin wash over the foreground mountainsides. With a warm gray mix (Light Blue Violet + Burnt Umber), soften the white sky areas.

7 Block in the closest mountains at the lower right and left corners with the same dark blue-gray mix you used for the mountain shapes in Step 1. Keep the edges and details of these closest mountains sharp and clean. Use the corner of your sponge to dab in the tree shapes. Load your sponge with Light Blue Violet and add slope shapes to the closest mountains. Add warmth to the slopes with Burnt Sienna here and there.

critique

Step back and take a critical look at your painting. Enrich the colors and finish the details in the closest trees with foliage green mix (Sap Green Permanent + Cadmium Yellow Medium). Brighten up the focal point in the center of the midground mountains with more Titanium White. Soften the sky color and set it back with more of the warm gray mix. Soften the slopes of the closest mountains by blending the Light Blue Violet color with vertical motions using the flat of the sponge.

1 HR 30 MIN

forever gold

IN THIS SPARE YET intriguing landscape, you will learn how to use some very simple tricks to give the illusion of vast distance in your paintings. This setting, where fields of grass have turned golden in the early autumn, provides interest in the near foreground (the lone tree) and the middle ground (the old fence and outbuildings). As the distance recedes, there are no more details and no more deep colors. The overall effect is of a vast and solitary place.

Light Blue Violet

Titanium White

Dioxazine Purple

Yellow Oxide

Raw Sienna

Burnt Umber

Light Yellow Oxide mix

Lightest grass highlight mix

Burnt Sienna

Dark foliage green mix

Medium foliage green mix

Light foliage green mix

Shadow green mix

Payne's Gray

Brilliant Purple

1 Mist your canvas with clean water. Wash in the sky with Light Blue Violet using the flat side of your sponge. Let the color fade to nothing in the center of the canvas.

2 Streak in cirrus clouds with the edge of your sponge and Titanium White. Blend out some of the clouds to be very thin and translucent and others a little whiter. To show cloud movement in the sky, make some of your strokes slightly diagonal, starting at the left and pulling upward toward the right.

1

2

3

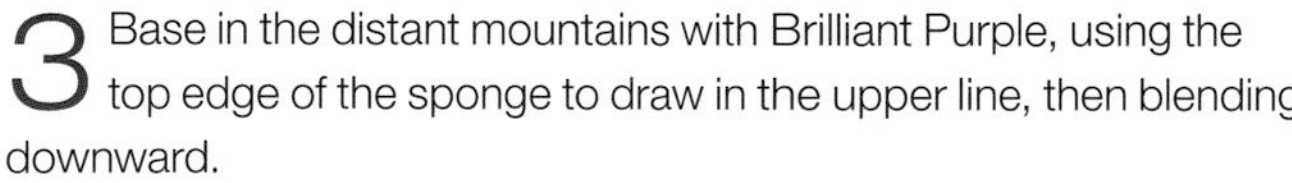

3 Base in the distant mountains with Brilliant Purple, using the top edge of the sponge to draw in the upper line, then blending downward.

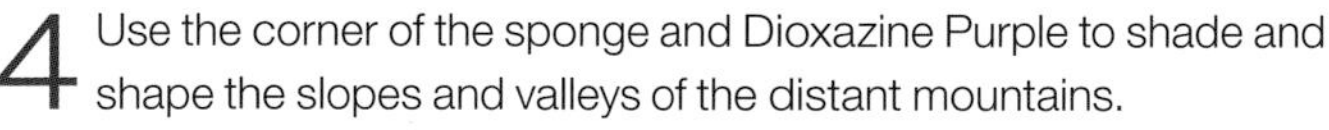

4 Use the corner of the sponge and Dioxazine Purple to shade and shape the slopes and valleys of the distant mountains.

4

5 Highlight the tops of the mountains with Titanium White. Blend out the white so it does not look like snow.

6 Lightly mist the bottom half of your canvas with clean water. Wash in the golden fields with Yellow Oxide using the flat side of your sponge. Work this color all the way to the base of the mountains. The color should be deepest at the very bottom of the canvas.

7 Using the light Yellow Oxide mix (Yellow Oxide + Titanium White), create the mid-ground field, bringing this lighter color down into the foreground in the center of the canvas.

8 Warm up the foreground fields on the right and the left sides with Raw Sienna.

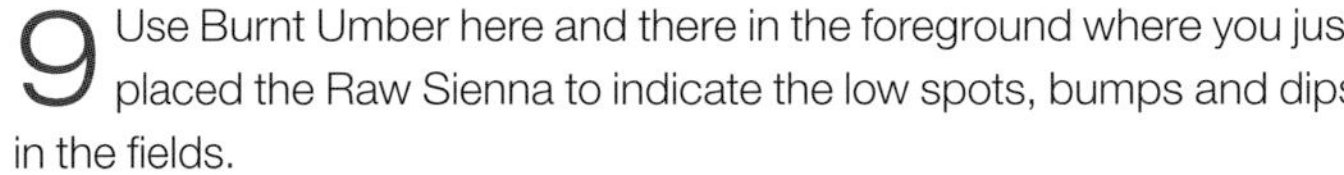

9 Use Burnt Umber here and there in the foreground where you just placed the Raw Sienna to indicate the low spots, bumps and dips in the fields.

10 Draw in the small outbuildings and the old wooden fence with Burnt Umber. Pinch the top edge and corner of the sponge tightly to create a point that you can draw with.

11 Using the same sponge with the Burnt Umber still on it, pick up Titanium White to shape and highlight the outbuildings. Leave some Burnt Umber showing to indicate shadows under the roof lines and along the bottoms of the buildings where they sit on the ground.

12 Detail the fence with Titanium White on the corner of the sponge to add highlights on some of the posts and a few of the rails.

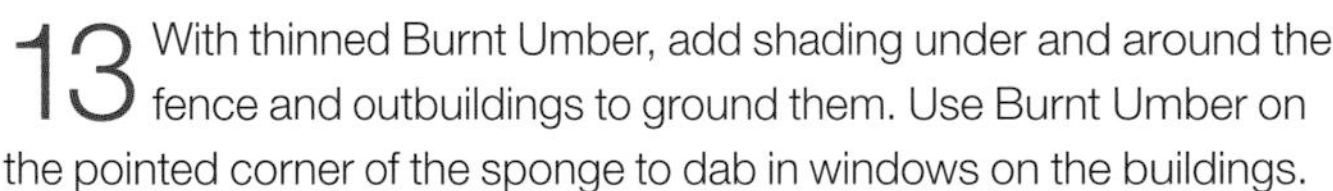

13 With thinned Burnt Umber, add shading under and around the fence and outbuildings to ground them. Use Burnt Umber on the pointed corner of the sponge to dab in windows on the buildings.

14 Indicate areas of dried grasses along the bottom of the fence, around the outbuildings and in the center foreground field using the lightest grass highlight mix (the light Yellow Oxide mix you used in Step 7 + more Titanium White).

15 Use Burnt Umber to place the trunk and draw the branches of the foreground tree. Highlight the top edges of the branches with Burnt Sienna.

16 Dab in the darkest leaves on the tree using the dark foliage green mix (Sap Green Permanent + Raw Umber). Since this is just the first layer of leaves, don't fill in too much. Allow the trunk, branches and background to show through the foliage.

17 Add the next layer of lighter foliage by dabbing on medium foliage green mix (dark foliage green mix + Cadmium Yellow Medium) on the tops and outside areas of leaves. Don't cover up the first, darkest layer completely—this is what gives shading and depth to the tree foliage.

18 Finally, add highlights here and there using light foliage green mix (medium foliage green mix + Titanium White). Remember to make the colors sparser as they get lighter. You should still be able to see some of the trunk, branches and background through the foliage.

19 Create the cast shadow on the ground beneath the tree with Payne's Gray. Make the shadow earthier in color by adding spots of shadow green mix (dark foliage green mix + Burnt Umber). Soften and blend out the shadows so there are no hard edges.

critique

Step back and take a critical look at your painting. Strengthen the white of a few of the clouds, and streak a little more Titanium White in the mountains to soften the edges and make them recede even further into the distance. This gives the illusion of vast space between the foreground and the mountains, where the fields of golden grass seem to go on forever. Use this trick in your paintings any time you want to make your background seem even more distant: soften the edges, remove the details and lighten the colors.

2 HRS

enticing palms

Raw Sienna

Unbleached Titanium

Light Blue Violet

Ultramarine Blue (Green Shade)

Light Blue Permanent

Ocean water green mix

Greenish yellow mix

Burnt Umber

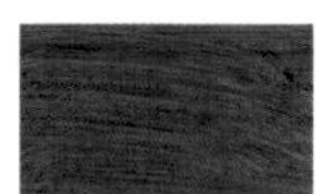
Dark palm green mix

Medium palm green mix

Highlight palm green mix

Payne's Gray

Dark foliage green mix

Medium foliage green mix

Light foliage green mix

Titanium White

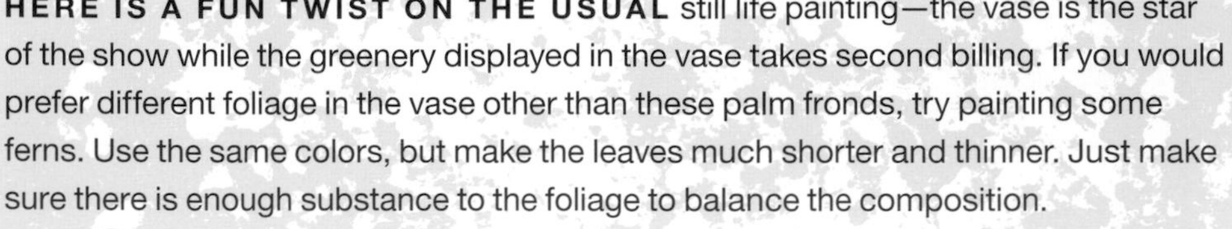

HERE IS A FUN TWIST ON THE USUAL still life painting—the vase is the star of the show while the greenery displayed in the vase takes second billing. If you would prefer different foliage in the vase other than these palm fronds, try painting some ferns. Use the same colors, but make the leaves much shorter and thinner. Just make sure there is enough substance to the foliage to balance the composition.

1

2

1 Lightly mist the canvas with clean water and wash in the background with Raw Sienna. Draw in the line of the tabletop with Unbleached Titanium using the tightly pinched edge of the sponge, then fill in with the flat of the sponge and a scrubbing motion.

2 Draw in the shape of the vase using the pinched edge of your sponge and Light Blue Violet. Fill in the middle with a scrubbing motion. Check the shape of the vase to make sure the sides are evenly curved and symmetrical.

3

3 Continuing with the vase, establish the colors of the sky, the horizon, the distant ocean water color, and the beach. Start at the top with Ultramarine Blue (Green Shade) for the top of the sky, Light Blue Permanent for the lower sky, ocean water green mix (Phthalocyanine Green + Cadmium Yellow Medium) for the distant ocean water, and Unbleached Titanium for the beach sand.

4

4 Sponge soft clouds into the sky with Titanium White, then add breaking waves on the beach. Streak in a little greenish yellow mix (ocean water green mix + more Cadmium Yellow Medium) into the water area to create distant waves.

5 Mottle Raw Sienna in the table area and on the beach under the breaking waves for shading. Draw in the palm tree trunk with Burnt Umber and begin the first layer of palm fronds with the same color.

6 Highlight the tree trunk with Unbleached Titanium. Add dark palm green mix (Phthalocyanine Green + Raw Umber) to the palm fronds and paint some grasses at the bottom of the tree trunk. Enrich the color of the palm fronds with medium palm green mix (dark palm green mix + Cadmium Yellow Medium) and lighten the grasses. Highlight the sunlit tops of the palm fronds with highlight palm green mix (medium palm green mix + Titanium White).

7 Shade the bottom and lower side edges of the vase with Payne's Gray and add curved reflective highlights on both sides with Titanium White. Mottle in some Payne's Gray cast shadows on the table underneath the vase.

8 Begin the large palm fronds displayed in the vase with stems of dark foliage green mix (Sap Green Permanent + Raw Umber + a little Payne's Gray) drawn in with the tightly pinched edge of the sponge. Stroke individual leaves on each stem starting at the base and pulling outward toward the tip, lifting off to form a point.

9

10

9 Enrich the green of most of the leaves with medium foliage green mix (dark foliage green mix + Cadmium Yellow Medium). Leave some of the background fronds dark for contrast and depth.

10 Highlight some of the leaves with light foliage green mix (medium foliage green mix + Titanium White). Remember, the lighter the foliage color, the sparser the application should be. You still want to see the dark and medium green leaves you painted in steps 8 and 9.

critique

Step back and take a critical look at your painting. The bottom of the vase needs more Payne's Gray shading to separate it from the table. The background above the table edge also needs more Raw Sienna shading to separate the table from the background. After the shading is applied, re-establish the sharp line of the tabletop using the tightly pinched edge of the sponge and Unbleached Titanium.

2 HRS 35 MIN

love awaits

Alizarin Crimson

Cadmium Red Medium

Cadmium Orange

Darkest red mix

Burnt Sienna

Purple-blue mix

Medium purple mix

Titanium White

Ultramarine Blue (Green Shade)

Cadmium Yellow Medium

Payne's Gray

Vivid Lime Green

Red-gray mix

Pink mix

Darkest leaf green mix

Medium leaf green mix

Highlight green mix

Dark shading mix

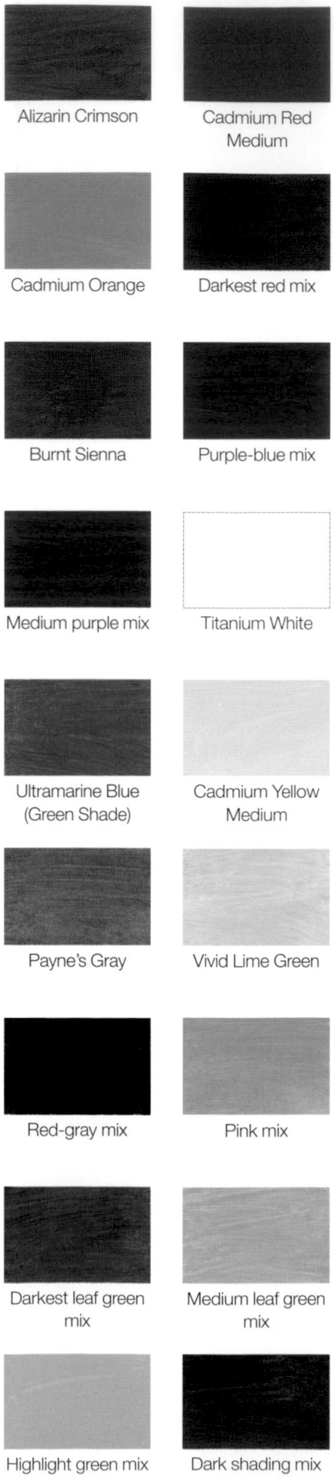

THE PRIMARY COLORS—RED, GREEN, BLUE—used in this floral still life make this painting a very strong statement, yet it's the bright white tulips you notice first. That's because the layered reds of the background and the tabletop contrast so vividly with the white flowers and not so much with the red tulips and azaleas. Even the cobalt blue glass vase steps back, as it should, letting the white tulips light up the reflections on the vase and the table.

1 Using Alizarin Crimson on the flat side of the sponge, wash in the first background color over the entire canvas and let dry.

2 Deepen the intensity of the red in most areas with a wash of Cadmium Red Medium.

3 While that's still wet, warm up some areas of the background with Cadmium Orange, leaving the first two colors showing as well.

4 Still working wet in wet, darken the right and left sides of the background and indicate the horizontal table area with the darkest red mix (Alizarin Crimson + Payne's Gray). Where this color is darkest, just apply a heavier application and don't blend out as much.

5

6

5 Tone down some of the intensity of the Cadmium Orange in some areas with Burnt Sienna, blending well. Leave a few spots where the orange is still bright.

6 Using the top edge of your sponge, draw in the shape of the blue vase and fill it in using the purple-blue mix (Ultramarine Blue + Dioxazine Purple). Apply medium purple mix (purple-blue mix + Brilliant Purple) in the center areas of the vase to bring them forward and to give roundness to the vase's shape. Use the edge and corner of your sponge and Titanium White to add reflective highlights to the glass vase and to shape the details. With straight Ultramarine Blue, strengthen the blue hue of the vase to emphasize that it is cobalt blue glass.

7

7 Begin the flowers by blocking in the basic shapes of the white tulips and white azaleas with Titanium White. Use a smooth drawing motion for the tulips, and a wiggly motion for the ruffled petals of the azaleas.

8

8 Shade just inside the tops of the tulips with Cadmium Yellow Medium, leaving a white edge showing on the back petals. Shade the bases of the tulips and the centers of the azaleas with Vivid Lime Green.

9

10

9 With thinned Payne's Gray, shade the lowest parts of the tulips where the light is not hitting them. Also shade some of the petals of the azaleas.

10 Go back in with Titanium White and brighten the whites of the white flowers, leaving little lines of the Payne's Gray showing to indicate petal separations on the tulips. Also, brighten the middles and outer edges of the open petals of the azaleas, leaving the Payne's Gray at the base of the petals to shade them and in the centers to indicate depth.

11

12

11 With the red-gray mix (darkest red mix + more Payne's Gray), block in all the red, pink and orange tulips and the red azaleas. This is a very dark color that will serve as the darkest shading color on the flowers.

12 With Cadmium Red Medium, use the edge and corner of your sponge to indicate the petals on the tulips, leaving lines of the red-gray undercoat showing through for petal separation. Use a zigzag motion of the sponge edge to indicate the ruffled petals of the azaleas. Maintain the red-gray undercoat for the tops of the tulips and the centers of the red azaleas.

13

13 Enrich the color of the red tulips and azaleas with Cadmium Orange.

14 With pink mix (Alizarin Crimson + Titanium White), highlight the red tulips. Add the stamens in the centers of the azaleas by dotting on Cadmium Yellow Medium, then Titanium White with the tip of your finger.

15 With darkest leaf green mix (Sap Green Permanent + Payne's Gray), draw in the tulip stems starting at the base of each tulip and drawing toward the vase. Do not cross over in front of any of the other tulips. Attach the stems to the bases of the tulips. Stroke a few very dark green leaves using the corner of your sponge.

14

15

16 Warm up the dark green leaves and add a few new-growth leaves here and there with medium leaf green mix (Cadmium Yellow Medium + Payne's Gray).

17 Highlight the leaves in a few areas with highlight green mix (Sap Green Permanent + Titanium White). With dark shading mix (Burnt Umber + Payne's Gray), indicate dark cast shadows on the table under and behind the blue vase.

critique

Step back and check your painting. If the bouquet looks too stiff and contained, open it up and let it spread out by adding more long, slender leaves, using the same colors as you did for the leaves in steps 15-17. Add a few reflective highlights to the table in front of the vase. If there are any areas where the bright background colors overwhelm the flowers, the easiest way to fix this is to knock them back with a few more well-placed leaves. Or just tone them down with a little Burnt Sienna.

1 HR 45 MIN

bonsai fantasy

THE ART OF BONSAI is thousands of years old and may take a lifetime to master, but you can re-create this art-form in about two hours using sponges and paint. Here is an interpretation of a bonsai cherry tree that is rather unusual in design. The light-colored background is applied after the cherry blossoms and leaves are painted, softening their edges and giving the painting a back-lit quality.

1 Mist the canvas with clean water. Wash in the background with Raw Umber on the flat side of the sponge and let dry. Block in the vase shape with the vase undercoat green mix (Raw Umber + Sap Green Permanent). Use a tight pinch of the sponge to draw the outside edges, then fill in with the flat of the sponge.

2 Use Unbleached Titanium to draw the front rim of the vase and to apply reflective highlights that indicate the shape and roundness of the vase. Don't forget to highlight the sides of the base too.

3 Enrich the subtle green color of the vase with areas of the medium green mix (Sap Green Permanent + a little Raw Umber). Shade the area where the vase narrows at the base with Burnt Umber. Draw the main trunk of the bonsai tree with tree trunk brown mix (Burnt Umber + Mars Black), using the top edge of the sponge to draw rough, bumpy bark.

4 Add curving, gnarled-looking branches coming off the main trunk, then even smaller curving branches coming off them. Highlight a few areas on the trunk and branches with Raw Sienna.

5

7

5 Begin placing in the leaves using the corner of your sponge with dark leaf green mix (Sap Green Permanent + Yellow Oxide) for the darkest leaves, and yellow-green mix (dark leaf green mix + Cadmium Yellow Medium) for the lighter leaves.

6 Again, using the corner of your sponge, draw in four- and five-petal cherry blossoms starting with the darkest color, Alizarin Crimson.

6

8

7 Working wet into wet, come back in with pink mix (Alizarin Crimson + Titanium White) and overpaint the Alizarin Crimson on most of the petals. Do the same with the bright violet mix (Prism Violet + Titanium White) to make a bright lavender, only this time overpaint just a few of the petals. Dot in the blossom centers with straight Prism Violet.

8 With Unbleached Titanium, mottle the background above and around the bonsai tree, using the edge of the tightly pinched sponge to work the color in among the flowers and leaves.

9 Blend the Unbleached Titanium out towards the bottom of the canvas, letting the original Raw Umber wash remain along the bottom. Let dry.

10 Load a clean sponge with Titanium White and mottle over the background again, letting subtle areas of the Unbleached Titanium mottling show through here and there. Again, tightly pinch the edge of your sponge to work the white in the openings among the petals and leaves. Wash some thinned Raw Sienna up from the bottom to warm up the lower background.

critique

Step back and take a critical look at your painting. The bonsai needs more green leaves worked in among the petals with the dark leaf green mix and the yellow-green mix used in step 5. Add some very thin twigs coming off the outsides of the bonsai to soften and air out the edges, using thinned tree trunk brown mix from steps 3 and 4. Finally, if the back inside rim of the vase needs to be sharpened, use the vase undercoat green mix from step 1 on the very top edge of the sponge to re-establish the line of the rim.

2 HRS 15 MIN

tropic pastime

A SKY FILLED WITH brilliant sunset colors reflects off the shallow water of a tropical beach as gentle waves roll ashore—how can you resist such a peaceful setting? Sunset skies come in many colors; see page 15 for another example. Make sure that whatever sunset colors you choose, they're reflected unchanged in the water beneath. Once the reflected colors are placed in the water, then you can go back in with Titanium White and stroke in the waves and whitecaps.

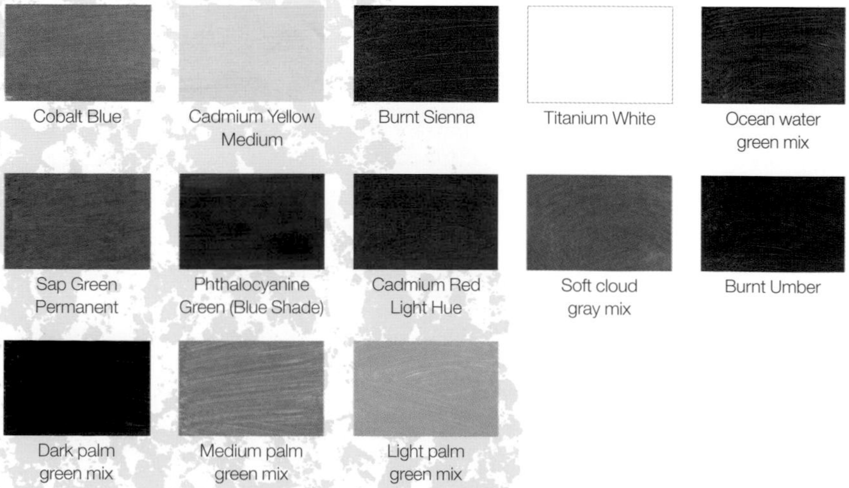

Cobalt Blue

Cadmium Yellow Medium

Burnt Sienna

Titanium White

Ocean water green mix

Sap Green Permanent

Phthalocyanine Green (Blue Shade)

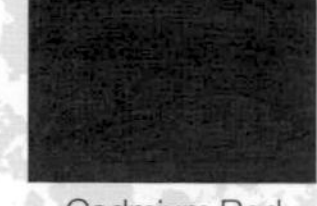

Cadmium Red Light Hue

Soft cloud gray mix

Burnt Umber

Dark palm green mix

Medium palm green mix

Light palm green mix

1

1 Mist the blank canvas with water to start. Wash in the blue sky along the upper quarter of the canvas with Cobalt Blue on the flat side of the sponge. The sky should be darker at the top of the canvas, fading out to very light blue as shown.

2 With Cadmium Yellow Medium on the flat side of the sponge, wash in the sunset colors of the sky along the middle third of the canvas, then add some Burnt Sienna in horizontal streaks here and there and blend out thoroughly to soften all edges.

2

3

3 Place in the clouds with Titanium White, keeping the upper clouds puffy and rounded, but streaking and flattening the lowest clouds near the horizon.

4 Load the top edge of the flat side of the sponge with ocean water green mix (Sap Green Permanent + Burnt Sienna) and use the edge of your sponge to draw a straight horizon line all the way across the lower third of your canvas. Blend downward to fill in, letting the green color fade away at the bottom of the canvas.

4

5

7

7 Add a rich reddish tone to the sunset colors with smaller streaks of Burnt Sienna, then add even smaller streaks of Cadmium Red Light Hue.

8 Using the edge of your sponge, apply short horizontal strokes of Titanium White starting in the lower sky for the lowest clouds and continuing down into the water for the distant waves. While the paint is wet, blend out these strokes with horizontal motions of your sponge.

5 With straight Sap Green Permanent on your sponge, streak in some darker green areas in the water. Then come back in with Phthalocyanine Green (Blue Shade) and add a bluish-green color to some areas. Leave the center area of the water alone—this is where the yellow reflection of the setting sun will go.

6 To get the light of the setting sun in the center of the painting, start with short horizontal streaks of Cadmium Yellow Medium in the sky and the water near the horizon line.

6

8

9 With Titanium White on the top edge of your sponge, paint the foamy breaking waves in the foreground (see page 16 for step-by-step instructions on painting breaking waves).

10 Shade the foreground beach at the very bottom of the painting with Burnt Sienna, keeping the color darkest just under the wave caps, and blending out towards the bottom.

11 Shade the undersides of some of the mid-sky clouds with soft cloud gray mix (Burnt Umber + Light Blue Violet). Use the same mix to shape the puffy clouds higher in the sky and at the top of the painting.

12 Draw in the palm tree trunks with Burnt Umber on the edge of your sponge. Start at the top of the trunk and draw your sponge downward. Widen the tops where the palm fronds attach to the trunks. Enrich the trunk color with Burnt Sienna, then use Titanium White to highlight the sunlit sides.

13 With dark palm green mix (Hooker's Green Hue Permanent + Burnt Umber + Mars Black) on the top edge of your sponge, draw in the darkest palm fronds first. Begin each frond at the trunk, arch outward to make the curve of the frond, then lightly drag the green color downward to create the leaves on each frond.

14 Repeat step 13 for the other two palm trees, but vary the size and shapes of the fronds to match the size of the trunks. Notice that the smaller tree on the far right edge of the painting has fewer and smaller fronds because the trunk is thinner than the other two.

13

14

15

16

15 Warm up the tops of the palm fronds where the sunset colors hit them with shorter curving streaks of medium palm green mix (Cadmium Yellow Medium + Mars Black).

16 Repeat step 15 for the other two palm trees, but use less of the medium palm green mix to provide color contrast with the larger tree.

17 Highlight the palm fronds on all three trees with light palm green mix (medium palm green mix + Titanium White). Use this highlight color sparingly, allowing the darker green and the medium green colors to show through for depth and contrast.

18 Come back in and enrich the palms with accents of Burnt Sienna, and darken and shade the centers with more of the dark palm green mix from step 13. Re-darken any fronds that may have gotten too light or washed out.

critique

Step back and take a critical look at your painting to see what it needs. Here, the setting sun is more distinctly indicated by adding streaks of soft cloud gray mix on either side, then brightening the center where the sun is with a little more Cadmium Yellow Medium. A few final whitecaps are added in the far distance where the sun lights the water along the horizon line.

2 HRS 20 MIN

early rising

AN EARLY MORNING SUNRISE warms the sky with yellow and burnt sienna colors that are reflected in the gently flowing water of a shallow river. This painting has a very calm and quiet feel because most of the colors are in the green, yellow and russet families. For interest, a few spots of brightly colored flowers are added but they don't spoil the overall effect of a peaceful and timeless landscape.

Light Blue Violet — Yellow Oxide — Burnt Sienna — Titanium White — Dark gray-blue mix

Dark green mix — Yellow-green mix — Light yellow-green mix — Bronze Yellow — Light bronze yellow mix

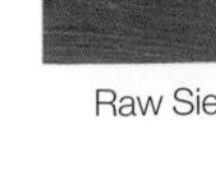

Brilliant Purple — Lightest grass green mix — Sap Green Permanent — Bright yellow-green mix — Raw Sienna

Burnt Umber — Darkest foliage green mix — Dioxazine Purple — Cadmium Red Medium Hue — Lightest greenish yellow mix

1

1 Mist the canvas lightly with clean water. Wash in the sky using Light Blue Violet along the top third of the canvas. Create the sunrise glow with a wash of Yellow Oxide in the middle third. Place a strip of Burnt Sienna between the Light Blue Violet and Yellow Oxide and blend well using the flat side of the sponge.

2

2 Load the top edge of the flat side of the sponge with Titanium White. Create fluffy cumulus clouds working wet into wet. Mist the canvas with clean water if your paint starts to dry out. This will help blend your colors and keep the edges of the clouds very soft and translucent. Brighten some of the cloud tops with a little more Titanium White. Don't overwork the clouds—you still want to see the sunrise colors of the sky through them.

3 Establish the foreground water using dark gray-blue mix (Ultramarine Blue + Burnt Umber) on the flat side of the sponge. Paint the entire lower third of the canvas and work up into the Yellow Oxide of the sky. The color should be darker at the bottom of the canvas. Map out the trees along the horizon and the small islands in the lower left and right with a dark green mix (Sap Green Permanent + Payne's Gray + Cadmium Yellow Medium).

4 Add more Cadmium Yellow Medium to the dark green mix to make a yellow-green mix. Lighten the distant tree line. Highlight the trees with small areas of light yellow-green mix (yellow-green mix + Titanium White). Create the muddy riverbank under the distant tree line with Bronze Yellow.

5 Highlight some areas of the riverbank under the distant trees using a light Bronze Yellow mix (Bronze Yellow + Titanium White). Accent with Burnt Sienna in a few places to shade and add depth to the muddy riverbank. The purple flowers under the trees along the banks are dabbed on with Briliant Purple. Keep these soft and indistinct.

6 Using your original sky colors of Light Blue Violet, Yellow Oxide and Burnt Sienna from steps 1 and 2, streak reflections of the sky colors into the foreground water. With the dark gray-blue mix used in step 3, shade and darken the shoreline to separate the riverbank from the water.

7 Add grasses along the left and right islands using the lightest grass green mix (Sap Green Permanent + Titanium White) and short vertical strokes made with the top edge of the sponge. Stroke the grass in from bottom to top. Let dry.

8 Place Sap Green Permanent here and there in the grassy areas to deepen the grass color and shade the lower parts. Then stroke the bright yellow-green mix in a few random places throughout the upper areas of the grass to highlight with the warm sunrise colors of the sky. Dab Raw Sienna along the edges of the islands to indicate the muddy banks where they meet the water.

9 Draw in the main tree trunks and the short branches coming off of them with Burnt Umber using a tight pinch of the sponge. Stroke in a few areas of Burnt Sienna over the Burnt Umber to enrich the color, then highlight here and there with Titanium White.

10 Dab in foliage along the branches and tree trunks starting with a layer of darkest foliage green mix (Sap Green Permanent + Payne's Gray). The next layer of foliage is dabbed in with the dark green mix used in step 3. Add some Titanium White to this dark green mix and sponge on the highlight foliage in a few areas. Finally, warm up the foliage with a few sparks of the light greenish-yellow mix. Re-establish the darkest shaded areas of the trees with the darkest foliage green mix. Be careful not to overdo the foliage—let the sky colors show through and don't cover the tree trunks and branches entirely.

11 With a small piece of natural sea sponge, stipple in the darkest flowers on the island at the left side of the canvas and under the trees at the right side with Dioxazine Purple and Brilliant Purple. With a clean sponge, stipple on bright yellow flowers with Cadmium Yellow Medium. Add a little Titanium White to the bright yellow for even lighter flowers. Finish with a few bright red flowers in Cadmium Red Medium Hue. Use the flower colors in different proportions for the two areas so they do not look like exact copies of each other. Vary the heights of the flowers too.

critique

Step back and take a critical look at your painting. Deepen the shading along the edges of the two islands where they meet the water with the dark gray-blue mix used in step 3. This creates cast shadows in the water and gives the illusion that the islands are grounded in the water. Thin Titanium White to highlight the lightest areas of the grasses. Doing so helps create balance with the white areas of the sky and gives the feeling that the tops of the grasses are touched by the light of dawn.

2 HRS 50 MIN

caribbean view

ONE OF THE MOST memorable things about a trip to the Caribbean islands is the color of the water. No one can forget the light greenish-aqua of the shallows near the beaches, the azure of the sky reflected in the straits, and the jewel-like cobalt blue of the deepest water. In this demo you will see how to re-create these colors, and how to tie a painting together using pink-tinged clouds and the pinks of a flowering tree.

1

1 Mist the canvas with clean water. Wash in the sky area with Light Blue Violet using the flat of the sponge. Streak in some clouds with Titanium White, then warm them up with light cloud pink mix (Alizarin Crimson + Raw Sienna). Shape the shadowed areas along the flatter bottoms of the clouds with thinned Payne's Gray.

2 Wash in the blue-green color of the water with thinned Bright Aqua Green, taking it all the way up to the horizon line. Use the edge of your sponge to draw in the straight line where the water meets the sky.

2

3

3 Wash over the blue-green water in a few places with Cobalt Blue Hue to indicate areas of deeper water. Use horizontal motions of your sponge and blend out well. Redraw the horizon line with this darker blue.

4 Block in the land masses, islands and the distant mountains with Burnt Umber, using the edge of the sponge to draw the shapes, then filling in with the flat of the sponge.

4

5

6

5 With the dark green mix (Sap Green Permanent + Burnt Umber), paint the green areas of the distant landmasses and closer islands, maintaining the Burnt Umber edges. Shape the green areas with medium green mix (dark green mix + Cadmium Yellow Medium), then with light green mix (medium green mix + Titanium White) to give the look of a variety of vegetation and the different angles of the slopes.

6 Establish the shorelines around the land masses with a base of Burnt Umber, then shape with Raw Sienna and highlight with Unbleached Titanium.

7 Deepen the blue water color with more washes of Cobalt Blue Hue in the distant water and Bright Aqua Green in the foreground water. With Titanium White, place some gentle waves coming in around the land masses and foreground island.

7

8 Begin the white sand beach area in the lower left of the canvas with a wash of Unbleached Titanium, letting it fade out as it meets the shallow water.

8

9 Shade and shape the beach with Burnt Sienna for the low places and dips in the sand. Highlight the high places on the beach area and dab on the foaming waves with Titanium White.

10 Place in the branches of the foreground flowering tree with Burnt Umber, using the edge of the sponge to draw the shapes. Mix Quinacridone Magenta and Dioxazine Purple to create a dark pink mix and place the darkest blossoms on the branches. Add another layer of blossoms with medium pink mix (dark pink mix + more Quinacridone Magenta) and highlight with a light pink mix (medium pink mix + Titanium White).

critique

Step back and check your painting. Re-establish the beach area with Unbleached Titanium and add another set of white foamy waves rolling in. Set the far distant mountains into the background with a haze of the original sky color (Light Blue Violet) and extend this blue to the left and right to darken this area of the sky. If needed, go back in with Titanium White and redefine the clouds.

1 HR 35 MIN

autumn splendor

Light Blue Violet

Titanium White

Darkest green mix

Burnt Umber

Medium green mix

Light green mix

Green-yellow mix

Raw Sienna

Brilliant Purple

Highlight grass mix

Tree trunk brown mix

Unbleached Titanium

Yellow Oxide

Highlight foliage mix

Cadmium Yellow Medium

Burnt Sienna

Medium grass green

THIS IS A SIMPLE STUDY OF HOW FALL FOLIAGE colors can be used to enrich the greens and browns of a landscape. The bright fall colors are used in the tree, as you would expect, but also in the field of grass, in the bushes at left, and underneath the yellow tree. Also in this demo you will learn a different way of painting blue skies and white clouds...by taking away paint rather than adding it. See step 1.

1

1 Mist the canvas with clean water. Wash in the sky area over the top three-fourths of the canvas with Light Blue Violet. While the blue sky color is still wet, rather than painting in the clouds with white paint, use a clean sponge to wipe out the blue color in the places where you want the puffy white clouds to be. Rinse the blue out of your sponge in a bucket of clean water every so often.

2

2 Now come back in with Titanium White on your clean sponge and strengthen the top edges of some of the clouds and brighten the whites in a few areas. Don't overdo this step—you will be refining the sky colors later after the trees are painted.

3 Block in the green tree shapes in the background as well as the foreground field with the darkest green mix (Sap Green Permanent + Raw Umber). Keep this first layer of tree foliage pretty airy—you will be adding more layers in the next few steps. The green of the foreground field can be solid; the grasses and highlights will be added later.

4 Place in the trunks intermittently among the foliage of the background trees with Burnt Umber. Warm up the foliage color of the background trees with medium green mix (darkest green mix + Cadmium Yellow Medium), then highlight with light green mix (dark green mix + Titanium White) along the tops where the sunlight hits the leaves.

5 With green-yellow mix (Sap Green Permanent + Yellow Oxide), apply areas of dried grasses in the foreground. Use the flat of the sponge to block in the general area of dried grasses, then use the top edge of the sponge to flick blades of grass upward, picking up some highlight grass mix (Yellow Oxide + Titanium White) on the sponge sometimes to indicate lighter, drier grass here and there.

5

6 Place in the bushes at the left with a base color of Raw Sienna. Dab on a bit of Unbleached Titanium for lighter leaves. Enrich the fall colors of the bushes with Burnt Sienna, and add a small dash of Brilliant Purple to shade underneath the bushes and to indicate cast shadows.

6

7 Draw in the trunk and branches of the bright yellow foreground tree with tree trunk brown mix (Raw Umber + a little Mars Black), and highlight the trunk with Unbleached Titanium. Start the first layer of fall foliage with Yellow Oxide, dabbing it on with a small piece of natural sea sponge.

7

8 Add the next layer of foliage with highlight foliage mix (Yellow Oxide + lots of Titanium White) dabbed on with the sea sponge. Don't cover the yellow foliage from step 7, allow it to show through. Although this may look like the tree is too white, don't worry. The shading in the next step will take care of that. Use the same highlight foliage mix on a regular sponge to add some very light grasses here and there in the field.

8

9 Brighten the fall color in the foreground tree with Cadmium Yellow Medium on a sea sponge, then shade and shape the tree with Burnt Sienna. Work on filling out the tree, extending the branches, giving it a good shape, and bringing it forward with your colors.

critique

Step back and take a good look at your painting. Dot in some fallen leaves under the foreground tree with Cadmium Yellow Medium and Burnt Sienna. Strengthen the shadows under the bush at the left with more of the darkest green mix and a bit of Brilliant Purple. Tone down the highlights of the bushes if needed with more Burnt Sienna. If the foliage of the background trees is too dense and takes too much attention away from the focal point of the yellow tree, dab in some Titanium White here and there to make "holes" in the foliage for the sky to show through and to make the trees a little more airy and open. Reestablish some of the cloud edges around the trees with Titanium White, and pull some lighter grasses underneath the yellow tree with medium grass green mix (light green mix from step 4 + more Sap Green Permanent).

1 HR 50 MIN

nanxi river

IN THIS PAINTING inspired by ancient Chinese landscapes, you will discover how satisfying it is to create something unexpected such as skies and water that have no blue in them whatsoever. Here, the blues and purples are in the mountains and provide complementary colors to the sky and river. Also, here are two different views of bamboo—closeup on the left, and in groves in the middleground of the river. There are many different textures here, and they're all painted with a sponge.

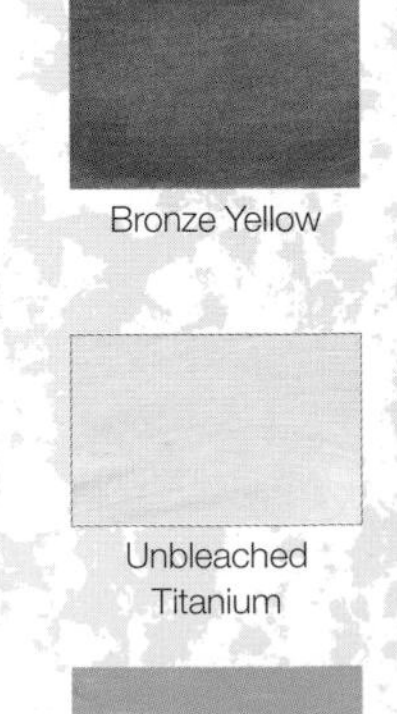

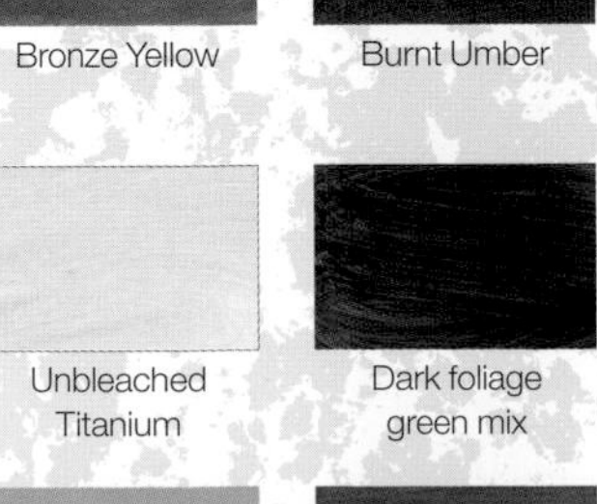

Bronze Yellow

Burnt Umber

Light Blue Violet

Brilliant Purple

Raw Sienna

Unbleached Titanium

Dark foliage green mix

Medium foliage green mix

Burnt Sienna

Light yellow mix

Light foliage green mix

Raw Umber

Yellow Oxide

Titanium White

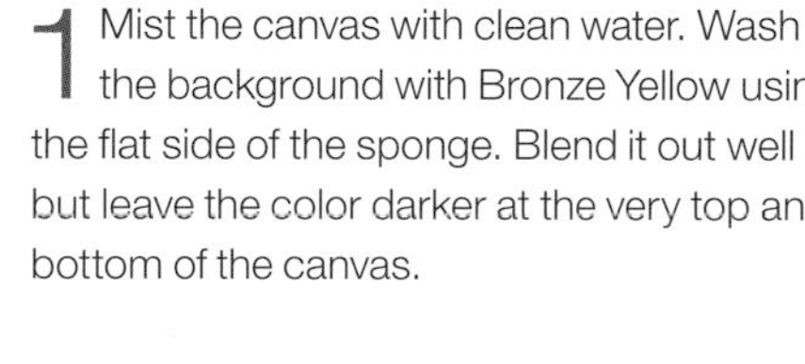

1 Mist the canvas with clean water. Wash in the background with Bronze Yellow using the flat side of the sponge. Blend it out well but leave the color darker at the very top and bottom of the canvas.

2 Block in the background mountains with Burnt Umber. Use the pinched edge of your sponge to draw the upper edges, then scrub with the flat of the sponge to fill in the color. Let it fade out at the bottom.

3 Wash some Light Blue Violet horizontally all along the bottom of the mountains, then blend the color upward to soften the steep slopes of the mountains with a misty look.

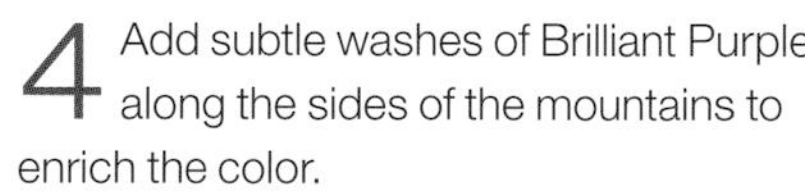

4 Add subtle washes of Brilliant Purple along the sides of the mountains to enrich the color.

5 Darken the sky with a mottled wash of Raw Sienna. Load the top edge of the sponge with Unbleached Titanium and scrub in some misty transparent clouds that overhang the tops of the mountains and drift along the mountain valleys.

6 With dark foliage green mix (Sap Green Permanent + Payne's Gray + Raw Umber), place in the bamboo groves on the far side of the river, dotting the tops of the trees to suggest leaves. While the green is wet, lightly pull the corner of your sponge downward to create the streaks of reflections in the river water.

7 With medium foliage green mix (dark foliage green mix + Cadmium Yellow Medium), draw in vertical lines to suggest the canes of the bamboo trees. Highlight the tops of the trees here and there with the same color.

8

8 Deepen the color of the foreground river with a little Burnt Sienna. Add areas of the dark foliage green mix into the river to imply moving reflections of the green bamboo groves.

9 Streak in short horizontal lines of light reflections in the river water with light yellow mix (Titanium White + Yellow Oxide) to show moving water. Paint these reflections right over the reflections of the green bamboo groves.

9

10 Place in the canes of the foreground bamboo with the dark foliage green mix, then pull some tiny leaves off the canes using the tightly pinched edge of your sponge and the corner.

11 Highlight and indicate the growth segments of the canes with a start-stop motion of the sponge, using light foliage green mix (dark foliage green mix + Cadmium Yellow Medium + Titanium White).

12 Within the green canes of the foreground bamboo, indicate a few older, drier canes with Raw Sienna and Titanium White double-loaded on the edge of your sponge. Let these colors be separate, don't mix, and as you draw the canes, the two colors will show.

critique

Step back and check your painting. Block in the landmass that the distant bamboo groves sit on with Raw Sienna and strengthen the shoreline with the light yellow mix. Adjust the line of the bamboo grove on the right to bring it forward. Darken the foreground river in the lower right corner with Raw Umber to indicate dips and waves in the river. Intensify the color of the river with areas of Yellow Oxide. Come back in with the light yellow mix and streak in short horizontal lines of reflections. Soften and blend out any reflections that seem too distinct or make the water look too active. The calmer the water and the further in the background it is, the longer and softer the reflections should be.

3 HRS

poppy vista

SOMETIMES THE MOST ordinary landscapes can be made extraordinary by the use of color, especially complementary colors such as the greens and reds in this painting. The colors of the poppies are repeated in spots throughout the green parts of the landscape—the grassy fields, the trees and the mountains—tying the painting together and making the scene look perfectly natural, yet with an indefinable glow and liveliness.

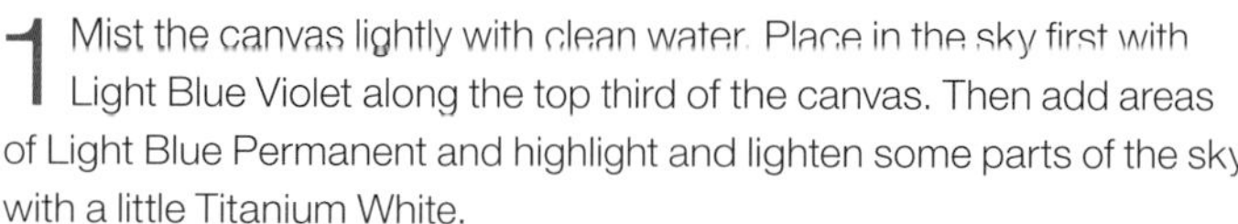

1 Mist the canvas lightly with clean water. Place in the sky first with Light Blue Violet along the top third of the canvas. Then add areas of Light Blue Permanent and highlight and lighten some parts of the sky with a little Titanium White.

2 Draw in the far distant mountains with Burnt Umber using the edge of the sponge to delineate the shapes of the mountaintops. Let the Burnt Umber fade out as you come down towards the middle ground. Place in the foreground fields with a dark green mix (Raw Umber + Sap Green Permanent). Blend this color well and let it fade out where it meets the Burnt Umber.

3 Shape the hills and valleys of the distant mountains with the dark green mix applied a little heavier than you did for the foreground fields. Add lighter areas of green on the distant mountains with a medium green mix (the dark green mix + Cadmium Yellow Medium). Highlight the lightest areas of the distant mountains with thinned Titanium White. (Thin the Titanium White by pulling it out of the paint puddle on your palette and working it into your sponge. Mist your palette with water if your Titanium White paint is getting too thick.) Soften the top edges of the mountains with the sky color and a little bit of Titanium White used very thinly. This should look like misty clouds overhanging the tops of the mountains.

4 Place the distant groves of trees with the dark green mix applied heavily. Warm up areas in the mid-ground grasses with yellow-green mix (dark green mix + Cadmium Yellow Medium). Add some areas of dried grass with Yellow Oxide. Highlight the mid-ground grasses with light green mix (dark green mix + Titanium White).

5 Block in the shapes of the tall, medium and short trees at the left and the shrubs at the right with the dark green mix using the edge and corner of your sponge. Apply this color pretty heavily as these are evergreens with dense foliage.

6 Load the top edge of your sponge with the light green mix from Step 4 and use a tight pinch to apply lighter areas of foliage to the foreground trees and shrubs as well as the trees in the distance.

7 Place the visible portions of the tree trunks in the foreground trees with Burnt Umber and a little Titanium White. Shade areas here and there in the trees and foreground shrubs with Burnt Sienna. Using the edge of the sponge and light vertical strokes, place in the foreground grasses with grass green mix (dark green mix + Yellow Oxide).

8 Highlight small patches of the foreground grasses with grass highlight mix (grass green mix + Titanium White). Use a medium pinch of the sponge as shown and stroke upward.

9 Load the top edge of the sponge with Burnt Sienna. Add shading underneath the distant trees. Indicate low places and areas of bare ground in the grassy field. Enrich the colors of the distant mountainsides and delineate the separation of the field from the lower slopes using horizontal strokes.

10 Place in the darkest color of the foreground poppies with Burnt Sienna using the corner of your sponge and a dabbing and wiggling motion to approximate the shape of the blossoms.

11 Over the Burnt Sienna poppies, dab on Cadmium Orange, letting the Burnt Sienna edges show on the blossoms. Dot Cadmium Orange here and there for drifts of poppies in the mid-ground grassy fields and next to the distant groves of trees.

12 Highlight the foreground poppies with little areas of Cadmium Yellow Medium. Don't do this on every blossom—just a few here and there.

13 Dot in the centers of the foreground poppies with Brilliant Purple. This color is complementary to the Cadmium Orange you used in step 11 and therefore will make the flowers "pop."

critique

Step back and take a critical look at your painting. Highlight the mid-ground grass areas behind the trees and the poppy drifts with the grass highlight mix. Enrich the foreground grasses in among the poppies with Sap Green mix (Sap Green Permanent + Yellow Oxide). Deepen the shading in the foreground trees with darkest tree green mix (Phthalocyanine Green + Burnt Umber). Use Burnt Umber to cool some of the greens and browns of the distant mountains and to reshape and sharpen the peaks as needed. Restate a few of the clouds behind the distant mountains with a little more Titanium White to help contrast with the mountain ridges.

2 HRS 15 MIN

watery lullaby

Blue-gray background mix

Warm gray mix

Payne's Gray

Brown-green mix

Burnt Umber

Unbleached Titanium

Deep water blue mix

Titanium White

Cadmium Yellow Medium

Light yellow mix

Burnt Sienna

Light Blue Violet

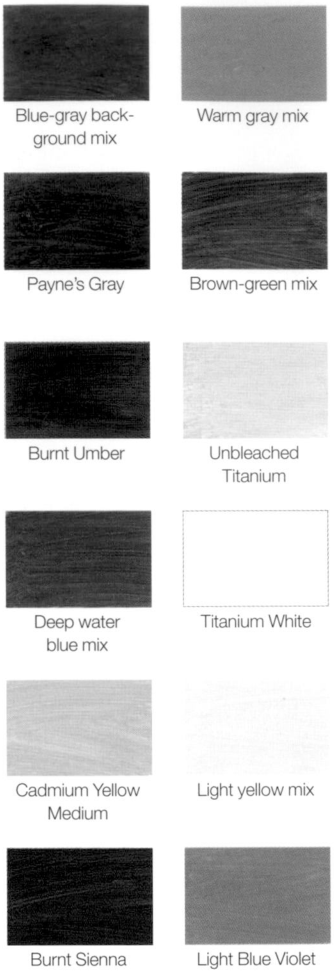

PAINTING FALLING WATER WITH A SPONGE is fairly easy and even fun—just let the sponge do the work for you! Dragging the flat side of the sponge downward in straight lines gives the look of falling water, and using very thin white paint gives the translucent, veil-like quality that most waterfalls have, especially tiny ones like these. The bright yellow leaves provide sparks of complementary color in an otherwise cool, low-key painting.

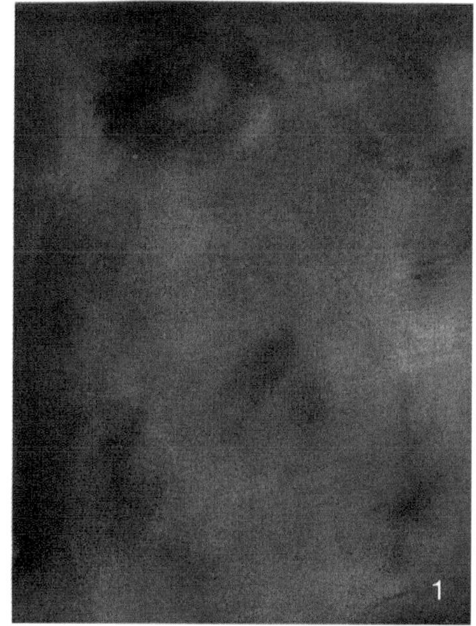

1 Wash in the background with the blue-gray background mix (Phthalocyanine Blue (Green Shade) + a little Payne's Gray). Mist the canvas first with clean water to help keep the paint moist and blend out your wash. Keep some areas around the outer edges darker.

2 Block in the rock shapes with the warm gray mix (Burnt Umber + Light Blue Violet + Unbleached Titanium), using the pinched edge of the sponge to draw the outer edges, then scrubbing on the color to fill in. Pick up plenty of paint for opaque coverage along the edges, but let the gray fade and blend into the blue background along the bottom edges.

3 Using the flat of the sponge and Payne's Gray, dab on some subtle texture on the rocks. Leave the tops of the rocks pretty free of texture.

4 Wash in some Payne's Gray shading around the edges of the rocks at the top. Let dry. With the brown-green mix (Sap Green Permanent + Raw Umber), shade and shape all of the rocks, leaving the warm gray color showing on the tops and some of the texturing on the sides.

5 Deepen the shading on the rocks with Burnt Umber, blending out the color so there are no sharp edges.

6 Highlight the tops and some of the sides of the rocks with Unbleached Titanium using a dabbing motion of the sponge.

7 Deepen the blue of the water in the lower two thirds of the painting with the deep water blue mix (Ultramarine Blue + Payne's Gray). Pull this color up over the bottom edges of the rocks to set the rocks into the water. Let dry.

8 Begin the foamy white water and little waterfalls by dabbing on Titanium White for the white water. Mist your sponge with water to thin the white, and pull vertical streaks downward to form the veils of falling water. Place these in several areas where the water would naturally fall over the rocks.

9 Blend out the white water in the upper part of the painting for a misty, foggy look. Streak in tiny little wavelets in the water between the rocks.

10 With Titanium White, draw in the tree branches overhanging the stream and rocks. Shade them and knock back the bright white with Payne's Gray. Block in the shapes of the bright yellow leaves on the branches and on the rocks with Cadmium Yellow Medium.

11 Highlight parts of the bright yellow leaves with the light yellow mix (Cadmium Yellow Medium + Titanium White). Add some dried brown leaves into the foliage by shading some of the yellow leaves with Burnt Sienna.

critique

Step back and check your painting for any final adjustments. Here the white of the waterfalls needs to be toned down a bit with transparent washes of Light Blue Violet. A few white branches need to be re-established to overlap some of the leafy areas. Touch a bit more of the brown-green mix onto the rocks to imply moss or lichen, and also to deepen the shadows in the water in the lower left corner where the rock casts a dark shadow.

2 HRS 35 MIN

mountain river bloom

CHERRY BLOSSOMS and misty mountain landscapes are quintessentially Asian and provide a delicate balance of textures and colors that are so enjoyable to paint, especially with a sponge. Mountain mists and low clouds can be easily placed in with very thin white paint on the flat side of the sponge, then blended out with the clean side until they are as translucent as you want. Try this technique with other mountain landscapes to give them mood and atmosphere.

1 Wash the entire canvas with Cerulean Blue, Chromium. As always, start by misting the blank canvas with clean water when you do a wash. Blend out well using the flat side of the sponge, but leave the top and bottom of the canvas a little darker blue than the center.

2 With opaque Burnt Umber, block in the landmass and mountain shapes, using the edge of your sponge to draw the top lines of the mountains. Scrub with the sponge to fill in. Thin the Burnt Umber by spraying your sponge with water, then block in the reflections in the foreground water, letting them fade away as they approach the distant shoreline. Make sure your reflections mirror the shapes of the mountains.

3 With the light foliage green mix (Sap Green Permanent + Yellow Oxide), place in the lighter green areas in the background landmass and in the water reflections while the Burnt Umber undercoat is still somewhat damp to make it easier to blend out the green. Then add darker green areas with Sap Green Permanent.

4 Highlight the toplit areas of the mountains with Raw Sienna to indicate the slopes and shape the rocks, then shade some areas with Burnt Sienna. Repeat these in the reflections in the water, using a lighter touch with the sponge and sparser paint.

5 Dab on the treeline on the far shore with the dark foliage green mix (Sap Green Permanent + Payne's Gray), then highlight the tops of the trees with the light foliage green mix. Dab in some drifts of red flowers in front of these trees and on the left side with Cadmium Red Medium Hue.

6 With your first blue, the Cerulean Blue (Chromium), deepen the blue of the sky along the top of the canvas, then in the foreground water, washing over the tops of the mountain reflections. Add small, very subtle areas of this blue to the mountainsides to bring the sky color in.

7 Load a clean sponge with straight Titanium White and place in the cloud shapes, using the edge of the sponge to draw the shapes, then scrubbing to fill in and blend out the white. Pull the white down over the tops of the mountains and down along some of the valleys to create a "mountain mists" look and to soften the edges of the ridgeline.

8 Work to blend and soften the cloud shapes in the sky, picking up more Titanium White on your sponge as you go. Using the edge of the sponge, streak in the wavecaps in the water, letting them overlap the mountain reflections.

9 Mist your sponge with water and soften the wavecaps with horizontal sweeps of your sponge. With the cloud pink mix (Cadmium Red Light Hue + Raw Sienna), warm up and enrich the color of the undersides of the clouds.

10 Shape the clouds with thinned Payne's Gray but don't overdo it to the point that they look like storm clouds. If the gray gets too dark, just wipe it off with a clean, damp sponge. Come back in with more Titanium White and reshape the cloud tops and brighten them to contrast more with the sky.

11 Draw in the branches of the foreground cherry tree with Burnt Umber using the edge of your sponge in a tight pinch. Draw finer twigs coming off the branches using the corner of your sponge and lifting off to a point. Highlight the tops of the branches with Raw Sienna in some places.

12 Begin the cherry blossoms by dabbing on the dark blossom pink mix (Alizarin Crimson + Burnt Umber) along the branches.

13 Squiggle in some Titanium White here and there wet-into-wet over the dark pink to lighten the cherry blossoms.

14 Accent with little spots of the bright pink mix (Alizarin Crimson + Titanium White). The leaves are based in with Sap Green Permanent, then highlighted with the yellow-green mix (Cadmium Yellow Medium + a little Sap Green Permanent). Use the corner of the sponge to pull these little leaf shapes out from the branches.

critique

Step back and check your painting. Warm up the foliage in front of the treeline on the far shore with Yellow Oxide, and tone down the red flowers on the left side to help set them into the background. Soften the white of the wavecaps in the foreground water by toning them down with thinned Cerulean Blue (Chromium). Soften the reflections of the mountains in the water by washing some very thin Titanium White over them.

1 HR 55 MIN

wetland dew

WETLANDS AND MARSHY areas are great places to study the effects of reflected light. The calm, shallow water acts as a mirror that shows all the colors of the sky and the surroundings. In this painting, the rich colors of sunrise have turned the water a reddish-pink, yet you can still see areas of blue sky color in the water, as well as reflections of the islands and distant landmasses. Use short horizontal strokes of thinned white to indicate tiny waves.

Sunrise red mix

Dark sky blue mix

Naples Yellow Hue

Titanium White

Burnt Sienna

Darkest foliage green mix

Medium foliage green mix

Yellow-green mix

Light grass highlight mix

Yellow Oxide

Raw Sienna

Light Blue Violet mix

Burnt Umber

Cadmium Yellow Medium

Raw Umber

Brilliant Purple

Unbleached Titanium

Light yellow-green mix

1 Mist the canvas lightly with clean water. Wash the entire canvas with the sunrise red mix (Cadmium Red Light Hue + Raw Sienna + Titanium White). Blend out well using the flat side of the sponge, but leave the color a little darker along the bottom of the canvas.

2 Darken the sky at the left and right sides with dark sky blue mix (Ultramarine Blue + Burnt Umber). Lighten the sky closer to the horizon with Naples Yellow Hue. Establish the lightest areas of the sunrise sky with very thin Titanium White. Work the area over with your sponge to blend everything out. There should be no hard edges anywhere. If your paint is drying as you work, mist the canvas with clean water.

3 Establish the treeline in the distance with Burnt Sienna. (I used Utrecht's brand of Burnt Sienna because it is redder and warmer than Liquitex's Burnt Sienna.) This area of Burnt Sienna allows the distant trees to look backlit by the reddish light of the rising sun.

4 With darkest foliage green mix (Sap Green Permanent + Raw Umber + Payne's Gray), overpaint the Burnt Sienna treeline in the distance, allowing the Burnt Sienna to show through in some areas between the trees and all along the top edge. With the same dark green, establish the wetlands and the little islands. Thin this same green with a spray of water on your sponge and lightly pull streaks downward from the distant landmass and the wetlands for reflections in the water.

5 Add another layer of color in the distant treeline and the wetlands with medium foliage green mix (dark foliage green mix + Titanium White). Add a touch of Yellow Oxide to this mix to make a yellow-green mix and enrich the color in these areas. Maintain the dark green edges of the islands. Add a touch of Titanium White to the yellow-green mix to make a light grass highlight mix and streak in the very lightest grasses. Accent some areas of the grass with fine streaks of Yellow Oxide in some places and Raw Sienna in other places to depict dried grasses.

6 With Light Blue Violet + a little Titanium White to make a light blue violet mix, use short, horizontal motions of the sponge to streak in reflections of the blue sky color in the water. Do the same in the background to separate the distant treeline from the mid-ground wetlands.

7 Base in the tree trunks with Burnt Umber using the top edge of your sponge in a tight pinch to draw the shapes. The foreground trunks on the right should be taller than the mid-ground trunks on the left, but leave room for the foliage at the top.

8 With darkest foliage green mix, dab in the first layer of dark foliage on the trees at either side of the painting. Use the same dark green to shade the edges of the wetlands and smaller islands and set them into the water.

9 Dab in the next layer of foliage on both trees with the medium foliage green mix you used in step 5. Pick up a little more Titanium White on your sponge and add the lightest highlights on the leftside tree.

10 Accent the foliage in the tree on the right with small spots of Cadmium Yellow Medium and an occasional spot of Raw Sienna. With thinned Raw Umber, tone down the redness of the water in the lower half of the canvas and indicate shading on the water next to the islands.

11 Begin the wildflowers with a layer of darkest foliage green mix. For the flower colors on the foreground islands, start with Raw Sienna, then add a layer of Yellow Oxide, then another layer with Brilliant Purple. The blue flowers are dabbed in with Light Blue Violet. The final highlights are Titanium White. Use a small piece of natural sea sponge to dab on the flower colors, and don't overdo it. You should be able to see all your flower colors in varying degrees when you finish.

critique

Step back and take a critical look at your painting. Lighten some of the grassy areas in front with light yellow-green mix (yellow-green mix + more Cadmium Yellow Medium). Pick up some Titanium White on the edge of your sponge and strengthen some of the wave lines in the water in the lowest third of the painting. Tone down the foreground water with a thin wash of Unbleached Titanium. Soften and fill in the foliage of the leftside tree with Unbleached Titanium and Sap Green Permanent on a natural sea sponge. Shade the water in the left foreground with thinned Raw Umber to indicate a shadow cast by the island and the tree.

moonlight rendezvous

1 HR 45 MIN

Ultramarine Blue (Green Shade)

Light Blue Violet

Titanium White

Brown-gray mix

Darkest green mix

Blue shading mix

Raw Sienna

Foliage green mix

Dark red mix

Cadmium Red Medium Hue

Dark tree trunk brown mix

Darkest tree foliage mix

Sap Green Permanent

Burnt Sienna

THE FINAL PAINTING TO BE DEMONSTRATED is a study of moonlight over water, an appropriate way to end this book and say goodnight. The setting is a quiet lakeside scene bathed in the cool white glow of the moon coming up over the water. The time of day is known as "L'heure bleu"—the "blue hour"—when the deep dark blue of the sky has not yet turned into the black of night. Blues, grays and dark greens provide contrast to the bright white moon.

1 Mist the blank canvas with clean water to start. Wash in the sky area and water area with Ultramarine Blue (Green Shade) using the flat side of the sponge. Let dry. Come back in with Light Blue Violet to lighten some areas in the sky and water, but leave plenty of the Ultramarine Blue still showing through.

2 With Titanium White on the flat of your sponge, place in lots of puffy white clouds in the top two-thirds of the canvas. Use the edge of the sponge in a medium pinch to delineate the top edges of some of the clouds and brighten the white in a few areas. The clouds at the horizon line should be flatter, more horizontal. Let dry.

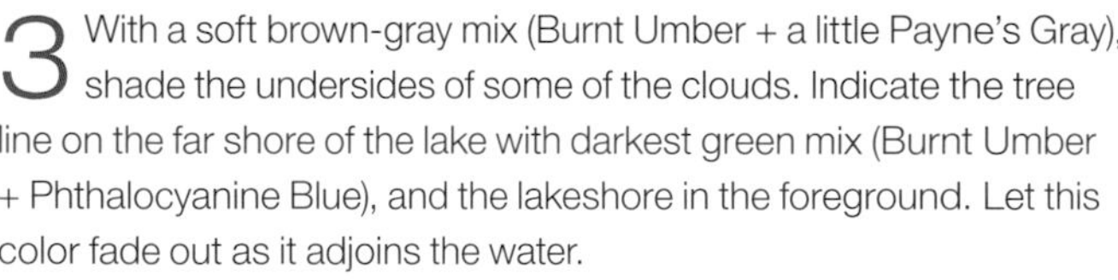

3 With a soft brown-gray mix (Burnt Umber + a little Payne's Gray), shade the undersides of some of the clouds. Indicate the tree line on the far shore of the lake with darkest green mix (Burnt Umber + Phthalocyanine Blue), and the lakeshore in the foreground. Let this color fade out as it adjoins the water.

4 Darken the shores of the lake with blue shading mix (Ultramarine Blue + a little Payne's Gray), and add this same color back into a few areas of the sky to darken it and give it a late-evening feel.

5 Begin the foreground foliage with dabs of Raw Sienna. Add green leaves and grasses with foliage green mix (Cadmium Yellow Medium + Payne's Gray). The red-leafed bush on the right is based with dark red mix (Cadmium Red Medium Hue + Payne's Gray), then highlighted with Cadmium Red Medium Hue.

6 Draw the trunks of the two main trees on the left with dark tree trunk brown mix (Burnt Umber + Payne's Gray). Use the corner of the sponge and darkest tree foliage mix (Phthalocyanine Blue + Payne's Gray + Burnt Umber) to dab in the dark, silhouetted foliage on the trees. Accent with a few spots of Sap Green Permanent and a few of Burnt Sienna to give some color to the trees. Maintain lots of openings in the foliage for the moonlight to shine through.

7 Place the moon behind the edge of the trees with pure Titanium White applied thickly. With the same white in your sponge, dot in areas of moonlight coming through the openings in the tree foliage. Streak in reflections in the lake water.

critique

Step back and check your painting. Tone down the upper parts of the sky with a dark blue mix of Ultramarine Blue + a little Mars Black, and use the same mix to add a cast shadow underneath the trees and to tone down the reddish color of the foliage in the midground. Soften the tops of the trees on the distant lakeshore with thinned Light Blue Violet to give them a misty look and to set them into the background. Tone down and soften the moonlight reflections in the water if needed so they don't compete with the focal point of the moon behind the trees.

resources

U.S. RETAILERS

Acrylic Paints

Liquitex Artist Materials
P.O. Box 246
Piscataway, NJ 08855
USA
Phone: 1-888-4-ACRYLIC
www.liquitex.com
Liquitex Acrylic Artist Color (High Viscosity / Heavy Body) in 2 fl. oz. (59ml) tubes

Utrecht Manufacturing Corp.
6 Corporate Drive
Cranbury, NJ 08512
USA
Phone: 1-877-UTRECHT
www.utrecht.com
Utrecht Artists' Colors Series 1 Acrylics (High Viscosity) in one-pint (16 fl. oz.) jars

CANADIAN RETAILERS

Crafts Canada
120 North Archibald St.
Thunder Bay, ON P7C 3X8
Tel: 888-482-5978
www.craftscanada.ca

Folk Art Enterprises
P.O. Box 1088
Ridgetown, ON, N0P 2C0
Tel: 800-265-9434

MacPherson Arts & Crafts
91 Queen St. E.
P.O. Box 1810
St. Mary's, ON, N4X 1C2
Tel: 800-238-6663
www.macphersoncrafts.com

U.K. RETAILERS

Crafts World (head office)
No. 8 North Street
Guildford
Surrey GU1 4 AF
07000 757070

Green & Stone
259 Kings Road
London SW3 5EL
020 7352 0837
www.greenandstone.com

Help Desk
HobbyCraft Superstore
The Peel Centre
St. Ann Way
Gloucester
Gloucestershire GL1 5SF
01452 424999
www.hobbycraft.co.uk

index

The BEST in painting instruction and inspiration is from North Light Books!

Painting Murals Fast & Easy
Discover a quick and easy way to paint gorgeous wall murals! With just a common household sponge and acrylic paint, you can create landscapes, seascapes, still lifes and more. Terrence and Theodore Tse show you how much fun mural painting can be, either directly on a wall or on canvas to display anywhere. With hundreds of full-color step-by-step photos and clear instruction in 21 complete demos, you'll learn these easy and innovative techniques in no time. No expensive equipment or painting experience is required!
ISBN-13: 978-1-58180-573-4, ISBN-10: 1-58180-573-X, paperback, 128 pages, #33030

Painting Landscapes Filled with Light
Capture the rich, illusive properties of light in your landscape paintings! In 10 complete step-by-step projects, beloved landscape artist Dorothy Dent shares her easy-to-master techniques for painting light-filled landscapes in different seasons, weather conditions and times of day. Dorothy's projects include both oil and acrylic painting demos, with advice for adapting the technique used for one medium to that of the other. Prepare to be amazed by the landscapes you create!
ISBN-13: 978-1-58180-736-3, ISBN-10: 1-58180-736-8, paperback, 144 pages, #33412

Fantastic Floorcloths You Can Paint in a Day
Want to refresh your home décor without the time and expense of redecorating? Then painting canvas floorcloths is for you! Choose from 23 projects simple enough to create in a few hours. Decorative painters Judy Diephouse and Lynne Deptula show you step by step how to paint designs ranging from florals to graphic patterns to holiday motifs, including some especially appropriate for kids' rooms. As an added bonus, there are 12 ideas for decorative accessories to inspire you to create a coordinated look. *Fantastic Floorcloths You Can Paint in a Day* makes home decorating as easy as picking up a paintbrush.
ISBN-13: 978-1-58180-603-8, ISBN-10: 1-58180-603-5, Paperback, 128 pages, #33161

Fast & Fun Flowers in Acrylics
Popular artist Lauré Paillex shows you everything you need to create fun, bright and colorful flowers of all kinds! You'll find more than 60 step-by-step demonstrations that give you great results in a jiffy. No demo is more than six steps long, and the convenient lay-flat spiral binding makes this a book you'll keep open on your painting for quick reference any time. From garden flowers to wildflowers, from spring bulbs to roses and orchids, you'll find just the flower you need for any project—or just for the fun of painting!
ISBN-13: 978-1-58180-827-8, ISBN-10: 1-58180-827-5, hardcover, 128 pages, #33503

These books and other fine North Light titles are available at your local arts & crafts retailer, bookstore, or from online suppliers.